Belinda Lawley

About the Author

TOM HODGKINSON is the author of *How to Be Idle*. Despite his success, he continues doing what he's always done, which is a mixture of editing magazines, writing articles, and putting on parties. He founded *The Idler* in 1993, and lives in Devon, England.

The Freedom Manifesto

How to Free Yourself from Anxiety, Fear,
Mortgages, Money, Guilt, Debt, Government,
Boredom, Supermarkets, Bills, Melancholy,
Pain, Depression, Work, and Waste

TOM HODGKINSON

HARPER PERENNIAL

NEW YORK ● LONDON ● TORONTO ● SYDNEY

HARPER ● PERENNIAL

Originally published as *How to Be Free* in Great Britain
in 2006 by Hamish Hamilton, an imprint of Penguin Books Ltd.

FIRST HARPER PERENNIAL EDITION PUBLISHED 2007.

Library of Congress Cataloging-in-Publication Data
is available upon request.

ISBN: 978-0-06-082322-1 (pbk.)
ISBN-10: 0-06-082322-4 (pbk.)

HB 07.14.2020

For Victoria

For Veronica

Contents

The Freedom Manifesto

Introduction

> *In every cry of every Man,*
> *In every Infant's cry of fear,*
> *In every voice, in every ban,*
> *The mind-forg'd manacles I hear.*
> William Blake, *Songs of Experience*, 'London', 1794

This is a book about good living, and at its heart is a simple truth: when you embrace Lady Liberty, life becomes easier, cheaper and much more fun. My intention is to show you how to remove the mind forg'd manacles and become free to create your own life. After finishing my last book, *How to be Idle*, I realized that idleness is, for me, virtually synonymous with freedom. To be idle is to live free. To be idle is to live by your own rules. To be idle is to unify what has been split up.

I have tried to bring together three strands of thought into a philosophy for everyday life; these are freedom, merriment and responsibility, or anarchy, medievalism and existentialism. It's an approach to life that is also known as having a laugh, doing what you want. The Western world has allowed freedom, merriment and responsibility to be taken from it, from ourselves, and substituted with greed, competition, lonely striving, greyness, debts, McDonald's and GlaxoSmithKline. The consumer age offers many comforts but few freedoms. Governments by their very nature make endless attacks on our civil liberties. Health and Safety is wheeled out as an excuse to extend government powers.

In seeking freedom, I would define myself as an anarchist. In anarchy, contracts are made between individuals, not between citizen and state. It proceeds from a view that people are basically good and should be left alone rather than from the Puritan view that we are all evil and need to be controlled by authority. In the Middle Ages, despite the hierarchies, we used to organize things for ourselves. The vast majority of the manacles discussed in this book had not been invented. Life was self-determined and full of variety.

What we need now is a radical redefinition of human relationships, one based on local needs rather than the greed of global capitalism. Our lives have been split into a million fragments, and our goal now is to bring them back together into unity and harmony. In this aim we are helped not only by the example of the medieval system and the anarchists and the existentialists but also by a whole series of humane figures through history. Witness will be borne by Aristotle, St Francis of Assisi, St Thomas Aquinas, the Romantics, William Cobbett, John Stuart Mill, John Ruskin, William Morris, Oscar Wilde, the back-to-the-landers, Chesterton, Eric Gill and the Distributists, Bertrand Russell, Orwell, the Situationists, the Yippies, the punks and 1970s radicals such as John Seymour, Ivan Illich and Schumacher. All form part of the long history of promoting the idea of cooperation, through which true freedom is possible, rather than competition. As we will see, there is a strong tradition out there of rejecting money, property and business as the primary objects of life. The aim is to stop looking to others to sort out our lives for us and instead to trust ourselves to do it. We are free spirits. We resist interference and we resist interfering with others.

In this book, I look at the barriers to freedom and how we can free ourselves from anxiety, fear, mortgages, money, guilt, debt, governments, boredom, supermarkets, bills, melancholy, pain, depression and waste. We ourselves have given these enemies power over us and only we can remove that power. It is useless to sit around moaning and hope that someone else is going to do that job for us. When we realize that these impediments are one and all mind-forg'd, then, lo! See the door to the garden of liberty swing open.

Life is about recapturing lost freedoms. Through school and work, we encourage each other to believe that we are not free and that we are not responsible. We create a world of obligations, duties and things to be done. We forget that life should be lived with spontaneity, joy, love. Here, I look to the past for ideas for the future. The Greeks looked back to the Golden Age, the Romans to the Greeks, Virgil and Ovid to a bucolic idyll. The medievals also looked back to the Greeks and a simpler life. Indeed, a feature of every age is its construction of an 'olden days' when people were happy and things were easier. Harking back to an imagined ideal past is not mere escapist nostalgia. It is, on the contrary, a method of moving forward, of deciding on our priorities in life. And the past is a far better place to look for ideas on how to live than the future, because the future is pure fantasy and the past actually did happen. The dream of a technological utopia of the future where machines do all the work is a nonsense.

How to be free? Well, like it or not, you are free. The real question is whether you choose to exercise that freedom: there is an essential nothingness at the heart of man. We have created our own universe. Life is absurd. God is love. We are free.

Death to the Supermarkets
Bake Bread
Play the Ukulele
Open the Village Hall
Action is Futile
Quit Moaning
Make Music
Stop Consuming
Start Producing
Back to the Land
Smash Usury
Embrace Beauty
Embrace Poverty
Hail the Chisel
Ignore the State
Reform is Futile
Anarchy in the UK
Hail the Spade
Hail the Horse
Hail the Quill
Love thy Neighbour
Be Creative
Free your Spirit
Dig the Earth
Make Compost
Life is Absurd
We are Free
Be Merry

1 *Banish Anxiety; Be Carefree*

Live merrily, oh my friends, free from cares, perplexity, anguish,
grief of mind, live merrily.
Marsilius Ficinus, quoted by Robert Burton in
Anatomy of Melancholy, 1621

Bring me my bow of burning gold!
Bring me my arrows of desire!
Blake, 'Milton', 1804

We don't care.
Punk slogan, 1977

When it comes to anxiety, I'm here to say: 'It's not your fault.'
Shed the burden: that dreadful, gnawing, stomach-churning sense

that things are awry mixed with a chronic sense of powerlessness is the simple result of living in an anxious age, oppressed by Puritans, imprisoned by career, humiliated by bosses, attacked by banks, seduced by celebrity, bored by TV, forever hoping, fearing or regretting. It – the Thing, the Man, the System, the Combine, the Construct, whatever we want to call the structures of power – wants you to be anxious. Anxiety suits the status quo very well. Anxious people make good consumers and good workers. Governments and big business, therefore, love terrorism – they adore it, it's good for business. Anxiety will drive us back into our comfort blankets of credit-card shopping and bad food, so the system deliberately produces anxiety while simultaneously promising to take it away.

The veritable stream of scare stories in the newspapers about rising crime makes us feel anxious. Newspapers set out to provide entertainment and gossip, stories that feed our need for shock and horror. They do it well. Flick through the *Daily Mail* on any given day and you'll find that nine out of ten stories are negative and unsettling. Every radio bulletin and every TV news show, every newspaper and many of our daily conversations drive home the same message: worry, worry, worry. It's a dangerous world out there, filled with crazy, suicidal, bomb-hurling terrorists and murderers and thieves and rotters and natural disasters. Stay home! Watch TV! Buy stuff on the web! Curl up on the sofa with a DVD! In the words of the Black Flag song 'TV Party': 'TV news knows what it's like out there, it's a scare!' As in George Orwell's *Nineteen Eighty-Four*, we are told that we are in a perpetual state of war – it's just that the enemy sometimes changes. We are no longer at war with the IRA; we are now at war with Al-Qaeda. Different enemy, same anxiety and same end result: mass powerlessness.

But if we bother to investigate these myths for a few seconds, they soon reveal themselves to be mere convenient fictions. According to the brilliant anxiety analyst Brian Dean, the truth is that crime rates have remained fairly constant for the last 150 years. Dean maintains that our fear of crime is vastly out of proportion to the reality. The truth is that we face far more danger from auto-mobile accidents and heart disease than from crime. Motor accidents kill ten people a day in the UK, and heart disease hundreds, but no one talks about banning cars or criminalizing the stress that puts a strain on the heart. The propaganda of insecurity, for Dean, is at the root of the problem: 'Our beliefs programme our rea-lities. If we believe that the universe is fundamentally *unsafe*, then we're going to experience perpetual anxiety – which isn't a good way to operate our brains.'

Our work, organized into the cursed jobs system, doesn't help, condemning as it does so many of us to meaningless toil. E. F. Schumacher was the great thinker behind the book *Small is Beautiful*. An anarchist and an idler at heart, he argued that the very enormity, the giant, impossible, dizzying scale of modern-day capitalism saps the spirit. He also believed that this enormity had made work into something pointless, boring, soul-destroying, something to put up with, a necessary evil rather than a pleasure. In his book *Good Work*, he argues that industrial society causes anxiety because, by focusing primarily on greed – or what the medievals called the sin of *avaritia* – it doesn't allow time for the expression of our nobler faculties:

7

Everywhere shows this evil characteristic of incessantly stimulating greed and avarice . . . mechanical, artificial, divorced from
nature, utilizing only the smallest part of man's potential capa-
bilities, it sentences the great majority of workers to spending
their working lives in a way which contains no worthy challenge,
no stimulus to self-perfection, no chance of development, no
element of Beauty, Truth, Goodness.

I say therefore that it is a great evil – perhaps the greatest evil
– of modern industrial society that, through its immensely
involved nature, it imposes an undue nervous strain and absorbs
an undue proportion of man's attention.

In the current scheme of things, when we're not working,
we're consuming. We leave the factory gates and pour our wages
straight back into the system at Tesco's. We suffer a strange split
in our roles in society between that of worker and consumer,
the oppressed and the courted. At least in the nineteenth century
people knew they were merely a pair of hands operating a
machine and that they were being exploited for another's profit.
Therefore, it was perhaps easier to rebel. The contract was
straightforward. Certainly, we all know that a vigorous culture
of resistance grew up among the workers in the nineteenth
century, the era of work and slavery. Now, though, the moment
we leave the factory gates and start to make our way back home,
we the are serenaded from all sides by advertising. The service
culture makes us into little princes surrounded by simpering
courtiers eager to curry favour so that we will give them our
cash or let them have their wicked way with us. They make us
feel important. The world of advertising practises its dark arts

of seduction. In *The Society of the Spectacle* (1967), the fantastically carefree Situationist Guy Debord put it like this:

> The worker, suddenly redeemed from the total contempt which is plainly showed to him by all the forms of the organization and supervision or production, now finds himself, every day, outside of production, and in the guise of a consumer; with zealous politeness, he is, seemingly, treated as an adult. At this point, the humanism of the commodity takes charge of the worker's 'leisure and humanity'.

The commercial world, then, treats us like celebrities – 'Because you're worth it,' it says. It flatters and kowtows to us and keeps on doing so right up until the moment when we hand over our credit-card details. Then we are cast aside and condemned to a purgatory of being held in a queue on a customer service line for all eternity. What fools we are.

The whole panoply of modern state control, also, is surely designed to make us feel nervous. The very institutions and devices that are sold to us as comforts and security measures create insecurity by constantly reminding us of dangers. Police; speed cameras; CCTV cameras; burglar alarms. Those two dark jailors Health and Safety are used by the interferers to foist ever more stringent attacks on our liberties. It's worth remembering, for example, that when the police force was proposed by Home Secretary Robert Peel in 1828, there was a huge outcry from the people, who complained about the attack on their freedoms that such an idea represented. Before the government-run police force, law-keeping was managed by locally elected constables. There is now a colossal machinery of state to deal with perhaps 50,000 hard-core criminals in the country, while the 60 million law-abiding citizens have to suffer. These devices are an attack on spontaneous enjoyment of life, on pleasure.

I am anti-crime, but not because I morally disapprove of law-breaking – in fact, I am attracted to criminals and the ASBO kids precisely because their criminality flags their refusal to submit to authority. Delinquency is a sign of life. I am against crime because it feeds straight into the government system: for every crime committed, there is a tenfold attack on personal liberties. One bomb leads to a thousand new laws. Governments love crime, as crime gives them a reason to exist – protection of the citizenry – and an excuse to control us. Therefore, the real anarchist should avoid criminal acts at all costs.

George Orwell's *Nineteen Eighty-Four* is becoming a reality in other ways, too. At the time of writing, the US government is trying to subpoena the records of Google, the search engine which can record everything we have searched for, thus gaining an insight into the innermost workings of our minds. The Internet threatens to turn from being a tool of liberation into a tool of surveillance, a spy in every home. I suppose the same thing could happen to our emails. Our most intimate conversations are being logged, recorded, saved, and they will be sitting for ever on some giant hard drive should the authorities need to look at them in the future. Big Brother is not only watching us but listening to us, eavesdropping on us and even peering into our brains and inspecting the contents of our very souls. What's more, we have submitted entirely voluntarily to this system. It was never like this with the Royal Mail. And now there is a new threat to our civil liberties in the UK in the form of ID cards, on which will be recorded our misdemeanours.

Anxiety and our being surrounded by anxiety-inducing agents is at the absolute centre of the capitalist project. That is why I say: *'It's not your fault.'* Everywhere, the same myth is perpetuated: you are just one object away from happiness. It could be the latest U2 album, a donation to charity, a more comprehensive insurance policy, a different credit card, a fabulous holiday, a better job, a faster car . . . However many times we are disappointed by the failure of this myth to bring us satisfaction, we keep coming back for more. In the words of CRASS founder, Penny Rimbaud, we 'feed the hand that bites us'. We remain unsatisfied. Capitalism is constantly and perpetually disappointing. The very thing that promises you freedom can quickly become the thing that oppresses you.

Anxiety is the sacrifice of creativity in the service of security. It is the giving up of personal freedoms in return for the promise, never fulfilled, of comfort, cotton wool, air-conditioned shopping centres. Security is a myth; it simply doesn't exist. This does not stop us, however, from constantly chasing it.

Some of us may find a sort of pleasure in anxiety and its opposites, just as some enjoy swinging from white to brown, crack to heroin, from the highs to the lows. I recently sat next to a genial man in his sixties in the dining car of a train. He asked if I wanted to have a look at his *Evening Standard*. I said, no, that newspapers made me feel anxious by parading a load of problems which I am utterly powerless to do anything about. He replied: 'Oh, I rather like feeling anxious. Then I have a drink!'

We are still scandalously encouraged by the medical drug-pushing establishment to believe that heart disease can be avoided by mechanical methods, i.e. stopping smoking or taking toxic pills, when it is perfectly obvious that although these might be contributory factors, the real cause of heart disease is an uneasy heart.

Idleness, doing nothing – *literally* doing nothing – can help fight anxiety. One strategy is simply to forget, to abandon your self and let things flow through you. Nietzsche recommends this:

> To close the doors and windows of consciousness for a time; to remain undisturbed by the noise and struggle of our underworld of utility organs working with and against one another; a little quietness, a little *tabula rasa* of the consciousness, to make room for new things, above all, for the nobler functions and functionaries, for regulation, foresight, premeditation (for our organism is an oligarchy) – that is the purpose of active forgetfulness, which is like a doorkeeper, a preserver of psychic order, repose and etiquette: so that it will be immediately obvious how there could be no happiness, no cheerfulness, no hope, no pride, no present, without forgetfulness.

By 'forgetfulness', Nietzsche means the skill of learning to live. Remembering can be an enemy. How often do we lie awake at night ruminating painfully on all the things that we have to do in the future and all the things in the past that we have done wrong? This to me is why a little moderate boozing is a splendid idea, as long as the quality is high. Real ale is compost for the soul. And this is also why it is important to read decent stuff. Put quality materials into your mind, quality ingredients. A diet of good writing, without crappy newspapers and magazines, which just make the anxiety worse, will produce quality thoughts and a self-sufficient, resourceful person. Feed your mind.

In gardening, the reduced-effort method of mulching the soil with rich organic matter rather than laboriously digging it every year is coming into vogue. This is the natural, low-work way. It allows nature to get on with it with minimum intervention from man. It is the same with your mind: mulch it with quality ingredients, books, food and beauty, and it will become fertile and produce useful and beautiful things. Mulching the mind also involves a lot less work than digging it up. Digging can actually be harmful, as it will bring weed seeds to the surface that otherwise would have lain dormant. These weed seeds will then germinate and produce a new load of unnecessary work.

We also need a diet of stimulating company, good cheer, merriment, feasting and fun. 'Good cheer' or, to put it in the modern vernacular, 'having a laugh with your mates', is one of the highest pleasures that life has to offer and can blot out those anxious feelings, largely by revealing that they are shared. Removing newspapers and TV from your life helps enormously. I have managed to cut down to one newspaper a week, which leaves a lot more time to concentrate on the important things in life, like drinking and music. Replace TV with friends, and newspapers with books.

For those of us 'in populous city pent', as Coleridge put it, I would highly recommend avoiding the underground and bicycling instead. I had two years of commuting in London by bike.

Fifteen miles of cycling a day, nearly two hours' worth, and what a joy it was. Cycling brings an exhilarating sense of freedom and self-mastery as well as a very enjoyable sense of not spending money. You coast through the city, in it but not of it, living it and not controlled by it. On buses and trains, you are sitting targets for the advertising hoardings. On a bike, you can simply sail past them. People cite 'danger' as a reason to avoid cycling, but this is a pathetic excuse and an example of the mean spirit that this book is fighting. So what if there's a little danger in your life? That's good. Wake up! If you can't face the idea of a bicycle, then leave a lot of time for your journey and sit on the top deck of the bus. This, too, can be a great pleasure, for the same reason: you float through the city, a detached observer. I have experienced moments of true joy when on the bus, moments when I could almost repudiate everything I have written above and truly believe that this is a wonderful world. Or walk! Walk through the parks and admire the noble gardens! But, whatever you do, avoid the underground. As my friend Mark Manning, also known as Zodiac Mindwarp, says, 'I can't sit staring in silence at people I don't know.'

Another strategy for dealing with anxiety is to ensure that your day is varied. One of the joys of living in the country is that there is plenty of physical work to do. Three or four afternoons a week, I trudge up to my vegetable patch and plant, dig, weed, cart muck or just stare. A diet of solely mental work is suffocating. 'It is obviously much easier for a hard-working peasant to keep his mind attuned to the divine than for a strained office worker,' says Schumacher. And this is proved by my neighbour, Farmer John. One of the great things, he says, about being a farmer, is the amount of quality thinking time you get. Another idea: *do not go to the gym.* Gyms are all mixed up with vanity and money, with the absurd quest for perfection. They are the consumer ethic transferred to the body. They are anti-thought, and their giant screens blot out our minds and divert us from our selves. Sometimes I think that life is becoming no more than staring at a screen. We stare at a screen all day at work. We stare at screens in the gym. Buses now have screens installed in them. There are screens on trains. Then we get home and stare at our computer screen before staring at the TV screen. For entertainment, we stare at cinema screens. Work, rest and play: all involve staring at screens. Screens make us into passive receivers. Smash the screen and find a pencil and a piece of paper instead. Goodbye, TV; hello, chalk!

The neo-Luddite Kirkpatrick Sale was on the right track when he smashed up a computer screen on stage. By parading a stream of other people's lives in front of us, screens remove the responsibility to create our own lives. We watch other people doing things instead of doing them ourselves. This makes us radically powerless, and powerlessness leads to anxiety. And anxiety leads to shopping. Shopping leads to debt. Debt leads back to anxiety.

Another simple solution to anxiety is to embrace a fatalistic theology. Catholics, say, are probably less anxious than Protestants. Buddhists are certainly less anxious than Jews. If you believe that there's nothing much that you can do that makes any sense other than to enjoy yourself, then your anxiety will fade. If you have that Puritan cast of mind and feel that you are terribly important in the world and it really matters what you do, then your anxiety will increase. Self-importance breeds anxiety (see Chapter 24). We must learn *not to care* – not in the sense of being selfish but in the sense of being carefree. Today, we advertise ourselves as 'caring' people and fling flowers at the graves of strangers in order to prove our 'caring' nature to anyone who might be looking. 'I'm a really caring person,' we say, a phrase that means precisely nothing other than that we burden ourselves with the problems of others with no practical beneficial effect whatsoever. Talk of being caring is cant.

So, free yourself of care. To become cheerful and carefree is your revolutionary duty as a freedom-seeker. Stop working; stop buying; start living. Feast, drink. Eat capons and good hams. Drink spiced wines and fine ales. Make your table groan with food. Make jam and chutney. Play the hurdy-gurdy. Get a piano. I have just converted my home pub into a music room. We found an old honkytonk piano which was practically free. So now we can have sing-songs round the old Joanna. Just as your anxiety is a product of your imagination, albeit influenced by the commercial world, so your imagination has the power to replace it with good cheer.

RIDE A BIKE

2 *Break the Bonds of Boredom*

Let others bemoan the maliciousness of their age. What irks me
is its pettiness, for ours is an age without passion . . .
My life comes out all one colour.
Kierkegaard

If contemporary science were more sophisticated and subtle, then I'm absolutely certain that it would rank boredom as one of the central killers in the modern world. The French writer Raoul Vaneigem, one of those anarchic work-avoiders called the Situationists and a friend of Guy Debord, wrote in *The Revolution of Everyday Life* (1967), 'People are dying of boredom,' and I believe this quite literally to be true. Greyness and boredom are not only enemies of merry living, they are murderers. It would not surprise me one jot if boredom were one day revealed to be carcinogenic.

Boredom was invented in 1760. That is the year, according to academic Lars Svendsen in his excellent study *A Philosophy of Boredom* (2005), that the word was first used in English. The other great invention of the time was the Spinning Jenny, which heralded the start of the Industrial Revolution. In other words, boredom arrives with the division of labour and the transformation of enjoyable autonomous work into tedious slave-work.

And we are very bored. Go into chat rooms and forums on the Internet between three and five in the afternoon and you will find hundreds of posts from office workers reading, 'Bored bored bored!' These pleas for help, these desperate entreaties from trapped spirits, are like messages in a bottle, sent out into the ether, into the the oceans of cyberspace, in the hope that someone out there is listening and that someone out there may be able to do something to help. The odds, of course, are low.

I recently helped compile a book called *Crap Jobs*. We had asked readers of the *Idler* to send in their stories of workplace hell, and one thing that struck me was how many people cited boredom as one of the worst aspects of working. They found the boredom almost literally unbearable and would resort to all kinds of tactics to overcome it: office sabotage, crude banter with co-workers, irresponsible acts. One of the problems is that many modern jobs require just enough concentration to prevent you from going off into a dream but not enough really to occupy your mind. Jobs which are totally mechanical can be preferable, for example, to call-centre jobs. Call centres bore their customers to tears, and they bore their employees to death. Low pay is combined with the psychic torture of not knowing what fresh hell the next call is going to present you with.

Our other recent publication was called *Crap Towns*, and again what was striking was that the *uniformity* of the modern town was often cited as one of the reasons for it being crap. Something awful has happened, which is that giant retail chains have turned our towns – once so vibrant, teeming and various – into identikit retail centres peopled by shopping zombies. A town today is little more than a circle of flats gathered around a vast, airless shopping mall. Our hearts sink when we walk down the high street. We are assaulted with brand names, colourless institutions that have replaced all the fun and difference of the old stores, the grocers, haberdashers, fishmongers, bakers, florists, cobblers and apothecaries. The drive for growth and economies of scale has driven the independent spirit away. Almost. Occasionally an old Victorian shopfront survives, and its beauty, elegance and sense of fun shines out like a rainbow. There are other rays of hope: yesterday I saw a sign in the town nearest to me which cheered me. It was in the window of a TV repair shop, another dying breed of service. The sign said: 'Old-fashioned service by the proprietor.'

To E. F. Schumacher's notion that 'Small is beautiful,' we could certainly add 'Big is boring,' as it is the sheer scale of modern institutions which makes them so impersonal, alienating and exhausting to the spirit. McDonald's is boring and my local Indian is not boring. Raoul Vaneigem wrote, also in *The Revolution of Everyday Life*, that quantity has conquered quality. We have become so obsessed by numbers and by bottom lines that beauty and truth have been knocked aside. Boredom is the very opposite of beauty and truth. Life has been sacrificed to profit, and the result is boredom on a mass scale.

One of the principal causes of boredom, it seems to me, is

the removal of everyday creativity from the people. This was certainly the problem as William Morris saw it. In *News From Nowhere*, Morris paints a post-revolutionary society, in 2005, in which everyone is involved in some kind of freely chosen creative activity. There is no money, and Piccadilly Circus is covered with fields. This is how he saw the fourteenth century, and whether or not he romanticized the Middle Ages is not the point: it exists as a worthy ideal. The Puritan Revolution began to introduce boredom to the masses. Even religion and the path to salvation became boring. In the Middle Ages, religion had been full of blood and gore and death. Churches were centres of economic activity and partying as well as of worship. The Church was a patron of the arts and commissioned local craftsmen to make adornments for its properties. The sermons were attended largely for their entertainment value; they provided real theatre. In medieval Florence, people would queue all night to see a great preacher and would then stream out of the church after the service, weeping copiously. All this drama and theatre was removed by the Puritans, who labelled the ways of the old church 'superstition' and 'idolatry'. In other words, all the pagan fun of the Catholic Church, which it had wisely kept, was taken away.

Politicians can also take a fair share of the blame for the perceived monotony of our lives. You don't hear governments coming out with lines like 'Tough on boredom. Tough on the causes of boredom.' The most stupefyingly boring of all governments – and all governments are boring by their very nature – was the Nazis. Lines and rows and columns, the absence of individuality, the imposition of a bureaucratic order on things, the systematic removal of everything interesting – particularly Jews, but also gypsies, vagrants, the workshy and political dissidents. The Nazis loved sending memos, filling in forms, filing, cataloguing, keeping everything neat and tidy. What the Nazis attempted was a great big tidy-up, like the Puritans before them, and that is why excessive tidiness must be resisted.

The main reason that so many people are so desperately bored is that boring people are in charge. The money-makers, the profit-driven capitalists, high priests of utter dullness, run the business side of things. And the bureaucrats, the form-fillers and health-and-safety enthusiasts, are running the government. They actually like boredom. Being alive would scare them. But it hasn't always been this way, and it need not always be this way. Once upon a time, not so very long ago, the boring people were sidelined as ungodly. In medieval times, particularly the earlier periods, those with bourgeois, money-making values were looked down upon by the warriors, clerics and peasants. 'There is something disgraceful about trade, something sordid and shameful,' wrote opinion-former St Thomas Aquinas. Happiness, he said, was to be found in reflection, not distraction:

> So, if the ultimate felicity of man does not consist in external things which are called the goods of fortune, nor in the goods of the body, nor in the goods of the soul according to its sensitive part, nor as regards the intellective part according to the activity of the moral virtues, nor according to the intellectual virtues that are concerned with action, that is, art and prudence – we are left with the conclusion that the ultimate felicity of man lies in the contemplation of truth.

Boredom is a form of social control. Contemporaneous with the emergence of boredom in the late nineteenth century, we find an attack on the notion of the plebs organizing their own fun. As we all know, art and entertainment in previous ages was a bottom-up affair. All dramatics were amateur, mystery plays were performed by the craftsmen's guilds; medieval artists were also craftsmen. But radical historian E. P. Thompson shows us how suspicious the authorities became of such democratic art production as the Industrial Age dawned and control of both work and leisure was taken from the people. He cites, in *The Romantics*, the well-meaning reply of a local posh liberal to an application by a factory man to put on a play in 1798: 'The play,' she worries, 'might have a tendency to do you harm, and to prepare you for following scenes of riot and disorder at the alehouse.' To Thompson, this anecdote proves the increasing 'fear of an authentic popular culture beyond the contrivance and control of their betters'. Thompson also blames a centralized education system and cites a letter written in 1911, surprisingly, by a former chief inspector of schools, which criticizes the education system for being boring: 'The aim of his teacher is to leave nothing to [the pupil's] nature, nothing to his spontaneous life, nothing to his free activity; to repress all his natural impulses; to drill his energies into complete quiescence; to keep his whole being in a state of sustained and painful tension.'

Boredom is painful. For Vaneigem, the pressure to become the same as each other exhausts our spirit: 'If hierarchical organization seizes control of nature, while itself undergoing transformation in the course of this struggle, the portion of liberty and creativity falling to the individual is drained away by the requirements of adaptation to social norms of various kinds.'

Lest we become too depressed, let us remember that the creative spirit lives on. On the Scottish Isle of Eigg near Skye, the whole island comes together for a drinking and music session every Saturday night. No one is paid; no one is hired. The music is performed for its own sake, not for profit. To fight boredom, we need to take control of our work and our leisure alike. The artist Jeremy Deller has spent many years travelling around the British Isles photographing examples of what he calls Folk Art. For Deller, this means acts of creativity which have been done more or less for their own sake created by ordinary people who would never consider themselves to be artists. This is art outside the art world, outside Cork Street galleries, museums, dealers and the Arts Council: outside, in other words, the worlds of money and bureaucracy. Examples include a giant owl made by a group of farmers, customized cars, doodles in the dust on the back of vans, a painting of Keith Richards on the back of a truck, a giant motorized elephant, gurning competitions. It's a wonderful project, because what it proves is that the free spirit is very much alive. It means, actually, that against all the odds, boredom has not completely destroyed us.

What can we do to fight boredom? Well, the very same system that has created it also promises to relieve us of it. We are bored by work, and then advertising promises to take our boredom away, once we have handed over our cash. This is called leisure, and the word is derived from the Latin '*licere*', meaning 'to be permitted'. Leisure, then, is what we are allowed to do in our 'spare time'. And it costs. In the UK, vast shops called Virgin Megastores sell piles and piles of prerecorded music and films. In their advertising, they claim to be mounting an attack on boredom. But we shouldn't allow them to relieve our boredom for us. We have delegated the relief of boredom; we have shirked our responsibility for dealing with it. In other words, we hand over our creativity to the professional musician or film-maker. We pay someone else to alleviate our boredom. We bore ourselves in order to earn the money that we will later spend in trying to de-bore ourselves. That absurd modern trend called Extreme Sports springs to mind. In order to feel alive, because most of the year we feel dead, we hurl ourselves from a bridge every few months. Falling off a bridge, or a few seconds of thrills, is thus supposed to compensate for a whole year of boredom. And the freedom to hurl ourselves from a bridge while tied to an elastic band is held up as one of the great triumphs of modern capitalism.

This whole universe of boredom is precisely what was being attacked by the Sex Pistols. I agree absolutely with Johnny Rotten – I don't want a holiday in the sun. I refuse your paltry offer of two weeks on a beach (boring leisure) as a break from fifty weeks in the office (boring work). In *Lipstick Traces*, rock 'n' roll critic Greil Marcus brilliantly relates the Dada movement to the Situationist movement, and both to punk. What they have in common is the rage against boredom, the desire, simply, to live. What all three movements share is the passionate belief that anyone can do it. We can all be creative and we can all be free. The first number of *Internationale Situationiste* announced in June 1958 that the world was about to change 'because we don't want to be bored . . . raging and ill-informed youth, well-off adolescent rebels lacking a point of view but far from lacking a cause – boredom is what they all have in common. The Situationists will execute the judgement contemporary leisure is pronouncing against itself.' Punk was about putting creativity back into the hands of the people; anyone can do it, they said and, to prove it, here are the three chords you need to write a song: E, A and B7. Do it yourself.

Well, I can go one better than that. Instead of the guitar, I urge you to take up the ukulele. This four-stringed marvel is very cheap, very portable and very easy to play. It is therefore even more punk than the guitar. Here are the three chords you need to play most songs:

Get a uke and you will never be bored again. You could even make some extra cash by busking. The uke is freedom. Indeed, the Ukulele Orchestra of Great Britain's first album is called *Anarchy in the Ukulele*, and aptly titled it is too.

Behind the attack on boredom is a radical desire to take control of our lives back from the giant organizations to whom we have more or less willingly entrusted ourselves. This is an act of gross irresponsibility on our part. But it is not too late. We simply need to discover our own creativity. The simple way to avoid boredom is to make stuff; already, there are the glimmerings of a new movement in this area, to which the success of US magazine *Ready Made* (www.readymademag.com) bears witness. My heart also soars when I see skateboarders. Having worked in a skateboarding shop for a year, I know what a radically creative and positive pursuit skateboarding is. It is a self-governing movement, a federation, with its own magazines, fanzines, competitions and businesses, all displaying a high level of ingenuity, independence and creativity. One of the latest companies on the scene is the brilliantly named Death Skateboards, who have the equally effective slogan, 'Death to Boredom', and three cheers for that.

PLAY THE UKULELE

3 *The Tyranny of Bills and the Freedom of Simplicity*

Despite previous reminders, our records show that we have still not received payment for your electricity bill. Your account details will now be passed to our debt collection representatives who will visit your premises to disconnect your electricity supply or install a pre-payment meter at your premises.
Letter to the author from Steve Hayfield,
Director of Revenue Management, SWEB, 2005

A liability order for non payment of the sum of £875.40 was issued against you by the West London Magistrates Court on 28.07.2005.
Letter to the author from Local Taxation Division, Hammersmith and Fulham, 'Serving our Community'

We have caught 172 evaders in your area in the last three months alone. Despite sending several reminders, we note that your address is still unlicensed . . . if you are using a television illegally, there is now a very real chance you could be taken to court and fined up to £1,000.
Letter to the author from Ross McTaggart, TV Licensing Enforcement Manager, 2005

Cultivate simplicity, Coleridge.
Letter to Coleridge from Charles Lamb, 1796

Every day, an avalanche of oppression lands on our doormats. Brown envelopes everywhere. Menacing typefaces. Plastic windows. Letters in red, purple, black. Requests for more money, generally printed in large type and in bold colours for the really stupid. The 'cogs tyrannic', as Blake put it, of bureaucratic machines roll on. If only we could escape from all these bills, we think, then we could take these weights off our feet and fly around wherever we wished.

The already enormous cost of everyday life is increased when you are lazy, like me. There is a tax on being disorganized. Those of us who want to live free, live idle, live, have a tendency – this tendency is labelled 'irresponsible' by the sensible people – to ignore all the bills, parking tickets, tax demands, bank statements, mobile phone bills and the rest of the unutterably hideous flotsam of modern life. We stuff them in a drawer, we postpone payment, we delay and procrastinate. We have better things to do, like blowing smoke rings at the ceiling.

But if you delay your payment, the bills start turning ever more frightening colours and the tone becomes gradually more threatening with each new reminder. In the phrase of the satirist Ian Vince, the letters are composed in a 'patronizing yet vaguely authoritarian manner'. The language is debased, ugly, cold, impersonal, guilt-inducing, and it really means: 'Get yourself together, you useless fool. You're letting the side down. Everyone else has paid. It's people like you who damage the whole system. Pull your socks up.'

The annual tax return exhibits a similar tone, a confusing mix of the helpful and the menacing. Here is a direct quote. First, there is the kindly, paternal note: 'If you need help, we are here – online, on the phone, or in person.' But this is immediately followed by the threat, printed in bold: **'If you make a false return you risk being charged penalties and interest.'**

And because of my tendency to neglect my financial affairs, I get stung with horrendous charges from the bank. The last couple of months, for example, have seen £300 deducted from my account for going over my overdraft limit, in some cases just for a day or two. And this is on top of their already punitive interest charges. I used to try to get these charges overturned and, occasionally, had some success. But now I can't be bothered. To write or phone and have any chance of getting through to someone who is not an automaton and then to succeed in claiming a refund – well, the chances seem too remote. So I don't even try. I merely make a half-hearted resolution to get myself sorted. Some deep, guilty part of me sees the charges as due punishment for my slackness. But then I read in the newspaper that my bank, HSBC, has just made an annual profit of nearly £10 billion. So it seems that they do more than handsomely from my uselessness around money.

The other day, the doorbell rang. It was Emma Brown (not her real name) from the Extable tax office. I sat down at the kitchen table with her. She explained that I owed £1,700, and if I couldn't pay it, then she would have to walk around the house looking at things, cars and tellies, to see if they could take them away. The word 'distraint' was mentioned. Now, I have no idea what 'distraint' means, but I do know that the word carries a palpable hint of menace. Luckily, I remembered that my accountant had recently told me I owed only £500 to the Inland Revenue. I checked my bank account and found that I had about £500 to go before I went over my overdraft limit. So she accepted a cheque for that amount and went on her way.

Now, I hadn't acted in a deliberately criminal fashion. I had simply been lazy, a trifle careless perhaps, absent-minded. But I was treated like a criminal. And everyone is at least a bit disorganized: you would have to be a robot not to be. The Nazis were well organized. So it is that all non-robots in society are attacked and fined. Nowhere is this self-hating process more evident than in the case of parking tickets. Woe betide the motorist who returns to their car ninety seconds late. They will be given a £30 fine. Neglect to pay this fine instantly, and it is doubled or tripled. I once ran up nearly a thousand pounds' worth of fines because I was late in reapplying for a residents permit, and it was only by going to a sort of tribunal, which I managed to sit through despite a crashing hangover, that I managed to get this fine reduced to £500.

Yes, they impose fines. The whole notion of a fine carries with it some memory of punishment for misdeeds. Rather than being a straightforward business transaction, or a legalized form of stealing, as it really is, a fine carries a moral component. A fine is something given by the authorities when you have done something wrong. God has punished you. If, for example, you are late with a tax return, then you are fined £100 – but by whose authority? If you don't buy a ticket for a train before you board, some companies make you pay the full, astronomical fare. And, of course, it's never anyone's fault. The system has a clever way of ducking responsibility for its own outrages. Probably the sheer scale of the companies works in their favour in this regard. 'I don't make the rules,' say our oppressors. 'I'm only following orders.' This chain of command exists to make us feel guilty if we get angry at a lowly clerk or call-centre operative and so renders us powerless.

In the Middle Ages, fines were imposed by the commune, the village, your local group, for transgressions of the rules. Medieval manorial records show that misdemeanours were constantly fined by the local community. 'John Aubrey did cause a nuisance by leaving his dungpile in the King's Highway. Fined 1s. But pardoned because a pauper.' The fine, though, was given by your neighbours, and the money went straight back into the communal pot, where it sat for communal works. Similarly in the case of the guilds: transgressions were fined, the money pooled and later used to host great feasts or dole out as alms. Now, the principle is the same – the fines will go to the council or local body. But the sheer scale of the institutions involved has removed any sense of collectivity or connection from the transaction: we simply feel aggrieved and hard done by. When I was in the magistrates' court the other day, waiting for my hearing on a charge of driving without insurance, a young couple entered. The man opened the door to one of the courtrooms, shut it and then bellowed out to his girlfriend: 'It's that old slag again.' There is no sense of involvement in the process of justice: for most, it is simply a case of the busybodies in authority – the old slags – wagging their fingers at the reckless youth.

Needless to say, it doesn't work the other way around. We are completely powerless to impose fines on the companies that have served us if they foul up in some way, which they often do. It's a one-way contract, designed to benefit the big guy and rob the little guy. Stealing from the poor and powerless is easy. As John Ruskin puts it in *Unto This Last*: 'The ordinary highwayman's . . . form of robbery – of the rich, because he is rich – does not appear so often to the old merchant's mind; probably because, being less profitable and more dangerous than the robbery of the poor, it is rarely practised by persons of discretion.' Truly it is easier to rob the poor: just look at Tesco's.

Ah, order! I have been trying and failing to get organized my whole life. I fail to invoice for money that is owed to me; I fail to chase up late payment; as a result, I lose and big companies win. It's true that the odds are stacked against us: *you* are alone at home, the poor poet, with your laptop and telephone, trying to do everything on your own. *They* have whole departments staffed with grimly professional drudges devoted to fobbing you off and avoiding you and frightening you into giving them your money. I think one problem is that we have been brought up to believe in the idea of a job, a salaried position in which your money worries are taken care of for you. We are dependent on employers.

We do not have the freelance mindset which is so important

to the freedom-seeker, the mindset that tells you to look after yourself. When you choose to live without nine-to-five working, you have to be better organized with regards to money.

G. K. Chesterton wrote an essay on the relationship between organization and efficiency: 'We have often been told that organization means efficiency,' he writes. 'It would be far truer to say that organization means inefficiency.' He argues that large organizations are necessarily and by their very nature inefficient because of the endless human chains involved. The bigger the organization, the more there is to go wrong. The small set-up is more efficient, he says. The most efficient way of producing a cabbage, for example, is to grow it yourself. It is more efficient to grow a tree for wood outside your front door than to rely on oil which is mined in Saudi Arabia, made into gas in a refinery somewhere, then piped through politically unstable countries until it finally reaches your house.

Book-keeping should be part of every freedom-seeker's self-sufficient education. Jenny Uglow's study of Enlightenment pioneers, *The Lunar Men* (2002), reveals that the sons and daughters of great men such as Erasmus Darwin and Joseph Priestley were taught book-keeping as a matter of course. This enabled them to look after their own affairs and avoid being at the mercy of those who cash in on chaos. Gandhi did this. It sounds extremely tedious, I know, but in his battles against the authorities and fights for freedom, he found it helpful to keep good accounts. But perhaps you can do simple things like writing down everything you have spent at the end of the day. It's astonishing how much this helps in keeping track.

My friend Dan Kieran has hit out against direct debits: he sees them as the enemy. Again, the direct-debit system profits from the lazy and disorganized. The *Sun* newspaper recently reported that £500 million a year goes out in direct debits which we have forgotten to cancel; in other words, we are no longer getting the service but we are still paying for it. So Dan will pay his bills by cheque or cash. This is a surprisingly difficult move to pull off, not least because the companies devote so much direct marketing to convincing you of the benefits of direct debit and, at first sight, it might seem foolish to think otherwise: surely direct debits make your life easier, because you do not have the hassle of receiving bills and writing cheques. But, in actual fact, the small act of taking responsibility for your bills by going back to the old-fashioned method of writing a cheque and putting it in the post produces a satisfying sense of being in control. It makes the transaction more real. Direct debits appeal to the tragic reality that we seem to prefer comfort to responsibility.

Bill-paying is not really so painful when you finally get down to it. I let all the bills and things I have to do, all the sensible stuff, hang over me and oppress me with their weight. But I find that when I actually sit down to sort out the pile of stuff, the process only takes about five minutes. What was all that worry about, I ask myself. That really wasn't so bad.

Another tip comes from angler and idler Chris Yates. Once or twice a month, he has an 'admin day' on which he suspends all other activities and sits down with his bills and invoices and slowly gets through them.

If you can't face getting organized, though, you could always get radically disorganized. You could systematically remove all the organizations from your life, root them out and throw them away.

You could avoid getting involved in the first place. The obvious way to be free of bills is to cancel the services the bills ask payment for. No Sky TV, no mobile phone, no Internet, no car. Gandhi, again, recommended simple living to those on the path of freedom. For example, he realized that he was spending a lot of money on laundry bills. If he needed less money, he reasoned, he would be able to spend more time on his voluntary work. So he did his own laundry. A comparison can be made with public transport. Instead of forking out on season tickets for the underground, why not buy a bicycle and cycle to your place of work?

In the States, this way of thinking has a name: the simplicity movement. And what does simplicity mean? It means self-reliance. The more bills you pay, the more you are asking others to do things for you, which in another world, you would be doing yourself. They sell themselves to you, all these bill-pedlars, with the promise that they will make your life easier. But they don't. They make it more difficult. Reducing your dependence on external services provides time and money. You can even make your own energy. It's time to bring back medieval technology: windmills and water power. Collect your rainwater. Install solar panels. Wind, flowing water, rain and sun are all free gifts from nature. It makes sense to use them.

Put simply, if you avoid consuming the products of the system, then you will not have to pay for those products. This way, you will save not only the money that you used to spend on umpteen services, you will also save on the time and mental hassle spent dealing with all those bills. The oppression will gradually depart from your doorstep. And you won't have to work so hard. Life will become cheaper and easier.

It's fascinating to note, by the way, how much Gandhi, who was in some ways the opposite of an idler in that he practised self-denial, has in common with extreme pleasure-seekers, like, for example, the gloriously carefree actor and wild man Keith Allen, who lives his life completely untroubled by conscience, guilt or any of the bourgeois virtues. But he also is given to simple living and a rejection of money and authority. It seems that the mildest and the wildest have more in common than might first be apparent. Certainly it is often also the most extreme pleasure-seekers who turn into the most extreme practisers of self-denial. It's common for pop stars who have done everything – drink, drugs and all the rest of it – to give everything up and drink lukewarm water and lemon and go to bed at nine thirty. The two paths are closely linked. Myself, I am a moderate, I go for the middle path. I never want to give up drinking and I have a tendency to excess, but lately I have been drinking in moderation.

However, the bastards can catch up with you. I was recently in a meeting with Keith Allen at which he was pitching his autobiography to a publisher. 'And why do you want to write this book?' asked the publisher. 'Tax,' came Keith's honest reply.

It is perfectly possible to create an uncomplicated, job-free life. Artists Penny Rimbaud and Gee Vaucher started CRASS, the anarchist punk band of the eighties. Forty years ago they rented a tumbledown house just outside London and renovated it and filled the garden with flowers, fruit, vegetables, sheds and arbours for quiet repose. Thanks to an open-house policy, which has ensured a steady flow of helpful residents and guests, they have been able to develop the house and grounds to a high standard with very little money. People power replaced cash. They keep things simple, they don't need jobs, and that gives them acres and acres of free mind-space to follow their own paths through life, to think, read, write, talk, drink, make art. Their income is virtually nothing, but they do exactly what they want and this, it seems to me, is a tremendous achievement. It proves that money and freedom are by no means synonymous. Gee said to me, 'I don't think I've ever paid tax. How much do you need to earn? £5,000 a year? I don't earn anything like that.' And a more bill-free and liberated household I have never seen.

CANCEL DIRECT DEBITS

4 Reject Career and All Its Empty Promises

Nowadays ambition and the love of a job well done are the indelible mark of defeat and of the most mindless submission.
Raoul Vaneigem, *The Revolution of Everyday Life*, 1967

There isn't a job good enough for me. There isn't a job good enough for anyone.
S. L. Lowndes, letter to the *Sunday Times*, 1982

Belief in the abstract invention 'career' is a middle-class affliction. The lower orders, wisely, don't quite have the same faith in progress and self-betterment as the bourgeois classes and neither do members of the aristocracy. The aristos are at the top, so they've got nowhere to go. Paradoxically, this gives them a humility that is lacking in the successful meritocrats of the middle classes. If you are to the manor born, then you do not have the self-satisfaction and pride of the self-made man. And at the bottom, the people don't see the point in striving for mortgages and security. But the middle classes as we know them today, the heirs of the Puritan tradition of money-making and self-denial, have elevated 'career' into the epicentre of their daily struggle. And now more than ever before, the middle classes attempt to impose their career ethic on everyone else. This is called 'government'.

The idea of a career is that it follows an upward path to some ever-vanishing point above you. It is the quest for self-perfection and the secular version of the Protestant's search for salvation. Career is a Puritan concept, it's a sort of lonely pilgrimage. It is a pilgrim's progress. Governments sell themselves by promoting the idea of 'equal opportunities for everyone to make the best of themselves' when really what they mean is 'equal opportunities for every slimebag to rat on his friends and colleagues in order to worship the false god of career advancement'. Your career is supposed to be something more than just a job: it defines and limits you, and it supposedly provides your creative and competitive fulfilment. Career is not just how you earn your bread; it is your life. But career advancement tends to be based on the model of survival of the fittest. In other words, your promotion depends on some other guy not getting promoted or even getting sacked. The competitive principle applied to work means that your success is achieved at the cost of someone else's failure. Big companies are hotbeds of intrigue and plotting for this reason. You start out doing work experience, you graduate to being bossed around by idiots, you become idiotic and, then, if all works out well, you end up being the idiot who bosses other people around. 'The carrot of happier tomorrows has smoothly replaced the carrot of salvation in the next world. In both cases, the present is always under the heel of oppression,' writes Vaneigem.

Meanwhile, your salary rises, and you buy bigger cars and houses, thus feeding other people's careers. Career precisely reflects the dynamics of other modern myths: it is a greedy monster, never satisfied, always wanting more. And career encourages what I consider to be a terribly unnatural self-specialization: in our urge to compete, we tend to try to become very good at one small thing to the exclusion of all others. This is called professionalism but could be more accurately labelled 'being useless'. The other day I asked my dentist if he was thinking of retiring soon. He said, no, because he wouldn't know what else to do. 'The problem with being a dentist is that you end up not being able to do anything else.' And if you can't do anything else, you become dependent on other people to fill your needs: culture is produced by experts, music by bands working for record companies, education by expert teachers, medicine by expert doctors. We are disabled. It will soon be difficult to put up a shelf without a degree in shelf-putting-up.

The dangers of such overspecialization were analysed in the 1970s by Ivan Illich. In such books as *The Right to Useful Unemployment*, Illich saw the professions as literally disabling. Every bit of power we hand over to a professional is a bit less power for ourselves:

I propose to call the mid-twentieth century the Age of Disabling Professions. I choose this designation because it commits those who use it. It exposes the anti-social functions performed by the least challenged providers: educators, physicians, social workers and scientists. Simultaneously, it indicts the complacency of citizens who have submitted themselves to multi-faceted bondage as clients.

The 'bondage of the client' is a powerful notion. To submit to the professionalism of another is to admit that you are weak in a particular area. So we cannot blame an external authority for our lack of freedom, because we are the ones who have given them this power over us or, in Illich's words, 'submitted ourselves'.

And very depressing it is that women, too, have fallen for the career myth. 'My career is really important to me,' say the solipsistic new career ladies. How on earth bossing around a little coterie of idiots at Asda can be more important than playing with your kids, hanging out with your friends and family or doing creative things at home is completely beyond me. Over the last hundred years or so, women have equated career with liberation. To escape the perceived boredom, tyranny and powerlessness of domestic life, which was certainly a reality in Victorian times, they have sought out work which will provide money and fulfilment. That is the promise. But what is the reality? As G. K. Chesterton wittily put it, 'I meet women who say they refuse to be dictated to, and they go and get a job as a stenographer.' Now, I am not saying that women should not escape oppression at home and seek freedom, autonomy, creative fulfilment, financial independence and so forth, but I am saying that these things are unlikely to be found in conventional full-time jobs and careers. Instead, it is surely better to create your own job.

In a recent edition of the *Idler*, we ran a piece from the well-known broadcaster Joan Bakewell. She wrote that she had made a conscious decision early in her working life to avoid having a career. She had no desire to become imprisoned by climbing up the corporate ladder at the BBC. Instead, she says, she found the thing that she wanted to do and just carried on doing that. In her chosen field, the idea of endless, unlimited progress didn't apply. Progress is a tyrant. Freeing yourself from a career-based model of working means freeing yourself from other people's expectations. Career is a path set down for you by some outside authority, whereas the truly free make their own path through the woods.

In *The Uses of Literacy* (1957), Richard Hoggart notes that ambition, competition and ideas of advancement are often absent from working-class attitudes to work, or at least they were in the fifties:

> Once at work there is for most no sense of career, of the possibilities of promotion. Jobs are spread around horizontally, not vertically; life is not seen as a climb, nor work as the main interest in it. There is still a respect for a good craftsman. But the man on the next bench is not regarded as an actual or potential competitor . . . 'keen types' are mistrusted.

The notion invades us that it is really only worth doing anything if it makes money or leads to recognition in the world. Mothers with children start to feel like their lives are being sucked up by childcare and domestic toil and that motherhood is not valued by their peers. You are only someone if you have a job.

Career is just posh slavery. And career is an institutionalized putting-off, a paradise deferred. We hold the abstract notion of a career in our heads as a kind of yardstick. Sometimes we are doing well against our self-imposed imagined career path; sometimes we are doing badly and other people's careers seem to be going better. We use career as a stick to beat ourselves with. And always we have our eyes on the next rung up the ladder.

But what is the alternative? Can we go it alone? Become our own boss? The gloomy Victorian poet and critic Matthew Arnold was, like many, many others of his generation, appalled at the nineteenth-century's elevation of work to a sort of religious faith. But it seemed to him that on the other path, the path of freedom, madness lay. The following extract is from a depressing poem called 'A Summer Night', where Arnold compares the two options:

> For most men in a brazen prison live,
> Where, in the sun's hot eye,
> With heads bent o'er their toil, they languidly
> Their lives to some unmeaning taskwork give,
> Dreaming of nought beyond their prison-wall.
> And as, year after year,
> Fresh products of their barren labour fall
> From their tired hands, and rest
> Never yet comes more near,
> Gloom settles slowly down over their breast;

And the rest, a few,
Escape their prison and depart
On the wide ocean of life anew.
There the freed prisoner, where'er his heart
Listeth, will sail;

And then the tempest strikes him; and between
The lightning-bursts is seen
Only a driving wreck,
And the pale master on his spar-strewn deck
With anguish'd face and flying hair
Grasping the rudder hard,
Still bent to make some port he knows not where,
Still standing for some false, impossible shore.
And sterner comes the roar
Of sea and wind, and through the deepening gloom
Fainter and fainter wreck and helmsman loom,
And he too disappears, and comes no more.

Is there no life, but these alone?
Madman or slave, must man be one?

Madman or slave, must man be one? Today, freedom-seekers
tend to be scoffed at and labelled cranks. With wild hair and
staring eyes, the hardy adventurer can easily go crazy. And
certainly, the odds seem stacked against the freedom-seeker. We
might say: you don't have to be mad not to work here, but it
helps. We think of Nietzsche, of Kerouac, who went home to
his mother, sad and bitter. We think of poor Coleridge, lost to

laudanum, rejected by his former ally, Wordsworth. Indeed, Arnold's poem seems to be saying that turning into a mad-haired loon will be your fate if you try to be free. Oh, woe, torment, eternal care, suffering!

It also helps to learn that today's madmen were the normal ones in medieval societies. In the early days, Christianity had opposed careers. 'Christianity tended to condemn all forms of *negotium*, all secular activity; on the other hand, it encouraged a certain *otium*, an idleness which displayed confidence in Providence,' writes medieval historian Jacques Le Goff in *Time, Work and Culture in the Middle Ages*. Yea, verily, idlers are more godly than toilers. Lazy men did not work because they trusted in God to bring them their daily bread. The country was full of begging friars. Unlike the Elizabethans and Tudors, the medievals were idle-friendly. The non-working mendicants played a vital role in society by offering people an outlet for their charity. It was a paradise for idlers.

Striving in your career is essentially anti-godly: it means that you are possessed of enough vanity to attempt to take your fate into your own hands. Laziness, on the other hand, puts you up there with the saints. 'The peasants' mistrust of the merchant and the noble's contemptuous haughtiness found a parallel and a justification on the ideological plane in the teaching of the Church,' writes the historian Aron Ja Gorevich in an essay on the medieval merchant. Career, then, is a Protestant invention and an ideal for living that would have been impossible in the more fatalistic Catholic medieval society. Everyday life back then was about being creative and doing lots of different things. God was creative and so work should be creative. This is why gardening, baking bread and brewing beer were the earliest forms of work to be approved by the Church. And when life was lived around the seasons, before electric light came along to make everything boring, life was rich and full of variety.

Looked at from a Taoist or existential point of view, career is a complete waste of time and energy. If all action is futile, all is vanity, life is absurd, and the world is a big nothing, then why not laze around or do what you want? Career takes a potential source of joy and turns it into a duty, obligation, almost a penance. Do you really want to have written on your gravestone, 'He suffered all his life'?

In the inelegant language of today, I would say that one answer is multitasking. Drink and smoke at the same time! But, seriously, you may have a vocation, a calling at the centre of your work life. In my case, this vocation, or my gift, if you like, is journalism. Ever since I was eight, I have been writing articles and producing magazines. But this central vocation does not mean that I should pursue this one area of endeavour and neglect other aspects of human activity. I also enjoy growing vegetables, spreading straw on the earth, keeping chickens, making things of wood, shooting baked bean tins with my air rifle, playing Pokémon with my kids, playing the ukulele. I don't do these things for money or career. I do them for their own sake. I find that three hours of paid work each day is enough to keep the wolf from the door. The rest of the day is given up to unpaid work or unpaid play.

To return self-sufficiency and creativity to our lives, we might operate some sort of business from home, a cottage industry, a creative production into which we can put as much or as little time and energy as we like, as much as suits us at a particular time in our lives. 'Learn a craft' is what I suggest to young writers who contact the *Idler*: carpentry or blacksmithing or gardening or upholstery; such pursuits sit alongside the life of the mind very well. It is wise to reject utterly as a piece of bourgeois propaganda the oppressive aphorism 'jack of all trades and master of none'. No: you can do lots of things. You can chop wood *and* carry water *and* write poems. You can combine small-holding with software design. One *Idler* reader is a classical tuba player who is also a trained plasterer. He loves both and both earn him an income. Why limit yourself to one small field?

One unhelpful solution thrown up by modern society is the dreadful aim 'work–life balance'. Oh, horrors! Quite apart from being an ugly, awkward and vulgar little phrase, there is some-thing rotten about the whole concept because it implies that work is bad and life is good. Well, make work good, make work into a creative pleasure, and you don't have to worry about balancing the good with the bad; all will be good. The idle utopia does not seek, with the trade unions, simply to cut down on unpleasant work. It aims to harmonize work and life into one happy whole.

Careers don't allow us to be fully ourselves; careers take as an index of success money and status rather than pleasure in work and creativity. 'Vocation', on the other hand, means 'calling', and it is a task that earns you a living and which you enjoy doing. In my case, my vocation is journalism; that is, communication. Eric Gill's was as a stone-carver, Blake's as an engraver, John Lennon's was writing songs, and so on. The vocation at the centre of your life does not mean that you do not do other things. A stone-carver might well write poetry, clean the house, make things out of wood and weed the vegetable patch as well as carve stone. But stone-carving is at the centre of his working life and it is through stone-carving that he makes a living.

We have a duty to look into our hearts and discover our vocation, find our gift. Once we have done this, we will find that other parts of life follow quite naturally. If we put vocation at the centre of our lives and not money-making for its own sake, then we will find that money will come. According to Max Weber in *The Protestant Ethic and the Spirit of Capitalism*, the medieval Catholic ideology around work was: 'Everyone should abide by his living and let the godless run after gain.'

Vocation is a community-based idea of work, it is a giving experience, whereas career is a selfish and competitive version of how to work. Vocation is steady and flat, whereas career is an upwardly sloping curve, stretching into infinity. With a sense of work as vocation, we can work steadily and happily.

A wonderfully positive notion of human work was given to me by the artist Joe Rush. In the 1980s, Joe was among the founders of a renegade artistic group called the Mutoid Waste Company, whose vocation was to create fantastic sculptures out of old bits of scrap metal which they found lying around. They would take an old beaten-up car and turn it into something magical and wonderful, a giant insect or a dinosaur, a skull or a bird. They lived the life of the mendicant friar, travelling to festivals and living in squats all over Europe. Their simple message was 'Be creative.' Joe's notion is that we are all born with a gift, and that it is up to us to find that gift and then explore it. 'You're gifted,' he says. 'It is a gift to you . . . and if there's anyone sitting out there getting jealous about it, it means they've not really gone out and looked for what their gift is.'

And how do you find your vocation, your gift? The answer is simply to do nothing for as long as you possibly can. In the same way that wise gardeners advise that the first step when taking over a new garden is to do nothing for a year, in order to see what grows there and only then to design your own unique, useful and beautiful garden, so I would advise taking a few months off, or even a year, if you can manage it. Most of the time we are too busy to step back and find out what we would like to do. Create some time for yourself and things will gradually become clear. Above all, stop trying. Career is a try-hard notion. The free of spirit have stopped trying and instead let things happen.

FIND YOUR GIFT

5 Get out of the City

For I was reared
In the great city, pent 'mid cloisters dim,
And saw nought lovely but the sky and stars.
Coleridge, 'Frost at Midnight', 1797

Escaping the city has been a long-cherished romantic dream. From the *Bucolics* of Virgil to the Romantic poets, and today in pop songs and folk songs, it's obvious that we all yearn for peace and that we're all trying to get back into the Garden of Love. The pastoral vision is there in the songs of Peter Doherty, with his talk of Albion and Arcadia and the shepherd's song. With good friends, good food and beautiful surroundings, out of the hurry and bustle of the metropolis, far from tube trains, from commuting, from bombs, from advertising, we could be happy. Wordsworth and Coleridge's revolutionary collection of poetry, *Lyrical Ballads* (1798),

emerged from a rural retreat: Coleridge at Nether Stowey in the
Quantocks in the West of England, and Wordsworth and Dorothy
in nearby Alfoxden House. They were joined there briefly by the
radical John Thelwall, and the three were viewed with great suspi-
cion by the locals and indeed by the government, who sent a spy
(later christened 'Spy Nozy' by Coleridge in *Biographia Literaria*,
1817) to watch them. This is how Thelwall wrote of those few
months in his 'Lines written at Bridgwater' (1797):

> Ah! Let me, far in some sequestr'd dell,
> Build my low cot; and happy might it prove,
> My Samuel! Near to thine, that I might oft
> Share thy sweet converse, best belov'd of friends! –
> Long-lov'd ere known: for kindred sympathies
> Link'd, tho far distant, our congenial souls . . .
>
> And 'twould be sweet,
> When what to toil was due, to study what,
> And literary effort, had been paid,
> Alternate, in each other's bower to sit,
> In summer's genial season; or, when, bleak,
> The wintry blast had stipp'd the leafy shade,
> Around the blazing hearth, social and gay,
> To share the frugal viands, and the bowl
> Sparkling with home-brew'd beverage: – by our side
> Thy Sara, and my Susan, and perchance,
> Alfoxden's musing tenant, and the maid
> Of ardent eye, who, with fraternal love,
> Sweetens his solitude

Mmm, I like the sound of that home-brew'd beverage. 'Alfoxden's musing tenant', by the way, is William Wordsworth, and the 'maid of ardent eye' his sister Dorothy. This sort of idyll is something that I have tried to create down here in our rented Devon farmhouse. With our own home pub and a larder full of ale, we invite friends to stay for good conversation and good drinking. It has occurred to me that my home pub really will be a haven of freedom, because now that smoking is to be banned in all public places, my pub, the Green Man, may be the only pub in England where smoking is encouraged.

Our poets and philosophers have always resisted the attempts by our political and commercial masters to impose robotic discipline.

As the Industrial Revolution dragged agonizingly on, it saw many and frequent protests against its effects in the form of attempts to establish ideal communities. These were efforts to create life along cooperative or communistic lines (and in those early days of political radicalism, the word 'communistic' had none of the nightmarishly centralized and grey associations it has today). William Morris, W. B. Yeats and D. H. Lawrence all dreamed of an earthly paradise, and it didn't generally involve living in a city. 'Wherever men have tried to imagine a perfect life,' wrote Yeats:

> they have imagined a place where men plough and sow and reap, not a place where there are great wheels turning and vomiting smoke . . . We wish to preserve an ancient ideal of life. Wherever its customs prevail, there you will find the folk

song, the folk tale, the proverb, and the charming manners that come from ancient culture . . . We must so live that we will make that old noble kind of life powerful amongst our people.

William Morris had a similar dream:

It seems to be nobody's business to try to better things – isn't mine you see, in spite of all my grumbling – but look, suppose people lived in little communities among gardens and green fields, so that you could be in the country in five minutes' walk, and had few wants, almost no furniture for instance, and no servants, and studied the (difficult) arts of enjoying life, and finding out what they really wanted: then I think that one might hope civilization had really begun.

In the 1970s, John Seymour had great success with his guidebook to living off the land, *Self-Sufficiency*. Like William Cobbett's *Cottage Economy* before it, Seymour's book is a work of positive philosophy and not merely a practical guide. Like Cobbett's, it is infused by his bloody-minded, independent and eccentric but wholly sane spirit. In Seymour's case, the decision to live off the land and escape the modern industrial system was taken for pragmatic reasons and was not done self-consciously. In his book *The Fat of the Land* (1961), he describes how he and his family were simply looking for a cheap way to live so he wouldn't have to do so much of his freelance journalism work. Getting out of the city, though, and living a country life, can be hard work. Rural isolation may seem romantic, but life is easier with friends and neighbours around. You need other people. In *Self-Sufficiency*, Seymour, like Yeats and Morris, dreams of a countryside society:

> I believe that if half a dozen families were to decide to be partially self-supporting, and settle within a few miles of each other, and knew what they were doing, they could make for themselves a very good life. Each family would have some trade or profession or craft, the product of which they would trade with the rest of the world. Each family would grow, rear or produce a variety of goods or objects which they would use themselves and also trade with the other families for their goods. Nobody would get bored doing their specialized art or craft, because they would not have to spend all day at it, but there would be a large variety of other jobs to do every day too. This partial specialization would set them free for at least some leisure: probably more than the city wage-slave gets, after he has commuted to and from his factory or office.

This is precisely my own hope for where I live: as the five houses in our hamlet gradually come up for sale, could I persuade friends to buy them and move down here? We could all have our own vegetable patches, some could have chickens, some pigs, some goats. You need friends and neighbours to do this sort of thing; to go it alone is too hard and too lonely. We could swap produce with each other and leave each other alone when we wanted to.

Ideally, you would bring an element of the city into the countryside. For some, cities are liberating. In the late twelfth century, a monk called Richard of Devizes wrote disapprovingly of the dissipation of London: 'No one lives in it without falling into some sort of crime . . . the number of parasites is infinite. Actors, jesters, smooth-skinned lads, Moors, flatterers, pretty boys, effeminates, pederasts, singing and dancing girls, quacks, belly dancers, sorceresses, extortioners, night-wanderers, magicians, mimes, beggars, buffoons: all this tribe fill all the houses.' Sounds fantastic, and not dissimilar from Dean Street these days on a Thursday night – in fact, it sounds identical, which is why I value my nights out there.

I grew up in London, went to school in London and spent the first twelve years of my working life in London with the night-wanderers, beggars and buffoons, and I enjoyed it very much. It was only towards the end that I started to find it limiting my behaviour. Your view of the city depends, I suppose, on whether you view commercial activity as liberating or imprisoning. In contrast to Richard of Devizes' appalled description of London above, a contemporary wrote approvingly of its commercial activity: 'The City of London . . . spreads its fame wider, sends its wealth and wares further, and lifts its head higher than all the others . . . the citizens of London are renowned beyond those of all other cities for their fine manners, raiment and table.' It's interesting to note medieval priorities here: refined manners, fine clothes and good food are right at the top.

Well, despite the undeniable attractions of the sorceresses and belly-dancers, and despite the wealth, I eventually decided that the country life beckoned. I found that, despite the inevitable hardships and bad weather and all the rest of it, what we did have was time and space. It's also easier to live on less money in the country, and that means less work. There is no doubt that my family is less money-orientated than before; the city seems to suck the notes from your pockets as you walk down its seductive streets. It's easy, I suppose, to be good in the country, because, as Oscar Wilde wrote, there are no temptations there.

City-lovers complain about the silence in the countryside. They miss the sirens. They complain, too, about the way everyone knows what you're up to. In the city, you can live with a certain level of privacy and anonymity. It's also undeniable that it's much easier in the city to find groups of like-minded individuals. The Arts and Crafts movement in the UK, while it adored the countryside, had strong links with London, and William Morris, for example, spent much time there on business.

It is possible to do both. You can create a healthy dialogue between country and city. You can retreat into the countryside to reflect and then come back into the city to act and to sell. You need the city in order to trade your goods, whether that is writing or stone-carvings or carrots. As St Thomas Aquinas says in the *Summa Theologica*: 'Both these lives are lawful and and praiseworth – namely, that a man withdraw from the society of other men and observe abstinence; and that he associate with other men and live like them.' The masons in medieval times, for example, would spend the winters on their smallholdings and the brighter months on the road working and trading. Grand country families of the eighteenth century spent the winters in London. The problem with cities is not the fact that they are cities but the fact that they are too big. The scale is simply dizzying, it is impossible. Any journey from one place to another within London, for example, seems to take an hour – although that problem is simply solved by the bicycle: sell the car, buy a bike.

A small city, though, can offer a fantastic degree of liberty. The medieval age offers us the example of the great free city states. From the twelfth century on, there was a giant democratic movement all over Europe to create cities of around 50,000–100,000 people which were self-governing and free of intrusion from the nobles. They were created by the new burghers who had grown fed up with the restrictions of life on the manor precisely for the purpose of living free. This culture is explored by Prince Peter Kropotkin in *Mutual Aid* (1902). It's a fantastically inspiring book by a great man. Born in 1842 to aristocratic parents, the iniquities of the serf culture in which he was raised turned him into a revolutionary and, from 1917, he lived mainly in Europe, including long spells in the UK. Oscar Wilde described Kropotkin as one of the two genuinely happy men he had ever met. *Mutual Aid* was published when Kropotkin was living in Bromley, Kent – a rather twee and suburban address for one of the greatest anarchist thinkers of all time.

In *Mutual Aid*, Kropotkin argues that medieval cities were deliberately founded on what would today be considered dangerously radical principles. They were set up in order to escape the rule of the nobles and to create an ideal working and creative community in which fairness, equality and helping each other were the dominant ethical principles. Rather in the same way that we are motivated by the values of competition and profit, the medievals taught the value of cooperation. They were heavily influenced by the rediscovery of Aristotle's *Ethics* (Aristotle was referred to as 'the philosopher', as if there were only one worth talking about) and by the Sermon on the Mount. It's important to realize that the changes did not just happen of their own accord; they were based on a philosophy and then a deliberate attempt to implement and communicate this philosophy. These cities had up to around 50,000 inhabitants, and they were bursting with schools, hospitals, baths, workshops and the most wonderful architecture. Work was organized around the guilds system. The cities had a natural limit on growth, because they were walled. It is in their cathedrals that Kropotkin and other medieval fans like Ruskin saw the passionate creative spirit of the enterprise express itself most fully. This is how Kropotkin describes the genesis of the medieval city:

> With a unanimity which seems almost incomprehensible, and for a long time was not understood by historians, the urban agglomerations, down to the smallest burgs, began to shake off the yoke of their worldly and clerical lords. The fortified village rose against the lord's castle, defied it first, attacked it next, and finally destroyed it. The movement spread from spot to spot, involving every town on the surface of Europe, and in less than a hundred years free cities had been called into existence on the coasts of the Mediterranean, the North Sea, the Baltic, the Atlantic Ocean, down to the fjords of Scandinavia; at the feet of the Apennines, the Alps, the Black Forest, the Grampians, and the Carpathians; in the plains of Russia, Hungary and France and Spain. Everywhere the same revolt took place, with the same features, passing through the same phases, with the same results.

Wherever men had found, or expected to find, some protection behind their town walls, they instituted 'co-jurations', their 'fraternities', their 'friendship', united in one common idea, and boldly marching towards a new life of mutual support and liberty. And they succeeded so well that in three or four hundred years they had changed the very face of Europe. They had covered the country with beautiful sumptuous buildings, expressing the genius of free unions of free men, unrivalled since for their beauty and expressiveness; and they bequeathed to the following generations all the arts, all the industries, of which our present civilization, with all its achievements and promises for the future, is only a further development. And when we now look to the forces which have produced these grand results, we find them – not in the genius of individual heroes, not in the mighty organization of huge States or the political capacities of their rulers, but in the very same current of mutual aid and support which we saw at work in the village community, and which was vivified and reinforced in the Middle Ages by a new form of unions, inspired by the same spirit but shaped on a new model – the guilds.

In thirteenth-century Florence, there were seven major guilds and fourteen minor guilds, or *arti*, as they were called. There were the Guild of Judges and Notaries, the Guild of Dressers and Dyers of Foreign Cloth, the Guild of Wool Manufacturers, the Guild of Silk Manufacturers, the Guild of Bankers and Money-Changers, the Guild of Physicians and Apothecaries and the Guild of Furriers, and then there were the minor guilds – Butchers, Shoemakers, Tanners, Masons, Oil merchants, Linen-drapers,

Locksmiths, Armourers, Saddlers, Carpenters, Innkeepers, Blacksmiths, Wine merchants and Bakers – and all lived together and more or less in harmony in a sort of anarchistic state, with the heads of the guilds sitting for two months at a time on the governing body of the city.

Could we re-create cities of a similar sort today? Shouldn't every town planner and architect be forced to read *Mutual Aid*? Clearly, we need to find a town of 50,000 people, 50,000 freedom-seekers, put a wall around it, declare it an independent republic and get on with things on our own. The medieval cities demonstrated to Kropotkin that, left to our own devices, we can do a much better job of organizing our affairs than any government. As the travelling hillbilly, punk and skateboarder William Elliot Whitmore puts it: 'We really all do share these same ideals, and your average citizen is good, but it's our governments that fuck things up.' The medieval-city movement also shows that a state of affairs where authority and competition are the organizing principles is not an inevitability, as is commonly thought by your pub philosopher.

What I would like to see, and what actually existed in medieval England, is a country consisting of small autonomous federations, of towns, villages, communes and hamlets. The very idea of central organization is absurd because it makes no allowance for difference across the country, different attitudes to life, different culture, different language, different customs, different climates, even different clothes. Centralization means uniformity, and that means boredom, and that means death (see Chapter 2). Imagine colonizing a small village or town with your mates and creating your own free society.

I wonder what sort of a change or crisis could lead to a new Western world and a new way of thinking? In the seventies, alternative thinkers used to talk almost hopefully of an oil crisis, but the oil still seems to be pumping out of the earth. When will it stop? I, personally, would welcome an oil crisis, because it might lead us back to wood as a source of fuel – wood, which is endlessly renewable; wood, which grows on trees, which is harvested, not mined. (I even like the idea of going around on horses and getting from country to country by boat.) As fuel costs rise, a demand for localized energy production has increased, and solar panels, heat pumps and fuel-cell companies are doing very well. Medieval technology such as water wheels and windmills are also coming back into vogue. We are beginning to realize that ideas such as renewable energy, far from being cranky, are simply sensible. And cheaper than relying on the hugely inefficient national grid. I imagine that producing some of your own electricity must inspire a feeling much like that of producing some of your own vegetables: a very pleasant and satisfying sense of freeing yourself, in part at least, from dependence on the centralized systems of distribution. Solar panels are anarchy in action.

Now, it's also actually perfectly possible to create a country life in the city or in the town, when by 'country life' one means, in the jargon of today, a sustainable life. My town-dwelling friend Graham Burnett introduced me to the Permaculture movement. This is an approach to living which originated in Australia with a man called Bill Mollison. The idea behind Permaculture is to set up systems of living that do not exploit the earth or other people, which coalesce with nature, fit in with your everyday life and your environment and are also low on hard work. Permaculture really is idleness in action. The *Permaculture* magazine, for example, is full of articles about people who have turned their suburban back gardens into veritable forests of fruits or city-dwellers who have produced all their vegetables from an allotment. It is a practical approach to life because it does not recommend that we all move to a smallholding in Wales and become self-sufficient. It shows how you can be free in the city. You can, for example, get an allotment. You can grow stuff on your windowsill. Dig up the bourgeois lawn and plant raspberries, gooseberries, blueberries, peach trees and pear trees. The other very appealing part of the philosophy is that it favours reflection over action: after the initial creation of a system, the highly productive Permaculture plot will largely look after itself. Permaculture is strongly opposed to hard work, because hard work can often mean excessive interference with nature. Therefore, it's ideal for idlers. I recommend it.

To regenerate our cities, all we need to do is to scatter seeds around the place. When you go for a walk, take seeds with you, poppies, rainbow chard, rocket. Plant them among the weeds in patches of wasteland. See what happens.

Here is John Seymour again:

> I can imagine, one day in the future, a highly sophisticated society, some of the members of which would live in towns of a human size, others scattered about in a well-cared-for countryside, all interdependent and yet in some ways very independent, the towns contributing to the country – the country to the towns. This would not be a very mechanized or industrialized society,

but a society in which the real arts of civilization are carried on at a high level, in which literature, music, drama, the visual arts, and the crafts that lead to the good life, are all practised and appreciated by all the people. This would not be 'going back', whatever that means. It would, if you like to think in terms of such imaginary progressions, be 'going forward', and into a golden age. Periclean Athens wasn't such a bad place, give or take a few slaves. If we could find a way to achieve the same result without slaves, we could have achieved something very worthwhile.

When it came to agriculture, the medievals were Permaculturists: systems were sustainable, there was no Nitram, no intensification: farms were mixed, land ownership was widely diffused, smallholdings were common, everything was recycled and reused without the help of local councils. Money stayed in local economies rather than being sucked out of it by supermarkets. There were no motor cars. Houses were self-built. Disputes were solved locally. There was no plastic packaging and therefore no waste. It was a Permaculturist's paradise. We now have the opportunity to take all the good ideas from medieval living without the hierarchies and the dominance of the clergy. One practical tip I can offer, by the way, is to carry a little pocket knife with you at all times. It's amazing how often this comes in handy whether in town or country. To have a small weapon on your person also gives one a very nice sense of independence and invulnerability. It must be like the feeling of having a sword at your side, a tradition that died away in the late eighteenth century.

So, once you have adjusted your attitude to your own life, whether we live merrily in the city or in the country doesn't really matter in the end. You don't have to leave the city to escape city life.

RENT AN ALLOTMENT

6 End Class War

Numquam libetas gratior extat
Quam sum rege pio.
(If to sweet freedom you would cling, submit unto a righteous king.)
Claudian, AD 370–c. 404

When Adam delved and Eve span
Who was then the gentleman?
traditional slogan of the rebellious medieval peasant

Our contemporary class system roughly reflects the tripartite system that was developed in early medieval times. The three classes were the peasants, the clerics and the nobles, or the *laboratores*, *oratores* and *bellatores*. The peasants worked on the land, the clerics read, wrote, reflected, prayed and looked after the poor, while the nobles went off and fought. Now, I would have been quite happy to be a member of any of those classes. They all sound a lot better than the options we have today: working class, i.e. doing a boring job and getting into debt; middle class, i.e. doing a boring job and getting into bigger debt; or upper class, i.e. lounging around, arguing with members of your family and gradually selling off your land and property to pay tax bills.

Yes, I would have been happy to be a peasant, a cleric or a noble. I suppose I am closest to the cleric in that my main occupations are reading and writing, but I like to think that I am a bit peasant-like in that I enjoy working the land in the form of my vegetable patch, and also a bit noble-like in that I enjoy lounging around and doing nothing. In one person, then, I aim to bring together the best aspects of each class. I suppose this is what is meant by bohemian.

The funny thing about the medieval system is that there was actually more equality, not less, than there is today. When you look at Manor rolls from 1100 to 1500, what is striking is that, economically speaking, there was a high degree of equality. Apart from the Lord of the Manor, everyone else was on the same level. This is the peculiar paradox of the medieval version of authority: it created more freedom. The clerics, of course, inspired by Jesus, insisted on the point that all men were equal in God's eyes; the prince was no better than the peasant. This idea was preached constantly to both noble and peasant, thereby bringing humility to the noble and nobility to the peasant. Certainly, says medieval historian Jacques Le Goff, there was a 'halo' over any activity connected with the land. To till the earth was to be close to God. And in the democratic Troubadour culture of the South of France, many poets argued that nobility was a matter of character not of birth, and was therefore available to the peasant, the burgher or the aristocrat. In England bondsmen would buy their freedom, and peasants became landowning yeomen, the class that Chaucer's self-confident, prosperous and generous Franklin belonged to:

> It snewed in his hous of mete and drynke,
> Of alle deyntees that men koude thynke.

Bishops, even, were drawn from all social backgrounds. There was a good deal more social mobility than is generally ascribed to the period, particularly in the later Middle Ages. And the medieval middle classes, like Franklin, were of a different breed to today's bourgeois, because they valued their freedom, as historian M. H. Keen writes: 'The prosperity of solid men of middle rank had . . . a profound effect on the English national character. They were what enabled Englishmen to resist tyranny.'

These days, we all work too hard for other people, doing uncreative and boring things. We have submitted to the tyranny of the work ethic. Even some of the aristocrats have got jobs these days, and they seem quite proud of it. The rule of the bourgeois through Parliament is the rule of the strong by the bland and the weak and, through that terrible law whereby the weak can sometimes conquer the strong, the awful, mushy whirlpool created by puritanical middle-class parliamentarians threatens to suck us all into its hellish sludge. The working classes are encouraged to upsize and join the middle classes through hard toil, and the upper classes are encouraged to become dull democrats themselves, to take jobs, work and be boring!

Now, proper old-fashioned working-class attitudes, such as those described by Richard Hoggart in *The Uses of Literacy*, are positive: they are based on the importance in life of neighbourliness, fun and friends over work and career:

> Whatever one does, horizons are likely to be limited; in any case, working-class people add quickly, money doesn't seem to make people happier, nor does power. The 'real' things are the human and companionable things – home and family affection, friendship and being able to say, 'Enjoy y'self': 'Money's not the real thing,' they say, and 'Life isn't worth living if y'sweating for extra money all t'time.' Working-class songs often ask for love, friends, a good home; they always insist that money does not matter.

These values to me are good values, and they are the ones under attack from the middle-classification of everything. Hoggart also points to a laudable live-for-the-moment attitude which contrasts with the 'sacrifice the now to the future' pension-planning attitude of middle-class life (brilliantly expressed, by the way, in 'She's Leaving Home' by the Beatles):

> . . . in general, the immediate and present nature of working-class life puts a premium on the taking of pleasures now, discourages planning for some future goal, or in the light of some ideal. 'Life is no bed of roses,' they assume; but 'Tomorrow will take care of itself': on this side the working-classes have been cheerful existentialists for ages . . . Pleasure is given high importance, sheets will

be mended rather than new ones bought but enough money will
be left for drinking and smoking . . .

Yes, yes, yes! As long as there's enough for beer and fags today,
then tomorrow can look after itself. I would rather have torn
sheets and a larder full of beer than be a teetotaller with new
bedlinen. I also love the providential attitudes described here.
And as for your plans for the future? Well: we all know the Jewish
joke: How do you make God laugh? Tell him your plans.

So, rather than class war, let's have class harmony, class
integrity, class respect, class peace. We have class but are not of
a class. We can help each other and learn from each other. I
happen to like posh people, in general. I like the aristocratic
tradition simply because so many aristocrats are anti-bourgeois.
They don't like work or, at least, they don't like what work has
become. There is still room up there for eccentricity and
difference. They look down on those who need to work and
instead they give themselves up to lying around doing nothing
– a noble pursuit, as I hope I have proved elsewhere – but they
will also get people together and do useful work in the community, they will patronize artists, open their doors, hold festivals
and be hospitable and charming, all of which are very important roles in a free society. I don't resent for a millisecond their
money or their houses, because I know that along with those
houses and that money goes an awful lot of hassle. I am grateful to them for looking after the splendid houses and gardens
and, if I can visit occasionally, then all well and good.

But our resentment makes it hard for us to escape. Resentment
can be a barrier to freedom. Whenever I give a talk about the

benefits of not working, a member of the audience always makes an enquiry, more or less politely put, about my class origins and whether I have a private income. The unspoken implication is 'It's all right for you to talk about being idle.' I explain that I do not have, nor have ever had, a private income, and that all the money I live on is earned by my own efforts in the marketplace. But, is that really anything to boast about? And why should we disregard someone's ideas if they do happen to have a private income? Many great intellectual breakthroughs and ideas and art and literature have come from the moneyed classes: Lord Byron, Marx and Engels, William Morris, Bertrand Russell – trustafarians all. Resentment of others – 'It's all right for you,' the feeling that life is just that little bit easier for everyone else around you – is the first manacle that must be cast off in the quest for freedom.

While I am an enemy of oppression and exploitation, I am not remotely in favour of dissolving all class boundaries. In doing so, you are left with a dreadful Protestant meritocracy, as there is in the States, where there is no excuse for not being a Master of the Universe, as Tom Wolfe described so well in *The Bonfire of the Vanities*. In actual fact, equality is a nonsense. Where all is equal, and there are equal opportunities for all, there is no excuse for failure. A class system will give you a built-in excuse for not bothering to work and simply enjoying life – if you need an excuse. And if you don't like the class you're in, move. One peasant, famously, became Pope. And being of a different class to another is not the same as being inferior to another: I am quite happy to belong to a different class to others, but I don't feel inferior to the upper classes or superior to the working classes.

It's actually terribly easy to escape from your class background

– whatever it is – by simply rejecting what the conventional, pre-prepared world has to offer and going off and creating your own world. This way, you will find like-minded comrades who are bound to you by their spirit rather than by their class background. There's no excuse for sitting around moaning about your lot. Yes, it might be true that terrible injustices have been done to you and your kind, but the way to escape the manacles of those injustices and to prevent their return in the future is not to moan about past trespasses but to rise above the whole thing and concentrate on living well. Bohemia can offer a way out of the strictures imposed by working- or middle- or upper-class backgrounds: each class, in its way, could be argued to be limiting to our freedoms. And in bohemian circles, lords and robbers mix with drunks, poets and musicians, people who have broken free of the ties that bind (if we allow them to do so).

The problem is not that people are different but that they do not respect differences. This is the problem with governments which claim to be ushering in a class-free society: what they really mean is a society where we are all the same – all robots, work-droids, automatons, like Charlie Chaplin in *Modern Times*. It's a society forged in their own tedious, colourless, gutless image.

Class difference adds colour to our lives. The knights and warriors and bishops have left wonderful works around the world for our delight: castles, gardens, churches. Children naturally seem to love kings and queens and stories of the knights of old. King Arthur was an aristocrat; he was not a Soviet bureaucrat. Monarchy can be fun. Robert Burton, in that brilliant seventeenth-century self-help manual and ramble *Anatomy of Melancholy*, outlines his own personal utopia, and he would actually keep class distinctions for the reason that it makes life more fun, varied and colourful. Burton attacks Plato's *Republic* for being boring:

> Plato's community in many things is impious, absurd, and ridiculous, it takes away all splendour and magnificence. I will have several orders, degrees of nobility, and those hereditary, not rejecting younger brothers in the meantime, for they shall be sufficiently provided for by pensions, or so qualified, brought up in some honest calling, they shall be able to live of themselves . . . my form of government shall be monarchical.

My utopia would probably include three levels of society, rather like medieval days, with knights, clerics and peasants. The warriors would be the aristocrats, and it would be their job to sit around doing nothing except for creating and tending beautiful gardens, having parties and festivals in their big houses, acting as patrons of the arts, and being hospitable, giving away food and beer. This is what the Eliot family of Cornwall do today. They use their splendid house and grounds as a meeting place and centre of artistic activity. The clerics would be the writers, poets, artists and so on. They would live like peasants, freely and self-sufficiently. And the peasants would be the craftsmen, the stonemasons, shoemakers, woodworkers, ceramic-makers, potters, blacksmiths. All three classes would be involved in the creation of music and architecture. The money-spenders, the thinkers and the craftsmen.

We would be able to use the aristocrats' libraries, wander round their gardens, swim in their pools. They would take over the role of the state and would do this in a personal way. No Arts Council, no Health and Safety inspectorate. We would bring back common land and common grazing. We would tear down the fences. We would need to de-enclose. Respect for difference would be the order of the day. There would be a prejudice against becoming robot-like, and we would pity efficiency and regularity. We would laugh at petty officials and drum them out of town. As Robert Burns wrote in 'The De'il's Awa' wi' th' Exciseman':

> We'll mak our maut, and we'll brew our drink,
> We'll laugh, sing, and rejoice, man;
> And mony braw thanks to the meikle black Deil
> That danc'd awa' wi' th' Exciseman

Federalism and respect. My way is not better than your way. No one thing is better than another. All things and all people are utterly different and utterly equal.

The real task is to find the enemy within, not without. As the beatnik thinker Alexander Trocchi put it, we need 'to attack the "enemy" at his base, within ourselves'. Class struggle itself feeds the middle class, because when you fight against something, you merely make it stronger. The answer is simply to ignore the things you don't like about the classes and concentrate on the things you do like about them. Class war is also a blind alley since it is a profoundly irresponsible attitude to life in that it says, 'If only those bastards hadn't screwed me, then everything would be OK.' Well, to an extent you allowed them to screw you, and you can choose not to be screwed. That way lies freedom.

It is our own complicity with the present way of organizing things that we must question. When we talk about anarchy, we do not mean a dissolution of order, a Mad Max environment where the most violent survive. We mean a decentralization of power; power to the people. D. H. Lawrence wrote that it is not a question of smashing the system but of putting a more humane one in its place: 'There must be a system; there must be classes of men; there must be differentiation: either that, or amorphous nothingness. The true choice is not between system and no-system. The choice is between system and system, mechanical or organic.'

It's interesting that he uses the word 'organic', which is today such a buzzword in foodie circles and as such easily dismissed as a middle-class fad. But 'organic' is a powerful word and, when we oppose it, as Lawrence does, with 'mechanical', its meaning becomes absolutely clear. Down with the robot, up with the human. Down with sameness, up with variety. Down with dependence, up with self-reliance. And so on.

As an idler and an anarchist, I love people from all classes who are fighting to be free. I love the aristocrats, I love the under-class and I love the bohemian bourgeoisie (of which I am one). I love the criminals and the drug addicts. If you want to join the elect, the colourful, the creative, it is very easy. Create your own life. Cast off resentment. Reject the idea of 'have-tos'. You don't have to do anything. You have free will. Exercise it.

BE BOHEMIAN

7 Cast Off Your Watch

The new movement is slowly, carelessly constructing an
alternative society. It is international, interracial, equisexual,
with ease. It operates on different conceptions of time and space.
The world of the future may have no clocks.
Tom McGrath, *International Times*, March 1967

Throw away your alarm clocks, I wrote in my previous book. Now I am asking you to throw away your watches, too. For some unfathomable reason, everyone seems to want an expensive watch. But isn't it mighty peculiar that what is in actual fact a symbol of slavery should also have become a status symbol? Wearing a watch indicates to others that you have bound yourself to the modern industrial tempo. Wearing an expensive watch means that you are proud of being bound in this way. It is, literally, a very expensive manacle. The watch is a golden handcuff. The bars of the cage are gilded.

We know from the historian E. P. Thompson and from Jay Griffiths, author of *Pip Pip: A Sideways Look at Time*, that our modern concept of time grew up alongside the consumer economy. In the early days, before anyone had thought of organizing and standardizing working practices, bells were used in monasteries to bring some structure to the daily round of praying, studying and gardening. Bells were later also used all over Western Europe to give notice of a local assembly. When you heard the bell, you were supposed to down tools, leave the fields and go into town for a meeting. Soon, clocks began to appear in the marketplace, with the function of imposing some kind of uniformity over working patterns. But time was still local and public. It was not the same time everywhere. Each town's clock would tell a different time, but each member of the community would share that different time. In a sense, with the public clock, time was free. It was free in the sense that you didn't have to buy a watch to know what the time was, because a public clock had been provided. And it was free because it was unique to the commune.

However, it is true to say that, even in the fourteenth century, we can see the beginnings of what Jacques Le Goff calls 'merchant time', the colonizing of time in order to make money more efficiently:

In 1355, the royal governor of Artois authorized the people of Aire-sur-la-Lys to build a belfry whose bells would chime the hours of commercial transactions and the working hours of textile workers . . . the communal clock was an instrument of economic, social, and political domination wielded by the merchants who ran the commune. They required a strict measurement of time, because in the textile business 'it is fitting that most of the day workers – the proletariat of the textile trade – begin and end work at fixed hours.'

Already, says Le Goff, the 'infernal rhythms' can be felt. In the medieval age, 'merchant time' fought with religious time. The dominant religious attitude was that time could not be sold. Here is the response of a fourteenth-century Franciscan monk when questioned on the issues of credit and interest:

Question: is a merchant entitled, in a given type of transaction, to demand a greater payment from one who cannot settle his account immediately than from one who can? The answer argued for is no, because in doing so he would be selling time and would be committing usury by selling what does not belong to him.

Nowadays, we have completely the opposite view: bankers and wealthy people are venerated. Time and money, which the medievals tried so hard to keep separated, have come together into one thing. How did the change happen? Well, as in other areas, I am going to blame that dastardly toiler and moralist Benjamin Franklin, who invented or expressed an entirely new way of thinking about time in the eighteenth century. Time was no longer a gift from God. Now, time was money. The following passage was written as a piece of propaganda for young men starting out in the world:

Remember, that *time* is money. He that can earn ten shillings a day by his labour, and goes abroad, or sits idle, one half that day, though he spends but sixpence during his diversion or idleness, ought not to reckon that the only expense; he has really spent, or rather thrown away, five shillings besides.

Remember, that *credit* is money. If a man lets his money lie in my hands after it is due, he gives me the interest, or so much as I can make of it during that time. This amounts to a considerable sum where a man has good and large credit, and makes good use of it.

Remember, that money is of the prolific, generating nature. Money can beget money, and its offspring can beget more, and so on. Five shillings turned is six, turned again it is seven and threepence, and so on, till it becomes a hundred pounds. The more there is of it, the more it produces at every turning, so that the profits rise quicker and quicker. He that kills a breeding-sow, destroys all her offspring to the thousandth generation. He that murders a crown, destroys all that it might have produced, even scores of pounds.

For Franklin, it is not only a moral duty to consider time as money, but the accumulation of money for its own sake has become a worthy goal. From being a means of exchange, time married to money begins to take on a life of its own. Profit becomes an abstract concept, a goal worth pursuing. There is no sense here of why profit is good or what will be done with the profit to benefit society. Goodbye, brotherhood of man; hello, lonely strivers.

So, if we believe with the evil Franklin that time is money, then it makes a sort of commercial sense to wear a watch in order to keep a constant account of where all that precious time is going and in order to help you avoid squandering it in the alehouse. From being local and public, time has become global and private. But when you are constantly aware of the time, you are not living in the moment, because you are planning your next move. You lose that delicious sense of time doing its own thing, or 'losing track of time', as the phrase goes. Losing track of time is that wonderful feeling when everyone forgets to be bound by the hours and instead lets themselves go. Suddenly, four hours can vanish in a flash. Take off your watch and you are literally free of time. If you want to know the time, go and find a clock or call the speaking clock; there are many ways of finding it out.

I am not arguing, by the way, for irresponsibility and lateness in our dealings with others. Since we have all agreed to live by one sort of time, then we should stick to it. Although, wouldn't it be nice, I sometimes think, to live by African time, where appointments are not made but rather just happen? The idea of making an appointment, to an African, or at least to an old-fashioned, rural African, would be ridiculous, because life is so unpredictable. An African supermodel used to be constantly late for her meetings in New York, as she simply could not get her head around the strict new relationship with time.

Now, although it is undeniably rude to be late, I try to give as vague a time as possible – for example, 'I should arrive between five and six.' I am also starting to learn to allow myself oodles of time to get to my next destination, as any hold-up could happen on the way. Or you might meet someone and get involved in a conversation. And if you are early, then great. I remember from Joe Orton's diaries that he would always be early for appointments, and that this would give him the opportunity for a leisurely wander around before he knocked on the door. He was not afraid of spare time. There are two sorts of people: those who enjoy delays and disasters, and those who get stressed out and start huffing and puffing, as if the huffing and puffing is going to make the slightest bit of difference.

It's probably impossible to free ourselves completely of clocks and watches and time, but we can quite easily change our relationship with time and become an equal to it rather than a servant of it. One tried and tested strategy for doing this is, of course, through drugs. Drugs can bend and stretch time and create their own new druggy logic. No heroin user, for example, is ever punctual. Drugs can make a minute last an hour or three days disappear in a few minutes. Their popularity is due to the fact that they offer a brief escape from slave-time, commercial time, time as a commodity in the sense that Benjamin Franklin described. They allow us to step outside the Construct, to dance or talk or meditate.

We allow ourselves to become slaves to time. Even the world of jobs is defined by its mere duration: the nine-to-five. I am a nine-to-fiver, a drudge, an automaton. What a miserable way to live. Always, time is bearing down on us, urging us to hurry up, do more, get organized. The clock is a giant admonisher, constantly ticking us off.

So how do we free ourselves from the grasp of clock-time? One simple answer is to deschedule. I have a tendency to cram too much into the day, and this is always a mistake. Be realistic.

Don't demand too much of yourself. Do less. Add space. Cut down your scheduled visits and meetings to an absolute bare minimum to make way for the more enjoyable and life-affirming 'things that just happen'. When you let things happen to you, life starts happening too. So, allow giant gaps between appointments. Allow giant gaps in your life, because your life is in the gaps. It's brilliant, for example, when things go wrong. Once, I was on the Isle of Eigg, and the ferry was cancelled three days in a row due to bad weather. This magically extended our trip and we had the perfect excuse to blow out our commitments back home.

We also need to abandon the slavish notions that 'There aren't enough hours in the day' and 'I just don't have enough time.' When we say we don't have time to do something, what we really mean is 'I prioritized something else.' People say, 'I haven't got the time to read/walk/play/cook/stare out of the window.' But they seem to have the time to watch hours of television every day. The sense of there not being enough time acts like a slave-driver at our heels, cracking a whip and telling us to get a move on. It is one of the triumphs of the capitalist project that the slave-driver is now inside us, which saves an enormous amount on the wage bill. Worse, we have been duped into spending our own money to buy a little slave-driver to go on our wrist. The White Rabbit is a slave to the queen, a fawning lickspittle. So, you see, it really is your revolutionary duty to throw away your watch.

It is also absurd to think that we are time-starved, since every one of us has precisely the same amount of time, as there are always twenty-four hours in the day. It is impossible for one person to have less time than another. So, instead of saying, 'I don't have enough time,' force yourself to say, 'I have plenty of time.' Sometimes the words can precede the reality. The sense of being time-starved is a motor for the consumer economy. If you feel that you are lacking time, then you will be easy prey for products whose advertising promises to 'save time', those labour-saving devices. The automobile, for example, saves no time in the long run. Ivan Illich once calculated that if you add up all the time you spend on a car, including the trips to the garage and the time spent earning the money to buy the fuel and maintain the vehicle, and divide by the number of miles you travel, then your average speed is 5 mph. You would be faster on a bicycle. Speed, paradoxically, eats up our free time. Therefore, if you want to save money, then submit yourself to clock time no longer.

I am making an effort in my everyday life to embrace disaster. This is easier said than done, but a disaster can be seen as an adventure if you let go of a too-strict self-timetabling. Disasters also break up the routine. The other day, my van broke down on the way to the station. Yes, I was late into London, but then I had a nice bit of free loafing time while waiting for the AA man. Living inside clock-time also seems to prohibit living in the moment because we are always worrying about what has to be done in the future rather than inhabiting this actual moment. We need to abandon merchant time and embrace natural time once more. Live by the seasons, embrace the time that stretches. Waste it no more in vain striving, television-watching and working. Let things happen and things will happen. Time is free, therefore all time should be free. We should abandon the expression 'free time', because it implies its opposite, 'slave time'. Time is a gift from God, and to say that it is the same thing as money is an act of pure evil. So remove that watch from your wrist, throw it into the river and dance down the street, free at last.

THROW AWAY YOUR WATCH

8 Stop Competing

*The principle of medieval trade was admittedly comradeship and justice,
while the principle of modern trade is avowedly competition and greed.*
G. K. Chesterton, *William Cobbett*, 1926

Since Darwin, whose theories emerged during a competitive
period in European history, we as a society have largely agreed
that the way forward is to compete with each other. The principle of 'survival of the fittest' is remarkably long standing and
successful not only as a biological theory but as an ethic for
everyday life. When fat cats debate in the media, they use the
phrase 'healthy competition' with the assumption that everyone
listening will agree that competition *is* healthy. It is an assumed
fact of life. Of course, it is no accident that Darwin's theories,
or at least a certain interpretation of them, came along when

such a justification was needed for a new and particularly rapacious form of capitalism. Now, you could be forgiven for thinking that we are stuck with this notion. The competitive principle conquers in business, and it governs schooling. It is even embedded in healthcare and public transport, with the government's blather about 'targets'. Employees within companies are encouraged to compete with one another. It is deeply ingrained in our consciousness.

The theory is that competition leads to good quality and reasonable prices of goods. But the reality is the opposite: unfettered competition, that is, commercial war, and the endless expansion that necessarily goes with it, inevitably results in monopolies, as one giant company gradually swallows up its failed competitors. An example of this is the amazing rise of Tesco's, the omniscient, omnipresent UK supermarket, which has destroyed communities, forcing local shops to close down, as they are unable to compete with the low prices. This in turn sucks money out of communities and into the pockets of the stock-holders. And businesses are proud of this: I remember countless business meetings at which someone has piped up, 'Well, we're not a charity,' to murmurs of approval all round. The shareholder system also exerts a downward pressure on quality, because mere quantity – more sales – becomes the important factor. Competition, in actual fact, kills variety. It leads to the establishment of giant enterprises, with labouring serfs at the bottom and magical whizz-kids at the top. It leads to chainstores swallowing up individual enterprises; it leads to the phenomenon, recently labelled 'clone towns' in the UK, whereby every high street looks pretty much like every other high street. It leads to the Starbucksification of the world, where the idea of freedom is reduced to the whole world being able to choose between a Starbucks cappuccino or a Starbucks mocha latte. Competition is an enemy of freedom and justice.

I have to admit to a fiercely competitive streak in myself. This became clear when I led a team from the *Idler* to a stunning victory over the *Financial Times* newspaper on BBC TV's brainy quiz show, *University Challenge*, in 2005. Although our victory was almost entirely thanks not to me but to Rowley Leigh, the literary chef, I was catapulted into a joyful mood. My girlfriend, Victoria, said that the victory had a wonderfully positive effect on domestic harmony: I was completely non-grumpy for two weeks.

So, if I love winning, how can I attack the idea of winning? Well, I think there are two very distinct types of competition – competition in the realm of play and competition in the realm of work. When competition is kept in the realm of play, then it is fun, completely pointless and enjoyed for its own sake. Who, for example, would want to give up playing darts, snooker and croquet? Games are ancient and they are fun. Thirteenth-century Catalan courts, for example, loved games and would throw oranges at each other for days on end. There is wonderful description quoted by Linda M. Paterson in her study *The World of the Troubadours*:

> The admiral had a board hoisted up very high, for next to the lord king Pere and the Lord King of Mallorca he was the most skilful thrower of all the Knights in the whole of Spain; and his brother-

in-law Lord Berenguer d'Etenca was equally good. I myself have seen both of them make a throw, but undoubtedly King Pere and the king of Mallorca were the most outstanding of all those I have seen throwing at the taulat. Both of them would always throw three darts and an orange; and the last dart would be as large as a short Saracen lance; and the first two would always overshoot the board by a long way, however high it was, and the last would hit the board. And after this the admiral ordered a round table to be arranged; and his sailors had two armed boats prepared, the flat-bottomed kind that go up river. On these you could see orange battles taking place; they had had a good fifty tree-loads sent from the kingdom of Valencia . . . The celebrations lasted more than a fortnight, during which time no man in Saragossa did anything but sing and make merry and play games and enjoy himself.

Two weeks of feasting and fun! Today, with our work-obsession, we have no idea what such a festival would be like. As the unusual German historian Johan Huizinga says in *The Waning of the Middle Ages*, modern man sees himself primarily as a worker, and this is the great change. No praying, no fighting, no working the land. Just work, hard work. Three days in a row is the longest we give ourselves over to mirth and merriment. Sometimes we give two weeks to that expensive form of self-torture called the holiday, but holidays involve more hard work, and they cost a lot, too. This is not to say that the playful, competitive spirit does not persist: we still have arm-wrestling, shows of strength, pub games, jousts and skittles. But when competition is held up as a guiding principle for ethical behaviour in the world of business and the world of work, then there is something seriously wrong.

In the same way that capitalists made a commodity out of time and then magically internalized clock time, so they also manipulated our competitive instinct, which might more properly be called simply a 'love of play', and used it to their advantage. If the slaves compete with each other, then there is no need for the masters to drive them on with physical force. It's so much easier. The chairmen of the board think it absolutely hilarious that their staff will work their guts out and compete with one another for low wages and with minimum supervision. It leaves them so much time for playing golf and chuckling together in boardrooms.

The urge to beat the other guy in business at all costs also leads to appalling treatment of workers in terms of low wages and poor conditions. The will to win and the need for endless growth, the result of the share system, leads to sharp practices, sabotage and a complete loss of pleasure in one's work. Ends conquer means. We know that this niggardly spirit was born in the Protestant age with the Puritans, with Benjamin Franklin, Wesley and the rest of those grey Republicans and promoters of boredom. But what is the alternative?

When I bring this subject up in the pub, people tell me that there is no other way; constant battle is the only way that life and work can operate. Other systems have been attempted – for example, communism – and have failed, therefore capitalistic scrapping and cruelty is what we're stuck with. You've got to be tough to survive in today's world, they say. This word 'survive', I also find particularly depressing. Have you seen all those awful self-help books with the word 'survival' in the title? *Families and How to Survive Them* and the like. Has life been reduced to a matter of mere survival? I personally don't see this as a very noble ambition. How to love, how to live joyfully, how to savour life – those should be our goals.

In any case, it simply isn't true that capitalism is the only feasible operating system. In *Mutual Aid*, Kropotkin makes a methodical study of examples from nature and from man where the principle of helping each other is the dominant factor. He studies examples of mutual aid among animals before going on to describe how primitive societies and even the lovely Barbarians had social codes quite different from our own selfish ones. For example, in certain primitive societies, the spirit of hospitality is so important that if you are walking through the forest alone and sit down to eat your lunch, you must first shout out three times to offer to share your meal with any passing stranger.

Medieval England, 'Merry old England', was deeply imbued with this spirit of hospitality. Indeed, the idea of a hospital was invented by the monks and nuns, who kept their doors permanently open and would look after any wandering beggar or citizen fallen on hard times, doling out beer, bread and bacon. Inspired by the Sermon on the Mount, they took the principle of charity, *caritas*, very seriously. In those days, it would have been morally impossible for a priest to step over what we now call homeless people. Workers gave 10 per cent of their produce or earnings to the local monastery, who in many cases would probably have been their landlord as well, and this 10 per cent tithe was primarily intended for poor relief in the local area. We looked after our own poor; we did not delegate this task to a distant coterie of bureaucrats.

The monks and priests constantly held before people the idea that striving was vainglorious, that it was wrong to get one over on your neighbour. The notion of a 'brotherhood of man' was powerfully promoted among the people. It's striking, for example, that St Thomas Aquinas constantly enjoins the reader to 'love God and your neighbour'. God and one's neighbour are practically equal in the grand scheme. We look after each other. That is the principle of charity as conceived by medieval man.

In the 1300s, of course, the Protestant ethic which later so thoroughly and disastrously infected Europe and America had not been invented. The principal concern of every man and woman was not how to make a lot of money but how to save their soul. And making a lot of money was almost a surefire way to go to hell: it is easier to pass through the eye of a needle than for a rich man to go to heaven. Jesus and the apostles lived lives of poverty, and the medievals' favourite philosopher, Aristotle, praised the *vita contemplativa*. This is why, although it was undeniably a mercantile period, the Middle Ages were profoundly split on their attitude to money-making and, indeed, the subject was a constant source of debate.

The new trade guilds of the twelfth century onwards were based on the notion of a 'just and fixed price' and also of the common good. The guilds needed to create a type of commerce and trade which was in keeping with medieval ethical codes, which were suspicious of hard work, trade and competition. The Lord's Prayer – 'Give us this day our daily bread' – is an anti-competitive creed, almost oriental in its fatalism. Certain forms of work had been deemed acceptable by the priests – gardening, baking and brewing beer – but work in general, particularly trade, was seen as another vanity. But then, attitudes began to change, as Jacques Le Goff outlines:

> Medieval men initially viewed labour as a penance or a chastisement for original sin. Then, without abandoning this penitential perspective, they place increasing value upon work as an instrument of redemption, of dignity, of salvation. They viewed labour as collaboration in the work of the Creator who, having laboured, rested on the seventh day. Labour, that cherished burden, had to be wrenched from the outcast position and transformed, individually and collectively, into the rocky path to liberation.

So, the task of the new guildsmen and merchants, who wanted to be free to work and to trade, was to set up complex systems of values which governed how they could work in ways that would not displease God. The principles of work were: that it should be creative, of high quality, that you should not do too much of it, you should agree prices, you should look after your fellow-craftsmen and there should be no competition. In other words, no exploitation. Night work, for example, was prohibited, as it might encourage unfair competition. Prices were fixed, and lending at interest, or usury, was proscribed, as before. The system was precisely anti-competitive. Membership fees and fines went into a common pot, which was used for splendid feasts, for the building of guildhalls and for alms.

This long period of cooperation was rudely destroyed by Henry VIII, who started to wreck the Catholic Church because he wanted to have sex with Anne Boleyn and fill up his coffers with ecclesiastical gold. The Reformation is generally taught as a regrettable necessity, but that of course is a Protestant view, and you have to ask whether, in swallowing it, we have been somewhat brainwashed. Here is how William Cobbett describes the process in *The History of the Protestant Reformation*:

> Now, my friends, a fair and honest inquiry will teach us that this was an alteration greatly for the worse; that the 'Reformation', as it is called, was engendered in lust, brought forth in hypocrisy and perfidy, and cherished and fed by plunder, devastation and by rivers of innocent English and Irish blood; and that as to its more remote consequences, they are, some of them, now before us, in that misery, that beggary, that nakedness, that hunger, that everlasting wrangling and spite, which now stare us in the face, and stun our ears at every turn, and which the 'Reformation' has given us in exchange for the ease, and happiness, and harmony, and Christian charity, enjoyed so abundantly and for so many ages by our Catholic forefathers.

While not exactly a Puritan, Henry VIII's plunder of the monasteries and his break with Rome suited the emerging Puritan element very well. Between 1500 and 1760, the Puritan faction in England – the serious, anti-fun people, the hard workers, the self-deniers, the Christmas-cancellers, the lonesome pilgrims, the Maypole wreckers, the Parliamentarians, the enemies of joy and spontaneous living – grew in strength until finally they became all-conquering and took over the whole country by means of the Industrial Revolution and the various acts of enclosure which privatized the land. They hated pomp, grandeur, gold and incense, so the fact that the churches had been stripped of their finery suited their austere tastes very well. Then the whole project backfired on them, because the logical next step after Protestantism is atheism: why should I believe in God?

But the memory of the communistic way of life that had prevailed before the Reformation lingered, and ever since the new ways began, we have rebelled against them and dreamt of more humane alternatives. It's fascinating to note that something similar happened in Mayan civilization in Mexico, at a similar time. According to the archaeologist J. Eric S. Thompson, the Mayans, like the medievals, believed that no one 'should strive for more than his fair share, for that can be attained only at one's neighbour's expense; consideration for others is all important.' This society was of course wrecked by the Conquistadors. Thompson quotes Mayan scribe Chilam Belam: 'Before the coming of the mighty men and Spaniards there was no robbery by violence, there was no greed and striking down one's fellow man in his blood, at the cost of the poor man, at the expense of the food of each and everyone.' It was the beginning, he says, of individual strife.

One of the first serious movements to protest against the new emerging order in Europe was that of the Diggers of 1649, who dug up the common land. Their leader, John Winstanley, a failed corn merchant, believed that people should 'work together; eat bread together.' They were rebelling against the new private land policies of the Tudor government, which had removed communal land from the villages, erected fences around it and put sheep in the fields. The Diggers, according to a court report, planned to:

> arise and dig and plough the earth, and receive the fruits thereof
> . . . their intent is to restore the Creation to its former condition. That as God had promised to make the barren land fruitful, so now what they did was to restore the ancient community of enjoying the fruits of the earth, and to distribute the benefits thereof to the poor and needy, and to feed the hungry and to clothe the naked.

Winstanley's deputy, John Everard, said that 'the time of deliverance was at hand, and God would bring his people out of this slavery, and restore them to their freedom in enjoying the fruits and benefits of the Earth.' The Diggers were behind one of the first revolts against the new Protestant order that was gradually infecting old England. Of course, things grew worse still after the Enclosure Acts of 1760 onwards, which were designed to remove the people from the countryside and force them into the cities, where they were needed as cheap labour in the new factories. A rural population of great variety and with much common land for grazing and collecting firewood was removed and gradually replaced by an arid countryside of huge fields of sheep. Sheep literally came to replace people, as they were more profitable, and nowhere was the process more brutally carried out than in the Highlands of Scotland, where socially ambitious lairds chucked the people off their crofts and left them to starve or to take their chances on the boats sailing to America.

The seventeenth century also saw the rise of the anarchic Ranters movement. In *The Pursuit of the Millennium*, Norman Cohn shows that the Ranters were the spiritual successors to the Free Spirit sects that had flourished across Europe in the eleventh, twelfth and thirteenth centuries. Like those sects, they argued that the pure of soul could do no wrong, and they could therefore sleep with their own sister on the church altar and it would not be a sin. The Ranters were anti-work: they held that all things should be held in common, that concepts of sin were not absolute but myths created by man in order to subject each other. They were the existentialists of their day, maintaining that nothing has intrinsic meaning and that any meaning is manmade. The itinerant preacher Laurence Clarkson (1615–67) wrote of Ranterism in his biography (1650). The philosophy is relativist in extreme; it's like reading Nietzsche:

> God had made all things good, so nothing evil but as man judged it; for I apprehended there was no such thing as theft, cheat, or a lie but as man made it so: for if the creature had brought this world into [no] propriety, as Mine and Thine, there had been no such title as theft, cheat or a lie.

Sin has its conception only in the imagination, he says. Everything is mind forg'd:

> Consider what act soever, yea though it be the act of Swearing, Drunkennesse, Adultery and Theft; yet these acts simply, yea nakedly, as acts are nothing distinct from the act of prayer and Prayses. Why dost thou wonder? Why are thou angry? They are

all one themselves; no more holynesse, no more puritie in one than the other.

Morality is manmade. It's a philosophy that goes back to the Sufis and the Free Spirit movement and that will stretch on to Nietzsche, Sartre, the Situationists and the punks.

The nineteenth century was peppered with attempts to wreck competition as an organizing principle. There was, for example, Robert Owen, the mill-owner turned philanthropist. There were the Chartist land colonies. There was John Minter Morgan, who envisioned 'properly constructed villages of unity and co-operation'. There was James Smith, who in 1833 put forward the creed of Saint-Simonism: 'Competition and antagonism must give way to association and community interests.' All sorts of societies sprang up: the National Community Friendly Society, the Association of All Classes (later amalgamated as the Universal Society of Rational Religionists), and the United Advancement societies. Cooperative colonies were started at Tytherley in Hampshire, and at Manea Fen in East Anglia.

In 1871, John Ruskin founded what he called the St George's Guild, which, to an extent, was based on the old medieval guilds. The idea was to create a community of craftspeople living along cooperative lines, and for the purpose he bought St George's Farm in Sheffield. His workmen, he said, were to be 'Life Guards of a new life . . . more in the spirit of a body of monks gathered for missionary service, than of a body of tradesmen.' The colony failed thanks to a lunatic self-declared seer called Riley, who tried to tyrannize it. But Ruskin's ideas and experiments were enormously influential, particularly on fellow medievalist

William Morris, who wrote: 'Fellowship is heaven and lack of fellowship is hell: fellowship is life, and lack of fellowship is death.'

Another great thinker in this area was the Christian anarchist Leo Tolstoy, who dreamed, Digger-like, of 'the founding of a new religion corresponding to the present state of mankind: the religion of Christianity but purged of dogmas and mysticisms; a practical religion not promising future bliss, but giving bliss on earth.' His idea was not benevolent state socialism – which, as we can see today, is a complete disaster mitigated only by a few helpful welfare projects – but self-government and the free cooperation of federated groups. Tolstoy's book *The Kingdom of God is within You*, which essentially intepreted Jesus' Sermon on the Mount as a manual for living without violence and without competition, had a huge impact on intellectuals of the day. He was the late-nineteenth-century equivalent of CRASS. A duo called J. C. Kenworthy and J. Bruce Wallace, inspired by Tolstoy, founded a group called the Brotherhood Trust in 1894. They started by opening a fruit and veg co-op that aimed to make money to buy land. Related cells opened in Hackney and Walthamstow and, in 1896, Kenworthy told a conference for the International Socialist Workers Congress that:

> The English nation is ready to give up politics as a weapon and turn to industrial cooperation on free Anarchist Communist principles . . . we are in the last stages of a corrupt civilization. A wrong conception of life, a belief that selfishness is the necessary law of conduct, had ended for us any wide perception of spiritual truth, and surrendered us to the grossest errors of materialism.

Kenworthy founded his little colony at Purleigh in Essex. Soon the colony grew to sixty-five people, and a reporter from the *Clarion* wrote: 'They have jumped the chasm from competition to Co-operation without waiting for the plank of social democracy and have arrived on the shores of anarchism.' They had 23 acres, 200 apple trees, 250 gooseberry bushes, cows and hens and all their own vegetables. They had their own printing press. Other colonies were also based on sharing principles. In Essex, there were Althorne, Asingdon and Forest Gate. More attempts were made to form Tolstoyan groups in Leeds, Blackburn and Leicester. Purleigh, though, failed – partly, as one member said, because it is in the nature of such experiments to attract nutcases who haven't fitted in elsewhere: 'There was much insanity at Purleigh. At least five who lived and stayed at the Colony while I was there, were subsequently put under supervision on account of their mental condition. Even those of us who kept our sanity did not always keep our tempers.'

In the 1920s, we find the attractive principle of Distributism being promoted by Catholic artists and intellectuals such as Chesterton, Arthur J. Penty, Hilaire Belloc and Eric Gill, the men my friend James Parker calls 'those fat Catholics'. The idea was that each household would have its own plot of land and that a guilds system would be reintroduced. We'll return to Distributism in our chapter on Forgetting Government.

Later in the twentieth century, we had the anti-materialistic hippie movement of the 1960s and 1970s, the Abbie Hoffmans and the Jerry Rubins and their battle against the tie-wearing 'squares'. The 1970s also saw genuine attempts to escape the nightmare of the industrial system on the part of pioneers such as John Seymour, the radical Catholic Ivan Illich, E. F. Schumacher, and the young Satish Kumar, who walked around the world and then settled in Hartland, a village in North Cornwall about an hour away from where I live. Satish now runs *Resurgence* magazine from Hartland and has a wonderful vegetable and fruit garden, which I went to visit recently. Today, the *Diggers' and Dreamers' Guide to Communal Living* lists around one hundred communities in the UK, and there are countless more people living in villages, growing vegetables, avoiding work and money, helping each other out and doing very nicely. The *Permaculture* magazine runs stories on communities around the world who have embraced self-sufficiency, crafts and communal living, such as the Tinker's Bubble community in Somerset or Ragman's Lane Farm in Gloucestershire. There are stories of people made redundant who embraced the principles, loosened their dependence on money and became self-reliant and are now thriving. Their biggest problem seems to be absurd planning regulations, which can make it practically impossible to build a shack in the woods, while monstrous out-of-town supermarkets are seemingly encouraged by local authorities. Planning permission granted for such eyesores is, I understand, often thanks to very slick presentations to councillors by the supermarkets, which promise jobs and services for locals.

Well, the inspiring examples above prove that there is not only one path through life, the path of job-debt-suffering. That may be the path presented to us by our schools and our media, but there are a million alternatives out there, each one more fun than the one set out for us and each one based on helping and sharing rather than competing. 'There's a better world a-comin can't you see, see, see,' sang Woody Guthrie, 'when we'll all be union and we'll all be free.'

There is great pleasure to be had in working in a community. The more you help other people, the more likely they will be to help you, and so it goes on in a friendly circle. Certainly, the system of full-time wage slavery works directly in opposition to any ideas of mutual aid, partly because it takes up so much of our time. When we get home from work, the last thing we want to do is go to a meeting of the Village Hall Preservation Society or feed the neighbour's dog. So, instead, we turn on the TV and allow ourselves to be advertised at for hours on end. We call it relaxation. Neighbourliness has been under attack for 500 years. The principle of competition has been dominant. But surely it can be seen to have been a complete failure, setting us all at each other's throats like dogs. Competition is a slave's creed. We think that by beating up the other guy we elevate ourselves, but, in fact, we are debasing ourselves to the level of a slave. To be competitive is a sign of submission as, really, it just means that we are carrying out the master's wishes. It is time to return to cooperation, neighbourliness, two-week feasts and giving stuff away.

Trade unions made the mistake of fighting management or, in other words, of competing with the bosses. The battle of union *versus* management is a negative one, because it is a battle between resentment and greed. The workers grumble and the bosses want more profit. All energy is dissipated in fighting, when that energy should be put to creative use. With the medieval guilds, union and management are united into one and the same thing, because the guilds are run by their members. Therefore, we need to start guilds. I have already started two: the Clerkenwell Freelance Writers Guild and the North Devon Diggers Guild. We plan to produce coats of arms and hold lavish annual feasts with our communal funds. We will help each other out in times of need.

START A GUILD

9 Escape Debt

A year ago I didn't have cent to my name. Now I owe $2 million.
Mark Twain

Banks are evil. This might strike you as a glib oversimplification of the problem of money and debt but, not so long ago, this was literally true. From the early medieval age and right up to 1500 and beyond, lending money at interest, or usury, was strictly off the agenda for anyone who was serious about his or her salvation. It was a sin, it was proscribed, it was evil.

The reason for the outlawing of usury was that time was a gift from God and therefore it could not be bought or sold. Christ, in St Luke's Gospel, says, 'Lend, hoping for nothing again' (6.35). Usury also went against Christian teaching because it involved the exploitation of a neighbour who had fallen on hard times, which is what lending money is all about. It was also seen as a lazy way to make money, since all you had to do to make a profit was to wait. Usury was not real work; it created nothing and it caused misery. Medieval churches abound with carvings of 'moneybags' money-lenders.

As a measure of how much things have changed, we should look at the story of Father O'Callaghan, the idealistic priest who tried to bring back the old laws against usury in the early nineteenth century, that great era of capitalist expansion. Of course, he got nowhere, as his ideas were completely unsuited to the avaricious ethic of the time. His first act, in 1819, after he became enlightened on this issue, was to refuse to absolve a corn-dealer on his deathbed until he had repaid all the interest he had made from his debtors. This practice was in keeping with medieval custom: according to Jacques Le Goff, 'moneybags' money-lenders, on their deathbeds, would pay back everyone they had ripped off for fear of going to hell. I suppose, in those days, at least it was easy to find a single accountable individual: in today's era of 'I'm only doing my job,' no one takes responsibility for anything.

Well, the corn-dealer repented and the money was paid back. But, following complaints from other usurers – or businessmen busy men, busybodies – in the area, O'Callaghan was reined in by his local bishop and finally disallowed from saying Mass. The poor, outcast O'Callaghan, who had simply made a statement which in 1200 would have been as uncontroversial as saying, 'Black is black,' roamed the world in search of more orthodox Catholics with whom to hook up. In this search he failed, and even the Vatican became fed up with him. William Cobbett, though, published O'Callaghan's book on usury, as it fitted in with his own sense that the modern industrial system actually enslaved rather than liberated people, with the ad line: 'It ought to be read by every man, and especially every young man, in the kingdom.'

Banking – credit notes and the like – was invented by the great Medici family in Florence in the thirteenth century. Somehow, they combined usury with being holy, probably because they were the Pope's bankers. The head of the family, Cosimo de'Medici, used to go for long walks with his priest to discuss the issues. He made up for his usury by lavishing huge sums on building projects and art. Big government debt came with war. When monarchies wanted to raise money for wars, they would borrow from a wealthy family like the Barings. The Barings would charge them interest on these loans, and so the country went into permanent debt. According to Cobbett, it was Henry VIII who started this system. In those days, though, the banks were relatively insignificant, as they merely had a hold on the government or the monarchy; now, these monstrous concerns own all our money. And that, of course, is in addition to our income taxes, which also go back to the banks as contributions to the interest on government loans which pay for past or future wars.

Today's banks make the most unbelievably enormous profits: HSBC declared profits of £10 billion in 2005. This puts a family like the Medicis on the scale of a corner shop by comparison. Truly, usury has been very profitable when practised on a highly organized, global scale. The banks tell us they are working selflessly for the benefit of their shareholders and their customers, thereby promoting themselves almost as charitable institutions, but of course this pretence of benevolence immediately crumbles when you find out that the people who are running the company are also the biggest shareholders in it and therefore have the keenest interest in its profitability. The men at the top of these firms are earning obscene amounts of money by enslaving the rest of us. It should be of some comfort to us that they are all going straight to hell, though of course it would be far more satisfying to see them suffer on this earth.

In the meantime, what can we do to free ourselves from this trap? How do we escape the bondage of debt? The point about usury is important, because it reveals the bankers in their true light, as venal and profit-centred rather than in any way paternalistic. It shows that the medievals were essentially anti-capitalist. As Jacques Le Goff writes in his study of the subject, *Your Money or Your Life*:

> The medieval usurer found himself in a strange situation. Within a history of the *longue durée* (a history of the deeply rooted and slowly changing), the usurer is the precursor of capitalism, an economic system that, despite its injustices and failings, is part of the West's trajectory of progress. But from all contemporary points of view, in his own day this was a man in disgrace.

So, the ordinary man in the street can feel morally superior to the bankers. The 'we look after you' self-advertising of banks is simply that: advertising, a marketing trick, a seduction technique. They are interested in maximum profits, and that is that. So you should never, ever feel guilty for having an overdraft; they merely use this guilt in order to make you feel you *deserve it* when they whack on a load of super-usurious charges, those admin fees and extra charges they steal from you without asking. These are *on top of* the interest they are already charging! They are the ones who should be feeling guilty – very guilty. I wonder what the thirteenth-century monks would have to say about their shenanigans? Well, we know. The thirteenth-century monk Thomas of Cobham wrote, 'It is clear that the usurer cannot be considered a sincere penitent unless he has returned everything that he has extorted through the sin of usury.'

Truly, the bankers are double- and triple-damned! The amazing thing is that we, the servile masses, act as though we are grateful when they grant us an overdraft! We tug our forelocks and say, 'Oh, thank you, kind sir! You're ever so munificent!' Well, there is in fact some debate in banking circles as to whether the various super-usurious overdraft charges and the rest are actually legally enforceable. Certainly, if you complain to your bank, as I did the other day about £130 worth of overdraft charges, they will often refund them. They are simply trying to get away with as much as they can and, although the odds seem stacked, because they are powerful and we are small, it is possible to stand up for yourself.

The other thing to get straight in our heads is that banks love you to be in debt. They adore it; they make so much money out of it. They trade in your debt; debts are sold on to investment funds and the like. That is why we are constantly encouraged to be reckless in our spending and put that dream holiday or car or new TV on the credit card. That is why the usurers spend so much money advertising their 'financial services' – and there's a euphemism for usury if ever I heard one – on the television. They batter you with these ads, and a lot of them are on kids' TV, with the effect that five-year-olds are going into the kitchen and saying to their mum and dad: 'Have you considered Ocean Finance? They're really nice people.' And, in fact, any ad for spending money, and most ads do encourage the spending of money, is a free ad for a bank, because the more you spend, the more they make. The latest thing is that evil supermarkets are also getting in on the usury business, offering loans, bank accounts and all the rest of the sorry range of so-called 'financial services'.

So, the very fact that we are daily actively, constantly and quite scandalously encouraged, nay, brainwashed, to get into debt by the culture all around us should in itself remove any guilt we feel about being in debt. You're supposed to be in debt! Debt makes the world go round.

But, yes, being in debt can feel like wearing boots of lead. It puts a mighty obstacle between our selves and our dreams. It is a bondage. It ties us down. We make debt-repayment a priority and postpone the thing it is that we really want to do. Therefore, we end up staying in our slave-jobs. 'I hate my job and would love to quit,' people say, 'but I owe five grand to the bank, so I can't.' In this respect, debt has been compared by many to a modern form of indentured labour. You get into debt, and then you are stuck in a job you hate in order to pay off the debt. This helps the system, as it means that most of us are more or less kept quiet and toiling. Debt also causes huge anxiety, health problems and breakdowns. Witness the recent rise of debt-counselling services.

The medievals were right: usury is bad. Why did we not listen?

Well, in my own experience, quitting your job is actually the *only* way to pay off that debt. The higher your wages, the bigger your debt. By a strange paradoxical process, working in a job seems to increase your debt rather than decrease it, as any wage slave will tell you. I have friends earning twice or ten times as much as I do, but they are in debt because they spend so much money. If you live and work at home, then you don't spend in the same way. Indeed, rat-race evacuees who used to go on John Seymour's smallholding courses referred to themselves as DFKs, which stands for Debt-Free Killers (the 'Killers' bit refers to all the slugs and snails they were wiping out). It is only by exiting the system that you gradually get rid of debt. Staying in the system, i.e. remaining dependent on it, will tend to increase debt, while freedom and self-sufficiency will allow you to snap your fingers at it. Again, I advise looking at the *Permaculture* magazine, as there is a lot of advice within its pages on how to get out of debt as part of the journey towards self-reliance.

The other option is not to care. The apparently enslaving nature of debt is in itself a myth. It will only enslave us if we allow it to do so. The subject of debt is frequently discussed on the *Idler's* web forum, where contributors will say: 'I'd love to live the idle life, but I've got this enormous debt.' I like in particular the rejoinder of *Idler* contributor Sarah Janes, who says: 'I don't think about my debt.' Similarly, the great eighteenth-century radical and free spirit John Wilkes was constantly in debt, but he never allowed the debt to come between him and the things he wanted to do. He did not allow the debt to become a disabling 'if only' in his mind. This is not to deny the very real effects of high levels of debt on our mental and physical health. I know what it's like, because I've been there, head in hands at the kitchen table, backs of envelopes and a calculator in front of me. But understanding that money really is mind-forg'd will help us to remove the manacles. We ourselves are complicit in the creation of the debt-and-money myth. Cease to believe in it, and it will no longer have any power over us. That's the first step.

You're very unlikely to be cast into the streets. One *Idler* reader became so worried about her debt that she went to her local Citizens Advice Bureau. They arranged with her creditors for her to pay back the trifling sum of £2 per month. Eighteen months later, out of laziness, she stopped making the payments. Since then, two years have passed, and she has not been hassled for the money. What an inspiring story! Presumably her creditors finally gave up and wrote the debt off.

To understand the essentially fictional nature of debt, it helps to understand the essentially fictional nature of money itself. For money, as the banker-turned-writer Edward Chancellor has argued, does not exist. It is not money, he says, but credit that makes the world go round. Credit, that strange quality that determines how much money you could borrow if you wanted to. Your credit is bound up with notions of your moral worth or other people's confidence in you. Damien Hirst's mother tells the story of when Hirst was starting out as an artist. He needed an overdraft, asked the bank for one and was flatly refused. But when he went back to the bank accompanied by his massively confident old Etonian art dealer Jay Jopling and let him do all the talking, the loan was granted.

It is credit, not cash, that makes wealth: apparently, rich people are often simply more spectacularly in debt than the rest of us. Debt, therefore, is not to be feared. When I look at my bank balances on the computer, the nature of money becomes clearer. Just numbers on a screen. How can those numbers affect my mental health unless I allow them to do so? My credit is the bank's debt and vice versa. It doesn't really matter.

The strange, elusive, flighty nature of debt was expressed superbly by Daniel Defoe, who attempted an explanation in his 'An Essay upon the Loans' (1710):

> I am to speak of what all People are busie about, but not one in Forty understands . . . If a Man goes about to explain it by Words, he rather struggles to lose himself in the Wood, than bring others out of it. It is best describ'd by it self; 'tis like the Wind that blows where it lists, we hear the sound thereof, but hardly know whence it comes, or whither it goes.
>
> Like the Soul in the Body, it acts all Substance, yet is it self Immaterial; it gives Motion, yet it self cannot be said to Exist, it creates Forms, yet has itself no Form, it is neither Quantity or Quality; it has no Whereness, or Whenness, Scite, or Habit. If I should say it is the essential Shadow of something that is Not; should I not Puzzle the thing rather than Explain it, and leave you and my self more in the Dark than we were before.

Again, the notion of credit is seen as completely formless, a sort of vapour that exists only in the mind, or by common delusion. Making solid, real things at home is an effective way of escaping from reflection on the impossibly abstract nature of money. To free yourself from the cycle of work-spend-debt-work, simply stop consuming and start creating. The money system has created an internal division inside all of us between the producer and the consumer. Every day, in the business world, the ordinary people of the country are referred to as 'consumers', which is in itself a terribly avaricious word. Think of the other meaning of 'consumption', a deadly disease of romantic poets, which consumed the body until it expired, having been sapped, drained, used up, emptied out. To be a consumer is to drain the world, to eat it, to stuff it into our faces, to wither it, to dry up its resources, to mine it of all its bounty; in short, to kill it. But being a creator or a producer, that is the very opposite.

We should aim to produce some of the things we consume. A simple and enjoyable tip, which I have mentioned before and will return to again, is to grow some of your own vegetables and fruit. In doing this, the split between producer and consumer is removed and we become whole again. I think this is what accounts for the very great and deep pleasure one feels when pulling up one's own carrots or radishes from the ground. It feels like something we are meant to be doing. It is an act of radical integration. I am planning to start a magazine for the anarchic gardener, which will be called *The Radish*. In it, we will combine practical advice on growing organic vegetables with the development of a radical political philosophy. We will be radical in all senses of the word, as, of course, 'radish' comes from the Latin '*radix*', meaning 'root'.

Above all, to be free of debt, we need to abandon our fear of poverty. I don't advocate true pauperism, in other words, being homeless and starving. But genteel poverty, having enough for needs and the bare necessities but limiting yourself when it comes to wants and desires, is a laudable state. Going back again to the Middle Ages, it is clear that being poor was actually considered to be a worthy thing. The poor were an important part of society. After all, Jesus and the Apostles were poor, and the mendicant orders sought to copy the apostolic life. The Catholic academic George O'Brien, in his 1923 essay 'The Economic Effects of the Reformation', points to the example of the wandering holy men:

> . . . even begging was dignified by the example of the mendicant friars. Europe was thickly covered with institutions for the relief of every variety of poverty and suffering, and the resources of the monastic establishments were supplemented by private alms, the giving of which was imposed as a strict duty on the owners of property. The Reformation, by its attack on the ecclesiastical foundations, deprived the poor of the former of these modes of relief, and greatly diminished the latter by its insistence on the doctrine of justification by faith alone.

Poor people were welcomed because, for one thing, they offered the opportunity for others to give alms, which was a religious and social requirement in the Middle Ages. Charity was at the centre of the quest for salvation. Also, as we mentioned earlier, to cease striving after gain was to put all your faith in Providence. People didn't feel pity for the poor, the poor were almost looked up to: it was as valid in the eyes of God to be poor as to be rich, perhaps even better. Saints made a virtue out of their poverty. Today, we make the horrible mistake of assuming that the poor want to be rich. We pity the poor and the homeless, and we assume that they want to enjoy the unholy race for gain, to become bourgeois themselves. Maybe, just maybe, they don't. And perhaps so-called 'poor' countries around the world don't want to join the bourgeois system either.

As O'Brien goes on to say:

> The most regrettable result of the change from the medieval to the modern system of poor relief is that it has rendered the receipt of relief despicable, and that poverty has come in modern times to be looked on as a disgrace. The desire of the reformers to put an end to mendicancy, and to ensure that, as far as possible, the Biblical injunction that none should eat but those who worked should be applied literally, led them to impute a certain degree of moral disapprobation to the receipt of alms except by the sick and disabled, and the poor laws of the reformed countries tended to take on a degree of harshness towards the poor, which was happily absent in Catholic days.

Today, though, the charitable impulse has been co-opted by giant companies which exploit the poorer people with bloated job-creation schemes. Charity is good but, under capitalism, our instinctive charitable nature is exploited. Working for a charity is today a career option for people who want to earn a lot of money while simultaneously displaying to the world that they are compassionate people. Aid and debt relief tend to come with strings attached; he who pays the piper calls the tune. Western countries offer debt relief to African countries, but only if they Westernize themselves, which is generally a shorthand for allowing the exploiters to go in and replace a self-sufficient rural economy with an urban, wage-dependent, industrial one. The satirical magazine *Whitestones* has written a pastiche of Live Aid's 'Feed the World' called 'Milk the World' which includes the line 'Money down the drain, Swiss banks overflow.' Today, charity can simply be a way of opening up new foreign markets for export. And institutional charity can wreck local businesses and difference. In Zambia, for example, home fashion industries have been completely destroyed because Oxfam have brought in cheap second-hand clothes from the UK.

Debt appears to be an enslaver, but once you realize it doesn't truly exist, you can be free from it, because how can you be enslaved by the product of someone else's imagination? Snap your fingers at the usurers. Why should you care about them? They are damned anyway! Sneer at their threatening letters, laugh at their puny figures on screens, chortle at their boring lives and at the damnation that awaits them!

CUT UP YOUR CREDIT CARD

10 *Death to Shopping, or Fleeing the Prison of Consumer Desire*

The best thing is to possess pleasures without being their slave;
not to be devoid of pleasures.
Aristippus, 435–356 BC

The warnings are all there in the Bible. Adam and Eve are living perfectly happily in the Garden of Eden. They don't work but neither do they consume. It appears to be a pre-agricultural era, where the food you need is simply plucked from the trees and hedgerows. (It's still possible to do this, by the way: the other day, we picked a bagful of sorrel and nettles while out on a walk, and Victoria made a delicious risotto.) If Adam and Eve were not hunter-gatherers, then they were certainly gatherers. But, then, consumer desire, or self-betterment, or the 'itch', as

Schopenhauer called it, appeared in the shape of the serpent. This capitalistic monster awakens in Adam and Eve the possibility that things could be better. Instantly, they are cast out of the garden and condemned to a life of toil, drudgery and pain. Wants supplanted needs, and things have been going downhill ever since.

Today, we are imprisoned by our desires, shackled by shopping. The will to shop is a corroding and enfeebling force. We desire a new pair of shoes, a new car, a new house, a new sofa, a new TV. We need money to buy these things, so we bind ourselves to an employer in order to get the money, or we get into debt by borrowing the money from one of the many institutional usurers in the marketplace. And this we call freedom. This, simply put, is the problem with desire. Our natural desire to live well and enjoy life is co-opted by the consumer system and turned into something materially based and enslaving. The waste is unbelievable: I recently heard a radio programme about the trade in second-hand Western clothes in Zambia. The idea that we had thrown this stuff away, in perfectly good nick, was literally unthinkable to the Zambians, and they assumed that we had sacrificed these things out of a charitable impulse. And shopping is just such a drag. I'd rather be drinking.

It seems obvious that if we could just extinguish consumer desires and stop shopping, we would get a lot closer to everyday liberty, simply because we wouldn't have to do so much work. This is not to say that one can't enjoy luxuries, it's just that we shouldn't take them seriously as a kind of goal in life. Don't make luxury into a meaning. The Greek philosopher and pleasure-seeker Aristippus was well known for his sense of detachment from things. He took his pleasures where he found them; he did not chase desire. He gathered rather than hunted. Aristippus was one of those lucky people who didn't care: he would have been happy in a hut or in a castle.

To be free from desire does not mean to renounce all pleasure and become a sort of joyless hermit. Recently, when giving a talk on creative idleness, I was asked whether I disapprove of TV-watching. I have to admit that there is a side of me that gets annoyed when my kids are watching TV on a sunny day but, on the other hand, who am I to remove a source of pleasure from someone else's life? I do not imagine a police force for the idle unplugging television sets across the country and telling people to pick up their ukuleles or spades instead. TV has led to some great works of creation, and a world without TV would be a world without *The Simpsons*. Having said all that, I have just telephoned Sky TV and cancelled our subscription and it really felt like I was socking it to the man. Why pay to have all that advertising and capitalist propaganda beamed into your home? Now, we will save £250 a year and watch DVDs instead.

The key is not to renounce all pleasures but to be a master of them. In our strange world, when it comes to pleasure, we seem to oscillate between binging and abstention. The Alcoholics Anonymous cult preaches total abstinence as the only solution to drink problems. This is achieved by attendance at an unending stream of meetings, and through team effort and the constant reciting of the rules of AA. But, to me, it all seems a lot of effort, and the philosophy behind AA seems to acknowledge that the desire for alcohol will never leave one. Is there not another way of dealing with drink problems? AA people say that one drink is one drink too many and a thousand is not enough, but couldn't there be an organization which encouraged moderate drinking? If I had to go to a meeting every day at which I had to confess my previous night's drinking, that would surely help me to cut down. The binge–abstain cycle may not be as intimately tied up with human nature as we think. Is it not possible that somehow we are encouraged to binge and abstain because that does the double job of keeping the cash flowing through the system (binging) and keeping us docile through self-flagellation and guilt (abstaining)?

It is important to distinguish between the actual physical pleasures produced by comestibles such as food and drink and the promise of pleasure produced by the marketing of mass-produced goods, objects. We desire things, we are attached to things, we believe that things will make us better. This process serves the *postponement* of desire which is one of the character-istic features, indeed a motor, of large-scale capitalism. The desire for things produces a restless craving, and this restless craving leads us into the world and into our schemes for better-ment. Of course, *things* have a built-in disappointment factor. I can still remember the slight sinking feeling I had as a boy when I was given a toy and it simply did not live up to the expecta-tion that had been created by its expensive TV advertising campaign. The fact that things are disappointing leads us not to abandon things, as it should, but to buy more things in the hope that the 'new and improved' thing will not disappoint like the previous thing. This is how capitalism works: through a constant stream of disappointments which encourages the spending of more and more money.

As I tell Victoria when she accuses me of being puritanical, it's not worthy and self-sacrificing to get rid of the desire for things, it is the bold move of a free spirit. It is an anarchist gesture, because the desire for things is what keeps the wheels of the slave-machine turning. If I didn't want a big TV, then no one would be forced to load them into the backs of lorries on minimum wage, or less, in the middle of the night. To be a restless robot is what is required by large-scale capitalism. Robot by day, restless by night and by weekend. And, of course, the more of us that lose interest in *things*, the less desperate we will be for jobs, and the fewer people will be available to load the vans in the middle of the night on minimum wage, or less. When you stop buying, you start living and you stop contributing to an exploitative system.

Intellectuals of all stripes have been aware of the problem of desire since the dawn of the Industrial Revolution. One of the key figures in the intellectual history of anarchism is William Godwin, best known these days for being the father of Mary Shelley, who eloped with Percy Shelley at the age of seventeen and wrote *Frankenstein* while on a debauched holiday in Switzerland with a few literary mates, including Lord Byron. Godwin is also known for being married to the great writer Mary Wollstonecraft, author of *A Vindication of the Rights of Women*, who very sadly died while giving birth to Mary Shelley. Godwin was an earnest man, lacking an instinct for fun, but a wise and humane thinker. His great work, *Enquiry Concerning Political Justice*, was first published in 1793, roughly thirty years after the invention of the Spinning Jenny and when we were well on the way to establishing the new consumer system. And his analysis of the manipulation of desire by the dominant powers is strikingly relevant today. What, Godwin asks, are the good things of the world?

> They may be divided into four classes: subsistence; the means of intellectual and moral improvement; unexpensive gratifications; and such gratifications, as are by no means essential to healthful and vigorous existence, and cannot be purchased but with considerable labour and industry. It is the last class principally that imposes an obstacle in the way of equal distribution. It will be a matter of after-consideration how far and how many articles of this class would be admissable into the purest mode of social existence. But, in the meantime, it is unavoidable to remark the inferiority of this class to the three preceding. Without it we may enjoy to a great extent, activity, contentment and cheerfulness. And in what manner are those seeming superfluities usually produced? By abridging multitudes of men, to a deplorable degree, in points of essential moment, that one man may be accommodated, with sumptuous yet, strictly considered, insignificant luxuries.

There we have it. I think the word 'inferiority' is a powerful one to describe consumer gewgaws. To work hard to produce useless items of nothing and then to make that the sole purpose of living – this is the insanity of desire. If you can remove the desire for such trinkets, then, very simply, you don't have to work so hard and are therefore to a significant degree freer than you were before. This is to say nothing of the grand exploitation of human beings which goes on in order to produce these gewgaws (what Godwin terms 'abridging multitudes of men, to a deplorable degree') in factories and mills, and still today in our supermarkets and distribution centres. This gives us a further inducement to overcome desire for pieces of crap, better cars or better homes. The process of improvement and envy and desire is nicely satirized in an episode of *The Simpsons* in which Marge is to be seen reading a magazine called *Better Homes. Than Yours.* A simple trick for the freedom-seeker is to stop buying glossy magazines, which make us feel bad and spend money.

If we can cut out Godwin's fourth category of good things, the gratifications which can only be purchased with excessive toil, then our lives can become very much richer. The first three good things are: subsistence, that is, food and drink and shelter; 'intellectual and moral improvement', which I take to mean books and friends, (friends are completely free and books can always be bought cheaply or borrowed from the library – or from friends); and inexpensive gratifications, which I take to mean tobacco and beer. So, put simply, if you have somewhere to live, enough money to buy or produce good food, friends, books and plenty of booze and cigarettes, then how bad can life be? These are the important things. All the rest is mere decoration, distraction, vanity, ostentation. But somehow the fourth category has taken over as the most important in our minds. This must stop!

This unmaterialistic attitude can be achieved on any income. What we need is *not to care*. How I love people who don't care, those free souls, the bright of eye. Not those who are cruel and selfish but those who are simply free of care or, literally, carefree. I have one friend who earns millions and another friend who earns less than £5,000 a year, but they have much more in common with each other than with many of the people in the middle, precisely because both are remarkably unmaterialistic.

They will give you their best suit, empty their cellars of wine when you visit. 'Some put their trust not in God but in vanities,' wrote St Thomas Aquinas, 'and what are these vanities? They are temporal goods, riches, honour and the like, *and indeed all things are vanity, every man living.*' But having these goods is neither here nor there; it is one's attitude to them that counts. Aquinas was also quite clear that you do not have to be an ascetic to be saved: 'Abstinence in eating and drinking has no essential bearing on salvation: The kingdom of God is not meat and drink . . . the holy apostles understood that the kingdom of God does not consist in eating and drinking, but in resignation to either lot, for they are neither elated by abundance, nor distressed by want.'

In other words, be cool. Once again, Aquinas is very close to the existentialists and the Taoists. It's a philosophy of non-attachment. Treat abundance and want with the same detachment. In the case of my own household, we were recently forced to reject consumer desire by a two-year period of involuntary poverty. Before this, I had been earning a big whack working as a consultant for large companies, doing advertising and publishing work. Suddenly, my income was reduced to an eighth of its previous level. I stopped reading newspapers, watched very little TV and moved out of the city. By economizing and cutting out the fripperies, we found that we were less exposed to false consumer desire than we had been before. To give up reading newspapers and magazines was partly a money-saving exercise, but it had the happy result of removing ourselves from the temptations of a million things. The odd thing was that the experience was satisfying and enjoyable. It did not feel like a miserable self-sacrifice.

Banishing TV was a good step. It is advertised as a service, but it's a method of simultaneously scaring us, diverting us from our own selves with entertainment, selling us products we don't need and making us believe in money as a sort of religion. Watching telly can also make us feel useless: we watch the experts doing things instead of doing them ourselves. It is far better, said Bertrand Russell, to do something badly yourself than to watch someone else doing it well. The Protestants who attacked medieval superstition and magic could never have dreamt of anything so magical and powerful and disabling as the television.

Of course, desire, or 'hunting after gold', existed before large-scale capitalism was invented. In the *Anatomy of Melancholy*, Burton tells the story of Hippocrates finding Democritus sitting on a stone, reading a book and cutting up animals, in order, he says, 'to find out the cause of madness and melancholy':

Hippocrates commended his work, admiring his happiness and leisure. And why, quoth Democritus, have you not that leisure? Because, replied Hippocrates, domestic affairs hinder, necessary to be done for ourselves, neighbours, friends; expenses, diseases, frailties and mortalities which happen; wife, children, servants, and such business which deprive us of our time. At this speech Democritus profusely laughed (his friends and the people standing by, weeping in the meantime and lamenting his madness). Hippocrates asked the reason why he laughed. He told him, at the vanities and fopperies of the time, to see men so empty of virtuous actions, to hunt so far after gold, having no end of ambition; to take such infinite pains for a little glory, and to be favoured of men; to make such deep mines into the earth for gold, and many times to find nothing, with loss of their lives and fortunes . . . They make great account of many senseless things. Esteeming them as a great part of their treasure, statues, pictures, and such like movables, dear bought, and so cunningly wrought, as nothing but speech wanteth in them, and yet they hate living persons speaking to them . . . when a boar is thirsty, he drinks what will serve him, and no more; and when his belly is full, ceaseth to eat: but men are immoderate in both – as in lust they covet carnal copulation at set times; men always, ruinating thereby the health of their bodies.

Raising great projects to mine for gold and then finding nothing is a precise metaphor for desire and activity today. Burton goes on to include 'checking desires' as one of the paths to freedom. Truly, fools are slaves:

'Tis Tully's paradox, 'Wise men are free, but fools are slaves,' liberty is a power to live according to his own laws, as we will ourselves: who hath this liberty? Who is free?

> He is wise that can command his own will,
> Valiant and constant to himself still,
> Whom poverty nor death, nor bands can fright,
> Checks his desires, scorns honours, just and right.

Freedom, then, exists in a sort of spiritual self-sufficiency. The truly free do not join the chase for riches or for honours because they know that along that road lies slavery. The truly free fear nothing. This was a similar thought to that of Aldous Huxley in his introduction to the *Bhagavad-Gita*: 'There will never be enduring peace unless and until human beings come to accept a philosophy of life more adequate to the cosmic and psychological facts than the insane idolatries of nationalism and the advertising man's apocalyptic faith in Progress towards a mechanized New Jerusalem.'

The *Bhagavad-Gita* contains sound advice on work and creation. 'The word is imprisoned in its own activity, except when actions are performed as worship of God. Therefore, you must perform every action sacramentally, and be free from all attachment to results.' In other words, we should concentrate on *means* rather than *ends*. Desire and modern capitalism preach that means are unimportant and that ends are all: 'I'm only doing my job.' We are a goal-centred society, whereas what the medieval age and the one anarchists dream of values is a life based around pleasure in the process rather than the fleeting and insubstantial pleasure of fulfilling a desire. You don't have to believe in God to see the truth of the above quote when it comes to work. Simply substitute 'with generosity' or 'with love' for 'as worship of God', and you get the same thing but in the secular version.

The existentialists had a useful approach to desire. For Sartre, desire is not something you could be free from exactly; rather, it is something that you embrace but without necessarily acting on it. This can certainly be true in the case of sexual desire. 'Say a massively fanciable woman walks into your life,' said Penny Rimbaud. 'To act on your desire would be to run the risk of completely wrecking your home life. So you act on it and embrace it, but in your mind. You go through the process

. . .' In the existential world, you invite the desire in, talk to it, allow yourself to be amused by its company, chat with it and, then, when it leaves, blow out the candle and go to bed. So, in order to be free from it and for it not to master you, it is important to acknowledge it in the first place and not simply to blank it out and pretend that it doesn't exist. I recently had the absurd dream of buying a Land Rover, for which I have no practical need whatsoever. I just like the look of them. I took one for a drive and, for about two weeks, it was as if I really did own it. Then the desire faded, with the happy result of me not spending money I didn't have on another encumbrance.

Well, so much for shopping. Next time you find yourself believing that shopping and choosing between brands is an expression of your freedom, just think of those zombie movies in which the living dead mutely walk in and out of shops and ride up and down the escalators. What a visionary that director was. Telly-watching makes us into zombies. So, first step: disconnect the telly. Now, underneath the desire to shop lies fear, and it's to conquering this particular threat to liberty that we now turn.

THROW OUT THE TELLY

11 Smash the Fetters of Fear

There is a charming tale of Tchekov's about a man who tried to teach a kitten to catch mice. When it wouldn't run after them, he beat it, with the result that even as an adult cat, it cowered with terror in the presence of a mouse. 'This is the man,' Tchekov adds, 'who taught me Latin.'
Bertrand Russell, 'Freedom versus Authority in Education', 1928

A chapel was built in the midst
Where I used to play on the green.
And the gates of this chapel were shut
And 'Thou shall not' writ over the door.
William Blake, 'The Garden of Love', 1793

I live in the middle of nowhere near the sea and, consequently, I drive past many tourists on the narrow lanes near by. As I pull in to let them pass, I always glance over to see whether they wave back to say thanks. One thing strikes me about these tourists, who are exclusively middle-aged or elderly, white and bourgeois, and that is their fear. More often than not, they will avoid eye contact, grip the wheel and stare in front of them at the road. They are not being rude, it's just that they seem terrified of being alive, too scared to glance up and smile or wave. They set up plastic chairs next to the boots of their cars on picnics, too frightened to walk a few paces away from their motorized security blanket. Full of nerves, like little rabbits, they move from one protected zone to another. The country-side is now merely a provider of views to the cowering suburbanites.

How much more fun life must have been when we went around on horses, chatting to strangers, leaning over gates, leaping over fences, singing with joy, being at one with nature, its animals and its weather. Thomas Hardy had a great nostal-gia for these old ways, before man became cowed and submissive. In *The Return of the Native*, he complained that a new, worried look was becoming the norm: 'The view of life as a thing to be put up with, replacing that zest for existence which was so intense in early civilizations, must ultimately enter so thoroughly into the constitution of the advanced races that its facial expression will become accepted as a new artis-tic departure.'

The freedom of being on a horse's back rather than in a car is absolutely palpable. Cars are a cocoon. The horse also, impor-tantly for me, can offer the rider the fantasy of being a medieval knight. Even though I tend to look rather ridiculous when I ride, wearing a bicycle helmet and wellies and sitting on a squat little pony not far off from a shire horse, I can still see myself as a Troubadour, Thomas IX de Martinhoe, riding to find my lady and looking forward to an evening of music and merriment, of good company, of swans, bustards, spiced wine and a roaring fire at the next castle . . .

Motor cars sell themselves as a mix of excitement and safety, a sort of Toad-like freedom of the open road mixed with womb-like promise. But they are one of the most deadly things about modern life and kill 3,500 people each year in the UK – that's ten a day, pretty much, vastly more than drugs or terrorism or AIDS or crime. Globally, traffic accidents are the ninth biggest cause of death (compared with war, coming in twenty-first, and violence, seventeenth). The things we cling to in order to protect us from life are the very things that will kill us, most likely. After a recent series of crashes, I found myself without a car, and so, instead of driving five miles to our nearest town, I walked, and what an enormous, thrilling pleasure that was and how un-dangerous, how full of joy compared to driving in a car, which is full of tiny terrors. Nowadays, we think it's normal to drive for four hours in a state of tension and fear, but it's crazy.

Like many of the problems I discuss in this book, fear is actually rather convenient to the smooth functioning of an orderly society. A docile population which is terrified of the authorities in their various forms, whether supermarket, bank, school or boss, and afraid of other human beings, will more likely depend on objects and institutions to give them guidance, solidity, security and a sense of meaning. If you are fearful, then you are unlikely to riot and very likely to work hard and spend hard.

Fear keeps us observing life rather than living it. We are spectators rather than participators. People would rather watch a soap opera than live in one. Indeed, when you come across a lively community in real life, people will sometimes say: 'It's like a soap opera round here!' What they are forgetting is that soap operas are supposed to be like life (apart from the obvious flaw that in soap operas no one ever watches soap operas). Like TV, cars keep life at a distance, as something to be looked at rather than lived: the view from the sofa, the view of the beauty spot glimpsed through the windscreen.

And at every terrorist bomb, at every *Daily Mail* front-page story about rising crime, at every strike and calamity, the directors and shareholders of the big insurance companies must rub their hands with glee. The profits of fear are considerable indeed.

Fear is a tool of control. It is fear of punishment that will keep a classroom quiet and make the teacher's job easier; it is fear of the sack that will keep the grumbling workers quiet. Fear is also an efficient controlling device. It also helps us to fulfil our roles as consumers. It is fear of life itself that keeps us spending in the arcades and typing our credit-card numbers into websites. It is fear that will prevent us from breaking out, fear that will stop us, like Chief Bromden in Ken Kesey's *One Flew over the Cuckoo's Nest*, from tearing the control panel from the floor in Nurse Ratched's ward, hurling it through the window and vaulting over the fence into the wild prairies, escaping into ourselves. Much easier to line up with the others and take the pills.

We might ask where fear comes from: our nature or our nurturing? Is it produced and conditioned in us or is there something innately fearful in man's breast? One source of fear is certainly the education system. Little children are fearless, imperious anarchists, and the education system works and works on them over a period of fifteen years to instil docility so that they won't complain too much when they end up with a boring job. Education is like pruning; it wrecks the natural growth of the tree in favour of a form that is useful to commercial society. Mass education in the late Victorian age arrived when there was an urgent need for clerks in the new expanding worlds of insurance and banking, the world inhabited by Tony Hancock in the film *The Rebel*. Today the 'Thing', as Cobbett called it, or the 'Combine', as Ken Kesey called it, needs us to be able, at the very least, to type our PIN into a machine, and for that we need a certain standard of literacy and numeracy. So you're taught how to type, click a mouse and shop in Tesco's – but not how to grab hold of life, to live it joyfully and fearlessly.

Perhaps the greatest obstacle to freedom is our own fear of freedom. You may remember that great scene in *One Flew over the Cuckoo's Nest* where McMurphy suddenly realizes that half of the inmates are on the ward voluntarily:

'Are you guys bullshitting me!'

Nobody'll say anything. McMurphy walks up and down in front of that bench, running his hand around in that thick hair. He walks all the way to the back of the line, then all the way to the front, to the X-ray machine. It hisses and spits at him.

'You, Billy – you must be committed, for Christsakes!'

Billy's got his back to us, his chin up on the black screen, standing on tiptoe. No, he says into the machinery.

'Then why? Why? You're just a young guy! You oughta be out running around in a convertible, bird-dogging girls. All of this' – he sweeps his hand around him again – 'why do you stand for it?'

Billy doesn't say anything, and McMurphy turns from him to another couple of guys.

'Tell me why. You gripe, you bitch for weeks on end about how you can't stand this place, can't stand the nurse or anything about her, and all the time you ain't committed. I can understand it with some of those old guys on the ward. They're nuts. But you, you're not exactly the everyday man on the street, but you're not nuts.'

They don't argue with him. He moves on to Sefelt.

'Sefelt, what about you? There's nothing wrong with you but you have fits. Hell, I had an uncle who threw conniptions twice as bad as yours and saw visions from the Devil to boot, but he didn't lock himself in the nuthouse. You could get along outside if you had the guts —'

'Sure!' It's Billy, turned from the screen, his face boiling tears. 'Sure!' he screams again. 'If we had the g-guts! I could go outside to-today, if I had the guts. My m-m-mother is a good friend of M-Miss Ratched, and I could get an AMA signed this afternoon, if I had the guts!'

We're all frightened little Billy Bibbits and Hardings and Sefelts, retreated, self-incarcerated, complaining endlessly about everything but too full of fear to do anything about it. We are, in the words of the song by those musical geniuses Suicidal Tendencies, 'Institutionalized', and it is institutions that are one of the very worst inventions of the last 250 years. The madman is no longer part of the village; he is in the asylum.

We've clipped our own wings. We can easily rage at school, like John Lennon in 'Working Class Hero', in which he rightly accuses the education system of merely pumping us full of fear in order to make us into scared little work-slaves frightened to put our heads above the parapet. In actual fact, that is probably why, much as I hate war, soldiers tend to be of a better quality than the average human being. They have seen hardships, they have suffered, they have overcome fear, and now they can stride into the world, unafraid of hunger or deprivation. They are self-sufficient and community-minded.

Our built-in stupidity is what makes us fearful. We can't do enough for ourselves and therefore rely on others to do things, and that makes us scared. We have also been told since the days of the Protestant revolution that we are more or less alone in this world, that we should trust nobody and suffer alone and in silence. How different from the old 'brotherhood of man' of pre-1500 days, where we were all in this together.

We also have to deal with the relationship between ego and fear, between self-importance and fear. We don't try to do things, because we are scared of doing them badly. So we don't do anything at all. It is rather like Withnail in Bruce Robinson's brilliant movie *Withnail and I*: 'I don't want to *understudy* Constantin,' he bellows self-importantly from the red phone box to his agent in London, 'I want to play the part!'

I prefer the existential idea, where you realize that everything is absurd, that one thing is not intrinsically better than another. Life is about nothingness, so go and create your own life and enjoy it. Everything is vanity, fiction, conditioning, self-created, mind-forg'd. Sartre's *Being and Nothingness* is a tough read, but it's full of beautiful passages and though abstract, the philosophy is a practical one. To me, it is not a million miles away from the oriental shruggery of Taoism, or even the fatalistic Christianity of Aquinas which teaches that you trust in Providence and don't bother striving. When Aquinas quotes the Bible as saying, 'All is vanity,' he may just as well be saying, 'Life is absurd.' All the rushing around and sweating for what used to be called 'honour and riches' and what is now called 'career advancement', it's all a complete waste of time. Worldly life is a fiction. Vanity and absurdity are the same thing – mere creations of man's imagination, utterly without meaning. Better therefore to get on with creating your own life. All three philosophies are also to their very core opposed to slavery, subjugation and exploitation.

This is why, although Tolstoy and Gandhi are persuasive on matters of war and non-violence, I would not be shy of using military metaphors for life. There is something genuinely noble about the warrior of old who is fearlessly and selflessly battling for a greater good than saving his own meaningless skin. That is why the ancients held up the example of *otium* (leisure) and *bellum* (war) as the noble paths in contrast to the scrabbling, vain, mean-minded bourgeois path of work and business. Put simply, the thinkers and fighters, the *oratores* and the *bellatores* have not had their balls cut off by Nurse Ratched. But the thinkers and fighters have all but disappeared today, or they have been reduced merely to the role of diverters. The Army says it is asked to do 'a job', so it goes and does 'the job'.

Rip up the control panel from the floor and hurl it through the window. We need to get out there with loud voices, cheerful smiles, waving at people. Say goodbye to those chills of fear, the Sunday night feeling, the dread before a meeting, the tightening in the stomach when we receive a letter from the Inland Revenue. Don't be scared of them! They are sent out by frightened little rabbits, Billy Bibbits sitting in airless offices, gazing out of the window, lost in sexual reveries, wary of losing their jobs. They don't exist!

This morning, I received a summons to go to court for driving without insurance. At first, I was terrified and indignant. Then I made the decision to laugh at it. It will be an adventure and, even if I do get banned from driving, so what? I'm trying to cut down on car use anyway. I understand that we spend something like £5,000 a year on our cars, and you can buy an awful lot of train fares and taxi rides for that sort of money. Come on, throw it at me! I'll pin the summons on the wall, show it to visitors. I laugh at your summons! Who cares?

What of fear in my pre-1500 medieval utopia? Well, the sorts of fears we've glanced at here were unknown because there were no governments or institutions of the sort we live with today. Fear, though, was a central part of life back then and that fear was a fear of God, a fear of not being saved. But this fear was of quite a different order to today's crippling, disabling fears. Medieval fear could be a positive force. According to Thomas Aquinas, fear was more of an abstract quality that was useful for salvation: 'For he that is without fear cannot be justified . . . the beginning of wisdom is the fear of the Lord.'

Aquinas here presents fear as a creative force rather than a destructive one. Fear was not a reason to shrink away from living, as it is today, and to find solace in shopping and TV. Fear is a sort of humility. He seems to say: acknowledge your fear and play with it, make use of it. Fear in the good old days of Merry Old England was something to engage with, eyes bright, bows burning with gold. Do not fear fear! Jump on that horse! Reject those tyrants, Health and Safety!

RIDE THE CHARIOT OF FIRE

12 *Forget Government*

*Man . . . has been taught to believe that men would tear each other
to pieces, if they had not priests to direct their consciences, lords to
consult for their tranquility, and kings to pilot them in safety through
the dangers of the political ocean.*
William Godwin, *Enquiry Concerning Political Justice*, 1793

*Democracy, as conceived by politicians, is a form of government, that is
to say, it is a method of making people do what their leaders wish under
the impression that they are doing what they themselves wish.*
Bertrand Russell, 'Freedom versus Authority in Education', 1928

*Please note. Persons wishing to obtain credit may experience problems
obtaining credit if their name does not appear on the Electoral Register.*
Letter from council to author asking for vote registration, 2006

Politicks are now nothing more than a means of rising in the world.
With this sole view do men engage in politicks, and their whole
conduct proceeds upon it.
Dr Johnson, in Boswell's *Life of Johnson*, 1775

I am an anarchist.
Pierre-Joseph Proudhon, 1848

In our Western, more-or-less liberal democracies, it rarely occurs to us that we might be able to live free of government. A vast, centralized state seems such an unavoidable reality that the most we seem able to hope for is to vote every five years for a very slightly different oligarchy to correct the worst excesses of the previous one. We cannot see beyond parliament as a means of organizing things. We grumble about the clowns in power and then elect a new lot of clowns. We believe in 'reform', that endless, futile process of meddling. Hope triumphs over experience.

Governments do too much and they do most of it badly. Governments, for example, are supposed to defend us from attack. But they don't do it very well. In fact, they encourage other people to attack us by attacking them first. Just look at Iraq. Terrorists have killed far fewer of us than we have killed ourselves by sending men to war. At the time of writing, 27,000 civilians have been killed in Iraq, and around 50 have been killed by Islamic terrorists in Britain. Governments appreciate terrorists, because they provide a good advertisement for the need for government, for its protection. They love wars, because they give government a reason for existing – to save us from the infidel. The enemy is created by the government, as George Orwell showed in *Nineteen Eighty-Four*. The alternative – anarchy, or self-government – is characterized as leading to lawlessness and disorder. But, as the pacifist and author of *War and Peace*, Leo Tolstoy, put it:

> . . . even if the absence of government really meant anarchy in the negative disorderly sense of that word – which is far from being the case – even then no anarchical disorder could be worse than the position to which governments have already led their peoples, and to which they are leading them.

There is also something rotten at the heart of government – and that is the simple fact that to be in power is a career option. You get paid for it. Plus, you get free taxis, swanky dinners, and people write about you in the newspapers. Politics is *Fame Academy* for the talentless, the *X-Factor* for boring men and women. Surely the fact that every politician is on a career treadmill and is constantly trying to earn more money and reach a higher position in the hierarchy is in itself enough evidence to damn the entire project? If our public servants, so-called, were unpaid and anonymous, then we might find it easier to trust them. Not so long ago, MPs *were* unpaid. John Wilkes, for example, never received a salary. Politics had not been so tragically professionalized. This is not to say, for sure, that many politicians are not well intentioned, but the well intentioned can do more harm than those who refrain from interfering. Doubtless, the Puritans meant well when they banned Christmas.

Politics is not the art of running a country, it is the art of persuading the people that they need a set of paid politicians to run the country. And in this dark art, our leaders are skilled and proficient. In order to keep themselves in power, they need to sell us the idea of themselves as our saviours and also to sell us the idea that we could not run things without them. In other words, they simply need to convince us that we are stupid and helpless. And this is what they work so hard to do. This is achieved principally by constant media coverage. Every newspaper, every radio bulletin, every TV news show, every news-based website: they are all crammed to bursting with coverage of party politics. It is the kind of free publicity that a PR for a private company can only dream of. And all these bulletins sell the inevitability and the necessity of government to us. They do it very well: most prime ministers would be very plausible sellers of second-hand cars – indeed, I don't doubt that most could sell you crack cocaine while persuading you that you were helping struggling economies and doing your health a lot of good into the bargain.

Moral campaigns like the so-called 'war on drugs' are simply carried out in order to convince us that the politicians have some sense of good and bad. The conventional reaction to the Holocaust is 'Never again'. We have a Holocaust Day, even, whose stated purpose is to prevent such evil ever coming to pass again. In congratulating ourselves that we are not literally sending Jews to camps and gas chambers, we avoid confronting the reality that we are sending other people to other forms of death and slavery today, right here, right now.

Then there is the spectacle of a general election. Every five years or so, the people, who have been more or less ignored by the politicians since the previous election, are suddenly bombarded with the notion that voting is very important. In an absurd piece of theatre, party leaders appear on television and are asked questions by groups of 'ordinary people'. This TV show, which is on for an hour every five years, is supposed to convince the viewer that we live in a democracy. Leaflets are dropped, earnest young candidates (career politicians on the make) come to the door promising that they will sort out the mess created by the current government. Newspapers are full of endless speculation and reports on the campaigns. I suppose that the whole thing can be enjoyed for a few moments as a piece of entertainment. The mistake is to think it has the slightest meaning or relevance to our everyday lives whatsoever. The election will happen, the fever will die down and things will go back to normal, the elected party doing whatever it feels like because it persuades itself that the people have elected it.

People who believe in parliamentary democracy of this sort only believe in it when their party wins. Otherwise, they would be delighted whatever the result, because if you really did believe in the majority vote being the right vote, then you would change your political allegiance to the will of the majority. But, instead, what happens is that the Tory voter simply complains when Labour wins and keeps his allegiance to the Tory party. The liberals in America are anti-Bush but they are pro-democracy. But if you are anti-Bush, then, in fact, you are anti-democracy. They don't see that it is not Bush who is at fault so much as the entire system. If you believe in democracy then you really shouldn't complain when the party which pulls in the most votes becomes the governing party.

The niggardly spirit of parliament communicates itself to the farthest reaches of the kingdom. The bureaucrats, the joyless health and safety police, have tentacles everywhere. I recently tried to organize a barn dance in my local village hall. A simple task, one might have thought. But no. After battling with piles of forms in order to get a Public Entertainment Licence so we would be permitted by the authorities to have eighty people dancing to a violin and an accordion, I eventually gave up, because, in order to get the licence for this one event, we were going to have to spend £1,400 to have an emergency lighting system installed, thanks to health and safety regulations. Well, £1,400 might be affordable to a big company, but our village hall funds, the profits of whist drives and slide shows, simply would not stretch. So what I did instead was to throw the party anyway but keep it private. I sent invitations to all the locals and all our friends. On the day itself, we suggested that people make a £5 donation so we could pay the bands, the Alabama 3 (acoustic version) and Louis Eliot. People brought their own booze. Victoria cooked a mighty ham, and we offered baguettes. We held it at tea-time and called it a tea dance so people could bring their kids. The party started at four, finished at eight thirty that evening. Everyone drank heavily, the room was filled with smoke, there was dancing, and farmers, hippies, neighbours and friends alike had a thoroughly good time. We even made a small profit, which went back into the village hall fund.

However, I could easily have given up, and that would have been as a direct result of recent government legislation, which removes power from localities, imposes the same rules across the whole country and makes it very, very difficult to put on a party. And the final insult is that we pay the government between a quarter and a half of our income for the privilege of being patronized and bossed around. We are obliged by law to spend an enormous amount of money in tax so that 650 parliamentarians can give full rein to their vanity and bustling self-importance. Even the supposedly put-upon medieval peasant was expected to put only 10 per cent of his earnings and produce into the local pot. If he resented that, what would he think of giving up to 40 per cent? And, in the days before standing armies and national debt, there was no central taxation. Your tithes went straight back into your local community rather than, as today, your tax being sucked off to London, wasted on the salaries of a load of ditherers and then returned to your local area having shrunk to almost nothing.

In the past, the Puritan tendencies of Parliament were often corrected to a degree by the more fun-loving monarchy. Now, sadly, the monarchy has lost any sort of power, and the old system of a parliament and a king has been replaced by government by the boring, a tediocracy. I rejoice when Prince Charles comes out with a cranky view. He opposes the bourgeois consensus and has the courage to express opinions that do not reflect the received wisdom.

There is a real alternative to elected governments. It is self-government, or anarchy, or running one's own affairs without relying on external authority. Anarchy, as I mentioned earlier, has a bad name. But, in fact, it is an eminently sensible and sane way of organizing things, because it stresses the importance of local solutions. Some of our most brilliant thinkers, as we've seen, men like William Godwin, Proudhon, Kropotkin, Oscar Wilde, Tolstoy and Gandhi, were anarchists. All of them saw the failings of big central government as a principle of social arrangement and sought to dream up alternatives based on individual liberty and a federal system of self-government.

This has worked in the past. We have only our own weakness to blame in submitting to governments. The first step is to recognize that there is a problem and to realize, in Proudhon's words, the 'insufficiency of the principle of authority'. Anarchy is about the creative spirit fighting the cowed spirit, and the battle has to start within ourselves. We need to recognize our own dignity, power and creative force in order not to allow our laziness and desire for comfort to prevent us from living how we want to live. Here is how Tolstoy defines it:

> Anarchy is a form of government or constitution in which public and private consciousness, formed through the development of science and law, is alone sufficient to maintain order and guarantee all liberties. In it, as a consequence, the institutions of the police, preventive and repressive methods, officialdom, taxation, etc., are reduced to a minimum. In it, more especially, the forms of monarchy and intensive centralization disappear, to be replaced by federal institutions and a pattern of life based on the commune. When politics and home life have become one and the same thing, when economic problems have been solved in such a way that individual and collective interests are identical, then – all constraints having disappeared – it is evident that we will be in a state of total liberty or anarchy.

Something very close to this was achieved in the later Middle Ages with the aforementioned Guilds system, as Kropotkin and others have shown. As we saw earlier, the ordinary people rose up across Europe, freed themselves from submission to the nobles, formed themselves into guilds and created their own free cities. The thirteenth century witnessed an amazing popular movement, which created a new ideal of freedom right across Europe, and the philosopher and friend of Bertrand Russell, A. N. Whitehead, in *Symbolism: Its Meaning and Effect*, claims that this sense of freedom lasted even into the seventeenth century:

> So far as their individual freedom is concerned, there was more diffused freedom in the City of London in the year 1633 . . . than there is today in any industrial city of the world. It is impossible to understand the social history of our ancestors unless we remember the surging freedom which then existed within the cities of England, of Flanders, of the Rhine Valley, and of Northern Italy. Under our present industrial system, this type of freedom is being lost. This loss means the fading from human life of values infinitely precious to it. The divergent use of individual temperaments can no longer find their various satisfactions in serious activities. There only remain ironbound conditions of employment and trivial amusements for leisure.

Spoken like a punk. Spoken like a Situationist. So what can we do? What can we do? What can we do in order, as the modern vernacular has it, to 'get our lives back'? What can we do to be ourselves, rather than trying to conform and contort ourselves into a uniform model? Well, we can start simply by ignoring government. The best way to smash the state is to take no notice of it and hope it goes away. We are constantly told by the media that not voting is a sign of 'apathy', while to me it is a sign of the absolute opposite. When you do not vote, as I don't, then something fundamental shifts in your psyche. You can no longer blame the government for your problems, as you have opted out of their system. Therefore, you start, in Kropotkin's phrase, to 'act for yourself'. You become responsible.

The first step, and it might be the only step, is the straightforward one of creating anarchy in your own backyard, your own anarchy in the UK. Right now, for example, there is a discussion on the *Idler* web forum about creating your own energy. Readers are recommending to each other various microtechnologies for the house that will reduce dependence on the big utility companies and cut bills. The reader who introduced the topic wrote:

> This is about saying bollocks to the ditherers at government level and getting on with doing whatever is do-able at private domestic household level, in normal suburban and urban houses, to help trim the rocketing fuel bills.

In other words, an anarchic approach to life is supremely practical. It is cheap and easy. Far from being an indulgent dream, it makes more practical sense than relying on external authorities to sort out your problems. Sitting around waiting for a revolution is unlikely to get results. And would revolution work anyway? A revolution presupposes a battle between two forces. One force will win, and that force will attempt to run the country via some kind of government – and we're back to square one. Therefore, the notion of a revolution is actually absurd. Revolution is merely a form of reform. We need to go more radical, more extreme than revolution, we need to go one step beyond. And the straightforward answer is to concentrate on ourselves and on local change. In short, we need to set a good example.

An important mental step in escaping the power of government is to understand that, to some degree, we ourselves are complicit with the problem. By not acting for ourselves, we allow others to act for us. In *Being and Nothingness*, Sartre says that it's no use sitting around moaning about your life, because that is to abdicate responsibility for it. And nothing external can make us think or act in certain ways unless we allow it to do so. In the existentialist world, where life is absurd, you may as well create your own life. 'To act', as I interpret it, is to accept that we are radically responsible for the creation of our own lives. Tolstoy made the same point:

> People construct this terrible machine of power, they allow anyone to seize it who can (and the chances are that it will be seized by the most morally worthless) – they slavishly submit to him, and are then surprised that evil comes of it. They are afraid of anarchists' bombs, and are not afraid of this terrible organization which is always threatening them with the greatest calamities.

And today we fear terrorism when the real enemy is our own government.

Instead of attacking the status quo – always a foolish idea, as attacking something tends to make it stronger (governments love opposition!) – it might be wiser to create our own societies alongside the current system and simply do our best to ignore the Thing altogether. In order to keep bureaucracy and taxes to a minimum, we will earn small amounts of money and instead do favours for each other. We don't want affordable housing, jobs and shopping centres. Those are slave's perks, handed down by authority, which may be more or less lenient according to whichever government fate has installed. What we want is to create our own little aristocracies, as D. H. Lawrence has it. We want soil, caravans and trees, smallholdings, vegetable patches, art and crafts. And beer and books. That's all. So, not a turning over but rather a mass ignoring of the dominant system might be our only hope.

Now, what about distributism, the idea that every family should have an acre or two of land. In the introduction to *Distributist Perspectives*, a collection of essays recently published by IHS Press, the contemporary Catholic academic Thomas Naylor writes:

> With the help of Distributism maybe it will be possible to (1) regain control of our lives from big government, big business, big cities, big schools, and big computer networks; (2) relearn how to take care of ourselves by decentralizing, and humanizing our lives; and (3) learn how to help others take care of themselves so that we all become less dependent on big businesses, big government, and big markets.

Distributism is anarchy. It is opposed to central control and to big business and it is in favour of self-direction and self-government. It says that 'small is beautiful.' It believes in human scale and sustainable systems. The objection that will be heard from the pub philosopher when the noble ideas of self-government, liberty and anarchy are raised is the old saw about 'human nature'. Left to our own devices, unregulated and uncontrolled by a central authority, we would fall to killing and raping each other. (By the way, have you noticed that, when about to utter a tedious platitude, piece of utter banality or shred of received wisdom, people always say: '*I* think . . .', with a great emphasis on the '*I*', as if they are about to utter an original comment based on long and deep thought and not a scrap of recycled propaganda picked up from the *Daily Mail*?)

As the guilds prove, the opposite is true. Government is a licence for people to kill and rape each other; government creates the killing and raping while pretending to prevent it. To repeat what Tolstoy says about government: '. . . even if the absence of government really meant anarchy in the negative disorderly sense of that word – which is far from being the case – even then no anarchical disorder could be worse than the position to which governments have already led their peoples, and to which they are leading them.'

You can see Distributism in action today in the allotment movement. All over the country, we are waking up to the possibilities of cultivating our own patch of land, for fun and food. Allotments are available from councils at extremely low rates, and any councillor reading this and wishing to make a name for him or herself should simply propose the creation of many more allotment sites.

Allotments bring power to the people. We can also see the self-reliant principles of Distributism alive and well in the Permaculture movement. There is no moaning here, no sitting around waiting for government to do something. In Permaculture, the emphasis is on what you can do to improve your everyday life now, to free ourselves from the iron grip of jobs, supermarkets, money and oil.

We need to create our own lives. 'I believe a man is happier,' wrote C. S. Lewis in his essay 'Willing Slaves of the Welfare State', 'and happy in a richer way, if he has "the freeborn mind" . . . and in adult life it is the man who needs, and asks, nothing of the Government who can criticize its acts and snap his fingers at its ideology.' Narnia is not so much a religious allegory, as is commonly thought, as a story about freedom. The White Witch is a symbol for Elizabeth I and her crackdown on fun, which attacked Merry England. In Narnia, you will remember, it is always winter and never Christmas. Mr Tumnus the fawn remembers the old days of dancing and merry-making. Gone is the variety of the seasons, gone feasting, gone dancing. Instead, mere uniformity. Thomas Cranmer's *Book of Common Prayer* was introduced in 1549, in the reign of Protector Somerset. With its banning of old religious festivals, it was introduced by an act of parliament called the Act of Uniformity, which I think speaks for itself: the old Catholic variety is attacked by the new Puritan uniformity.

We are, in fact, all free. It is just a question of whether or not we choose to exercise that freedom. We make the choice. I am here to remind you that you can be free if you so wish, for this is a simple fact that is more or less hidden from us. We are told we are slaves and we accept it because we can't be bothered to be free. Instead, we sink into work-slavery and shopping-slavery. Freedom is a finger-click away. Truly, the manacles are mind-forg'd.

STOP VOTING

13 *Say No to Guilt and Free Your Spirit*

Most of us are beholden to other people's expectations. But other people's
expectations didn't exist for me. So long as I was happy, that was all that
mattered. This gave me a wonderful advantage over other people my age
because, unfettered by conscience, I did exactly what I wanted.
Keith Allen, 'A to Z of Life', *Idler*, 2005

A man who has conscience is himself the Devil and hell and purgatory,
tormenting himself. He who is free in spirit escapes all these things.
John of Brünn, adept of the Free Spirit, *circa* 1320

In our heads we keep a sort of conscience account. Every pleasure has to be repaid with a goodly portion of guilt. For every
act of the free spirit within, the chained spirit wags a finger and
imposes a penance. When we have done something that we are

told is wrong, we torture ourselves with self-loathing, recrimin-ations and resolutions to behave better in the future. Guilt also drives us to do work that we do not enjoy. Readers of the *Idler* write in saying that they would like to be more free of work, but how can they deal with the guilt? Sitting around doing nothing, they say, makes them feel guilty. Therefore, they play the role of devil to themselves, lambasting themselves with diabolical little toasting forks, prodding and goading.

Guilt doesn't work. It is a disabling emotion not an enabling one. It is negative; it holds us back. I have always found guilt-inspired resolutions to be singularly ineffectual, for the simple reason that I always break them. And if we are to believe Nietzsche, then guilt is the emotional counterpart to debt. When you are guilty, you feel you owe someone something. And, indeed, he says, the commercial transaction may even pre-date the emer-gence of guilt into the emotional arena:

> The feeling of guilt, of personal obligation, had its origin . . . in the oldest and most primitive personal relationship, that between buyer and seller, creditor and debtor: it was here that one person first encountered another person, that one person first *measured himself* against another . . . the major moral concept Schuld [guilt] has its origin in the very material concept Schulden [debts].

This explanation of the origin of guilt suggests that guilt is not something innate. Also, for Nietzsche, the concept of guilt emerges when we draw a distinction between intention and action. 'I didn't mean to do that,' we will say. In this sense, guilt is then a total abstraction, for it presupposes that doing is different from choosing. The whole idea of guilt is based on the assumption that, inside us, there is a split between two warring factions – for me, Good Tom and Bad Tom. Bad Tom does something bad, and then Good Tom makes him feel bad about it. One day, we hope, Good Tom will conquer Bad Tom. But he never does. So the battle goes on, but the battle weakens our spirit, and this is one reason why guilt is debilitating.

It is irresponsible to feel guilty about past actions, because it means that you are likely to disavow responsibility for things you do. When we say, 'I feel really guilty about that,' it means that we reject the side of us that did that thing, whatever it was. Therefore, the guilt-free among us – and they do exist – are actually the most responsible of beings and not the most irresponsible because, if you take responsibility for your own actions, then you will not feel guilty about them.

A sign that guilt is not an innate emotion but something culturally produced can be found in the example of infidelity. A man who is unfaithful to his girlfriend may feel pangs of guilt. But when he has split up with that girlfriend, the guilt over the infidelity vanishes and, indeed, he may feel the opposite emotion – he might feel quite pleased with himself. It is obvious too that small children do not feel the burden of guilt. Guilt is something we learn to feel.

In our intimate social relations, as in our relations with the wider community, other people are constantly trying to foist a sense of indebtedness on to us. If you are given a dinner, you are supposed to send a thank-you card. Gifts are given with unspoken conditions about the level of gushing thanks which must be produced by the recipient. Events like Christmas become a maze of reciprocal obligations. Our heads become so full of all the things we ought to do that we are in danger of forgetting the things we need to do. We then send letters out of guilt rather than out of a genuine desire to express gratitude, and this is surely unhealthy, because then the letter becomes merely the discharge of a debt and not an expression of love or friendship.

We are asked to suffer for our sins. In the case of an infidelity, for example, the suffering is supposed in some way to atone for the misdeed. Funnily enough, in medieval times, fines replaced guilt. Manor rolls are full of men and women being fined for 'fornication'. Here are some examples from fourteenth-century Foxton:

Alice Gosse fornicated with William Overhawe; fined 6d.
Asselota, daughter of Alan Asselote, fornicated when at day-work of the reeve.
Alice Fenner fornicated with John Taylor out of wedlock; let her be distrained until she pay the fine.

Back then, instead of suffering for your sins, you just had to pay a fine into the communal kitty. One payment settled your account. In the same way, usurers would be saved from damnation if they paid back the money they had extorted before they died. Clearly, what happened is exactly as Nietszche wrote: a financial payback for misdeeds was gradually replaced by an emotional one; material obligations pre-date the emergence of moral burdens. In medieval Catholic times, you paid the fine and then got on with your life. In the Puritan version of things, money was no longer recompense for an immoral act; you had to pay by suffering. Nor could you pay back through confession; that wasn't good enough for the Puritans. You had to become a better person. Now, instead of repaying our debts, we are forced, like Christian in *A Pilgrim's Progress*, to carry the burden around on our backs on our endless quest for perfection.

But, insists Nietzsche, 'To ask it again: to what extent can suffering balance debts or guilt?' What difference does it make? My suffering makes no difference to anyone else. It is a negative; it is completely pointless; it has no practical benefit to anyone. Guilt can be synonymous, as Nietzsche says, with 'the icy No of disgust with life' – which is what the 'Just Say No' campaigns remind me of. We do something fun, then another part of us feels disgusted. Guilt is a nay-saying to life, and what the conscience-free have in common is an uplifting grabbing hold of life in all its awkwardness.

Most of us have the two tendencies fighting it out inside us. I once asked my friend Hannah if she was going to the party of a mutual friend, which was taking place on a Monday.

'Oh, I don't know,' she replied. 'There's the Monday-night rule.'

'The Monday-night rule?'

'Yes, you must know it. The rule that says you can't go out on a Monday night.'

Hannah, out of guilt for giving in to too much pleasure at weekends, had invented this rule as some sort of penance for her indulgent behaviour. She had split herself into two: the medieval roustabout, the 'eat, drink and be merry' Hannah on the one side, and the hard-working, pleasure-shirking Hannah on the other.

Guilt is an invention, it is manmade. We choose to allow ourselves to feel guilty; guilt is optional. And often we merely want to put on the appearance of feeling guilty to a friend or enemy in order to avoid an accusation of being thoughtless or uncaring. To express guilt seems to be the correct thing to do. 'I've been feeling really guilty for not coming to your party,' we might say. The guilt is expressed. And the answer that we are hoping for, more often than not, will come right back on cue: 'Oh, don't worry. It's fine.' Our guilt has repaid the debt. So now we have been released from the guilty feeling. Guilt is also a way for us to express to others that we are a person of good conscience. 'I feel really guilty about getting drunk last night,' we say, when in actual fact we feel no guilt whatsoever or, at least, we could *choose* to feel no guilt. When people say to me, 'I drank too much last night,' I always reply, 'I drank exactly the right amount.'

Some people are free of guilt. They are very unusual, but what they share is a Nietzschean Yes-saying to life and a powerful lack of conscience which enable them to do what they please. My friend the late Gavin Hills was untroubled by feelings of guilt and never felt indebted to others. This did not mean, however, that he behaved immorally or inconsiderately. In fact, he was quite an upstanding gent when it came to doing good (not in a busybody sense, but in making good things happen). He looked after lame ducks in his life, people who had somehow lost the way, but he never spoke of these lame ducks, and his friends only found out about them when he died. The free-wheeling pleasure-seeking actor Keith Allen is guilt-free; he does what he wants and therefore has never suffered from resentment. Far from being irresponsible, Gavin and Keith exemplify a radical responsibility in their refusal to submit to guilt, because guilt is, in a sense, a cop-out. And there is something marvellously heroic and liberating, about the total rejection of guilt. As Hazlitt wrote of the great libertine and poet John Wilmot, the Earl of Rochester, 'his contempt for everything that others respect almost amounts of sublimity'. Wilmot simply rejected conventional wisdom and bourgeois reality. We could say the same about contemporary libertine Peter Doherty: there is something spectacular and impressive about his total disregard for accepted morals and behaviour.

This sort of conscience-free living has a long tradition. Ancient Rome and Greece are full of it and, then, there is the example of the strange heretical sects of Europe which rebelled against guilt and good conscience because they saw them as a means of control rather than innate impulses. This was the case, for example, with the Sufis, as reported by Norman Cohn in *The Pursuit of the Millennium: Revolutionary Millenarians and Mystical Anarchists of the Middle Ages* (1957):

Towards the close of the twelfth century various Spanish cities, and notably Seville, witnessed the activities of mystical brotherhoods of Moslems. These people, who were known as Sufis, were 'holy beggars' who wandered in groups through the streets and squares, dressed in patched and parti-coloured robes. The novices amongst them were schooled in humiliation and self-abnegation: they had to dress in rags, to keep their eyes fixed on the ground, to eat revolting foodstuffs; and they owed blind obedience to the masters of the group. But once they emerged from their noviciate, these Sufis entered a realm of total freedom. Disclaiming book-learning and theological subtleties, they rejoiced in direct knowledge of God – indeed, they felt themselves united with the divine essence in a most intimate union. And this in turn liberated them from all restraints. Every impulse was experienced as a divine command; now they could surround themselves with worldly possessions, now they could live in luxury – and now, too, they could lie or steal or fornicate without qualms of conscience. For since inwardly the soul was wholly absorbed into God, external acts were of no account.

A wonderful philosophy, which allows you to embrace sensual pleasure while being free from it. A similarly amoral and anarchic approach was pursued by the Free Spirit mystic Henry Suso of Cologne, who in 1330 wrote an account of a conversation he had one Sunday afternoon with a bodiless image:

Suso: Whence have you come?
Image: I come from nowhere.
Suso: Tell me, what are you?
Image: I am not.
Suso: What do you wish?
Image: I do not wish.
Suso: This is a miracle! Tell me, what is your name?
Image: I am called Nameless Wildness.
Suso: Where does your insight lead to?
Image: Into untramelled freedom.
Suso: Tell me, what do you call untramelled freedom?
Image: When a man lives according to all his caprices without

distinguishing between God and himself, and without looking before or after.

In this context, guilt can be seen as a mind-forg'd manacle, as it tends to work to prevent capricious behaviour. Guilt, therefore, is on the side of authority rather than freedom. It is the boss within. Guilt also means an avoidance of the present: it is all about regret concerning actions in the past helping to strengthen resolve to improve behaviour in the future. Government presents the same reason for itself existing: without government, our so-called natural impulses would be given free rein, and the world would descend into anarchy, bloodshed and looting. So, guilt is a sort of 'government of the mind', as the film-writer Bruce Robinson put it.

The answer? Lower your standards! Take it easy! Embrace merriment! Accept disorder! One of the very many difficult legacies of Puritanism is the notion of perfectionism. The Catholics, for all their corruption and easy morals, at least were easier on themselves. The Puritan sets himself impossibly high standards of behaviour and then beats himself up when he fails to meet them.

But if you lower your standards and make it easy on yourself, then you will give yourself fewer opportunities to feel guilty. The higher your moral standards, the greater the guilt. Remove all moral standards and you will become completely free.

SAY YES

14 *No More Housework, or the Power of the Candle*

It is just as irksome to have a servant as to be a servant.
D. H. Lawrence, 'Education of the People', 1918

Few tasks are more like the torture of Sisyphus than housework,
with its endless repetition: the clean becomes soiled, the soiled is
made clean, over and over, day after day.
Simone de Beauvoir, *The Second Sex*, 1949

A certain aversion to housework – cleaning, washing up, doing the laundry, mopping floors, making beds – seems almost to be an innate characteristic of man, and certainly of the lazier among us. In the early medieval age, when we looked down on manual labour, this prejudice was no less powerful: Aquinas, for example, put dishwashers at the bottom of the scale of professions, because they had to deal with dirt. The Greeks and Romans delegated such unpleasant toil to the slaves. In George Orwell's *Down and Out in Paris and London*, the *plongeurs* are the lowest of the low, far below the relatively aristocratic waiters and cooks in the Parisian kitchen hierarchy. And, if you make the mistake of going to seek a job in your local Jobcentre, the only job ever on offer seems to be the one that no one wants: kitchen porter.

In the capitalist system, the conventional way of dealing with the problem of housework is to try to earn enough money to pay someone else to do it. Cash will deliver us from toil. The middle-class Victorian household was full of servants, and even the lowliest country vicar employed a housekeeper. The smart Victorian wife became a flopping, swooning, useless, trussed-up ornament who was not allowed to toil; in this, she was quite different from the businesslike Georgian wife.

One solution promoted by machine-based societies is to buy machines to do the work for us. Dishwashers and washing machines are today seen as essential parts of the household. But, to take the example of the dishwasher, does it really lighten the load or does it just persuade us to part with our money because of its artful promise to 'make our lives easier'? We bought a dishwasher two years ago and, at first, rather like having a human helper, it seemed a gift from the gods. What a brave new world, that has such machines in it! You put the plates and cutlery in it and, an hour later, they come out all clean! That's the idea, anyway. The reality is rather different. Unless you clean it every day and keep it filled up with the right special salts and whatnot, it stops cleaning and, worse, it returns the plates with the dirt firmly encrusted, necessitating cleaning the plates again under the tap. Dishwashers don't wash the difficult things like porridge-covered saucepans or greasy oven trays. You have to do those yourself. Then there are the ecological issues to consider: how much detergent and electricity are you burning up in order to have your pots mechanically washed? Consider also the enormous effort that a dishwasher entails: rinsing the plates, filling the thing up, buying all the pills and potions it needs, and then – horrors – emptying it! Finally, you need three of everything, because the thing you need is in the dishwasher. Wash up by hand, and all these problems are avoided.

Machines, as we will see later, add to the loneliness and isolation that is one of the central problems of modern life. The wife is at home alone with the washing while hubby whoops it up over pub lunches with co-workers and friends. He has worked to buy her all these machines to make her life easier so it seems churlish for her to complain. But something seems wrong. This thought hit me on a recent visit to Mexico. Each week, near where we were staying, vast gangs of women would take their washing out to the river and spend a couple of hours doing it together while the children played in rubber dinghies. This struck me as a far more pleasurable way of doing the laundry than switching on a machine and humping sodden loads of washing into baskets and into other machines, all on your own. Boring work is always far less boring when shared with others. The other day, we sat in our basement in the *Idler* office and spent five hours sending out the subscription copies to our readers.

We stuffed envelopes, licked stamps, took sacks of mail to the post office. Because there were four of us working together, we chatted all day and had a very pleasant time. The job was also done fairly quickly. In the past, we paid a poor underling to do this work. It would take him three days of lonely toil, and we would have to pay him for his time. This way, the job was accomplished far more quickly, far more cheaply and far more enjoyably. The only barrier to this way of working is ourselves: as editor of the mag, I used to think myself above the task of stuffing envelopes. I wanted to delegate it to an inferior. Now I have decided to enjoy the process.

There is pleasure in humble work: if you seek enlightenment, then chop wood, carry water, as the old Chinese wisdom has it.

It is better to do things for ourselves. D. H. Lawrence, in his essay 'Education of the People', makes a powerful argument against the employment of cleaners and the like for those who wish to be free. For Lawrence, freedom from servants means freedom from servitude. In the following passage, we see the same wide-eyed, star-gazing quality that we see in Coleridge who, when dreaming of his poets' commune 'on the banks of the Susquehanna', wrote, in a letter to Robert Southey, 'We shall have no servants!' No servants means more freedom, not less. Lawrence goes on:

> No man is free who depends on servants. Man can never be quite free. Indeed he doesn't want to be. But in his personal immediate life he can be vastly freer than he is. How? By doing things for himself. Once we wake the quick of personal pride, there is pleasure in performing our own personal service, every man

sweeping his own room, making his own bed, washing his own dishes – or in proportion: just as the soldier does. We have got a mistaken notion of ourselves. We conceive of ourselves as ideal beings. For the rest we are lively physical creatures whose life consists in motion and action. We have two feet which need tending, and which need socks and shoes. This is our own personal affair, and it behoves us to see it. Let me look after my own socks and shoes, since these are private to me.

Let us each become jacks of all trades. Every man, woman and child should be able to cook, clean and change a plug. We are in danger of becoming a radically useless world of computer-game players. Freedom lies in self-sufficiency, says Lawrence:

> Self-dependence is independence. To be free one must be self-sufficient, particularly in small, material, personal matters. In the great business of love, or friendship, or living human intercourse one meets and communes with another free individual; there is no service. Service is degrading, both to the servant and the one served: a promiscuity, a sort of prostitution. No one should do for me that which I can reasonably do for myself.

The next problem, having dispatched our army of servants, is how to do the cleaning in such a way as not to feel we are oppressing ourselves. We tend to internalize the role of servant. We split ourselves into two beings: resentful Victorian servant and bullying Victorian master. The internal master says to the internal servant, 'Come on, man, do the washing up! Pull your socks up! Tidy your study!' And the internal servant reacts with grumbling resentment and even with outright sedition. Everyone knows the liberating feeling of saying to ourselves, 'Bugger it: I'll do the washing-up in the morning.' Due to our collective memory of more or less enslaving others to do the work we don't want to do, we nowadays enslave ourselves. Or, worse, we enslave our partner. Relationships can easily turn into a battle in which one partner tries to boss the other around. The wife will nag the husband to help more around the house; and when he does start helping around the house, he feels he has a right to start telling his wife what to do. Therefore turmoil ensues.

So the only answer, therefore, and this is a difficult one to pull off, is to *learn to love the washing-up*. In the words of Lawrence:

> The actual doing of things is in itself a joy. If I wash the dishes, I learn a quick, light touch of china and earthenware, the feel of it, the weight and roll and poise of it, the peculiar hotness, the quickness or slowness of its surface. I am at the middle of an infinite complexity of motions and adjustments and quick, apprehensive contacts. Nimble faculties hover and play along my nerves, the primal consciousness is alert in me. Apart from all the moral or practical satisfaction derived from a thing well done, I have the mindless motor activity and reaction in primal consciousness, which is a pure satisfaction. If I am to be well and satisfied, as a human being, a large part of my life must pass in mindless motion, quick, busy activity in which I am neither bought nor sold, but acting alone and free from the centre of my own active isolation. Not self-consciously, however. Not watching my own

reactions. If I wash dishes, I wash them to get them clean. Nothing else.

Make drudgery divine, as George Herbert had it. What we need is a poetry of domestic work, a new form, the 'domestic pastoral', something which raises the status of doing mundane chores. We need rock songs extolling its virtues: 'Do the Dirty Dish' by The Cramps, 'I've Just Found the Sock I was Looking for' by U2. Let's make washing-up cool. I am planning a lifestyle article with my friend Nick Lezard. We invented a new demographic category, the Dobo, which stands for Domesticated Bohemian. The Dobo has a wild past but now has a family. He or she is still occasionally given, however, to a night of hedonism. The wildness is still in there. Hence the need for a literature celebrating domesticity.

An odd paradox is that it is possible, however strange it might seem, to find freedom in service – that is, in helping other people. Who is more free, the man with a million pounds and three servants or the man who serves him? Wooster or Jeeves? Gandhi had an ideal of public service but also had servants at different stages in his life. Some people, it seems, like being servants. George Harrison once said of Mal Evans, the Beatles' roadie, that he embodied the eastern ideal of freedom through service. It was in helping others that he found himself.

If we were all taught to look after ourselves, Lawrence argued, then we could have a more diverse culture. Everyone could work, dress, eat and sleep in a way that suits them and not in a way which suits the industrial model of regularity: 'Oh, if only people can learn to do as they like and to have what they like, instead of madly aspiring to do what everybody likes and to look as everybody would like to look.' We must reject Puritan uniformity. Sew hearts on your sleeves, tie ribbons to your ankles!

Embrace your own self and you will start to act originally, that is, authentically and with your own style. When you have your own garden, for example, you can plant exactly what you like. So why do we all copy everyone else, and why do all suburban gardens look the same? Here is the redoubtable Violet Purton Biddle in her 1911 book *Small Gardens and How to Make the Most of Them*. Substitute the phrase: 'human being' for 'amateur gardener' and 'life' for 'garden', and Mrs Biddle's words seem wise indeed:

> 'Be original!' is a motto that every amateur gardener should adopt. Far too few experiments are made by the average owner of a garden: he jogs along on the same old lines, without a thought of the delightful opportunities he misses. Each garden, however small, should possess an individuality of its own – some feature that stamps it as out of the common run.

As with gardens, so it is with life: we fear experiment. The word 'experiment' is actually a very useful one. Instead of actually doing something seriously, you tell people that you are experimenting. 'Did the Beatles take drugs?' I used to ask my parents when young. 'Well,' they would reply. 'They *experimented* with drugs.' But, apart from the value of the word as a euphemism, it is fun to make your life into a series of experiments. If the experiment fails, it doesn't matter – try another one. When we moved to the country, we only intended to stay a few months.

It was an 'experiment'. Now we have been here for four years, and we are still experimenting. In a world where you are constantly asked to be 'committed', it is liberating to give yourself the licence to be a dilettante. Commit to nothing. Try everything.

In gardening, as in housework, it is best to do as much as possible yourself. This is easy for us, as we have quite a small garden, and even that seems like a burden at times. But to learn about flowers and plants and soil and to look after them, and plant them, and eat them: life doesn't offer a much more pleasurable, useful and satisfying activity. When I was young, I never understood gardening, as I was only interested in drinking. Now I see that all those middle-aged and elderly gentleman and ladies in their garden were actually having a great time, when I just thought they were being boring. My life has improved enormously, as now I am interested in gardening *and* drinking: two pleasures, where formerly there was only one. And the two go together very well: there is nothing like a good beer after a couple of hours of digging, and there is nothing like a couple of hours of digging after a night of drinking. It does wonders for the hangover. In fact, one *Idler* reader wrote to us to say that he deliberately gets hangovers for the pleasure of getting rid of them by gardening in the morning.

The bourgeois model of living, which is to get 'help', as servants are euphemistically called, is flawed. What you want is not paid help but unpaid help. In 1900, there were fifteen people living in the remote farmhouse where I now live. The couple had ten children, and there would be 'men in the house', who lived and ate with the family before getting married and going off on their own. It is obvious that in many eighteenth-century households, the servants were treated well and respect went both ways. Dr Johnson, for example, at his house in Gough Court, had five or six people living with him. They were not exactly servants, but they shared the work. His 'servant' Francis Barber, of whom a famous portrait by Joshua Reynolds hangs in Johnson's house to this day, ran away to sea, and Johnson paid for him to be released. Servants would often inherit an annuity on the death of their master. William Cobbett talks of the loss of the old respect between master and servants: he writes in *Rural Rides* that the labourers in farms were well looked after and everyone used to eat together. The labourers sat with the master. The Victorian notion of servants' quarters, the back stairs, 'upstairs, downstairs' sort of segregation, had not been invented. Slaves, even, in ancient times, were often part of the family and, of course, they had the opportunity to become free men. Before the First World War, the estate of St Germans in Cornwall had 128 people living on it and from it. Now, there are two or three. The best stately homes would have been run as a sort of commune, where all the members shared the work and the bounty.

Perhaps we cannot go back to happy relationships between servants and masters. It is better, indeed, to rid our minds of that imprisoning duality. Help without hierarchy, that should be the aim. And helping each other. There is no doubt that many people lighten the load. When we have big Sunday lunches, everyone helps with the preparation of the food, or they bring salads or bread. Everyone lends a hand with the serving of it and then with the washing-up afterwards. We also try to have friends to stay often, as burdens are considerably lessened when there are a few of you mucking in. In those circumstances, such toil can be quite enjoyable. When you can chat while doing it, it becomes fun.

One problem with domestic work is that the television, that promoter of impossible perfection, upholds an absolute standard when the state of one's house should really be a matter for individual judgement. I myself am guilty of trying to live up to some sort of absurd, absolute 'standard' when it comes to cleaning, which surely cannot exist, however many times my mother tells me that it does. I tell myself this is because I can't stand the chaos, as if the chaos actually creates more work. If we all cleaned up as we went along, then we'd have more idling time.

One answer, of course, would be a general lowering of standards or, rather, an elimination of the whole notion of standards in the first place (my mother would disagree). In the UK recently, we've had to suffer the spectacle of a TV show, and related books, called *How Clean is Your House?* Two guilt-inducing fascist matriarchs travel around the country shaming the nation into cleaning up.

As in many areas of life, I blame the Victorians for our current ills. It was in that dark, rational age that the idea that 'cleanliness is next to godliness' took form as a kind of morality: good people have clean houses; bad ones have dirty ones. But there is nothing morally good about cleanliness, just as there is nothing morally bad about its opposite. Indeed, we have the example of the 'dirty saints', who held it vain to wash, and the Knights Templar, I understand, never changed their underpants, for similar spiritual reasons.

Excessive tidiness outdoors, moreover, is commonly accepted these days as ecologically unsound. In organic gardening and Permaculture, the gardener is encouraged to leave wild spots to create habitats for wildlife and for nature to do its own thing. In *The History of the Countryside*, academic Oliver Rackham deplores what he calls 'the Vandal hand of tidiness', that suburban urge to tidy everything up. 'Every year,' he writes, this urge to clean up 'sweeps away something of beauty or meaning.' Tidying, he describes as 'all the little, unconscious vandalisms that hate what is tangled and unpredictable but create nothing'. What Rackham really loves is an old, overgrown hedge. In the book, he mentions Hooper's Rule, which says that you can determine the approximate age of a hedge simply by taking the number of different species in a thirty-yard stretch and multiplying it by one hundred. So, for example, the gloriously untidied hedge in my vegetable garden boasts sloe, elder, hawthorn and holly, which means it must have been first established around 1600.

The obsession with whiteness doesn't help. Why, I wonder, are baby clothes so white? A speck of dirt and they are flung into the washing machine. The insistence on everything being spotlessly white creates a lot of unnecessary extra toil. Wouldn't brown wool be a more sensible fabric, something that can absorb or even hide the mess? White plastic kitchen units, too, need constant cleaning, where wood will absorb little stains and spills. Brown wood is less work to keep clean than white plastic. I rarely clean our pine dresser, whereas the Ikea units seem to need constant wiping. Wood absorbs the dirt, while dirt sits on top of white plastic until you can be bothered to wipe it up. Sheets have to be spotless. It is as if we are pretending to live in a

Victorian manor house with nine servants, but we have to do all the work alone. No wonder every woman and most men are constantly knackered by housework. All this cleaning creates huge piles of work, eating up time which could be more fruitfully spent staring out of the window or hoeing between the cabbages.

It was in Victorian times, too, that we invented the terrible light bulb, which shines its pitiless, unforgiving glare on to our dirt and mess. How much different things must have been in the Georgian era, when everything was lit by candles. We would not have seen the dirt, and so there would have been less cleaning to do. White clothing was not so popular; therefore less laundry. The idea of crisp sheets smelling of lavender, changed every day, was a Victorian invention essentially designed to show how rich you were because you could afford lots of staff to do the laundry. The same goes for massive expanses of manicured lawn: these arid areas of flat greenness did not exist before the eighteenth century, nor did tennis courts and croquet lawns. Everything was a bit rougher, and that meant less work. Houses used to smell nicer, too: we had lavender instead of Mr Muscle.

When it comes down to it, cleaning may simply be a lighting issue. If you want a cleaner house, simply turn off the lights and fire up a candle. Electric light is the enemy. We need to reject the cold, harsh spotlight of Edisonian rationalism and embrace the warm, flickering, beautiful, forgiving, irrational light of the candle. Under candlelight, there isn't such a need to keep everything so spotless, simply because the dirt doesn't show up. The idea of common standards to which we all have to adhere is a tyranny. Set your own standards. Do as you please. Look after yourself.

We need to change our language around this problem, and my suggestion is to stop calling it 'housework' and start calling it 'housecare'. That means you are voluntarily looking after your home rather than working on it out of a sense of duty to some abstract house-cleaning authority wagging its finger at you.

I'll leave you with an *Idler* proverb: instead of complaining about the mess, light a candle. Then you won't see it.

LIGHT A CANDLE

15 Banish Loneliness

Society has parted man from man,
Neglectful of the universal heart.
  Wordsworth, *Prelude*, 1850

One of the most terrible effects of the Reformation and then
the Protestant revolution was the introduction of loneliness on
a grand scale. The old medieval Catholic theology encouraged
a collective approach to life. For them, it was a literal truth that
God was other people; we were all in this together. If the things
you do benefit the whole of society, then you are working for
God and for your own salvation. Thus the emphasis on charity
and hospitality. As in primitive societies, it would be frowned
upon to turn a hungry wanderer from your door. Monks and
nuns opened 'hospitals' which provided hospitality in the form

of beer and bread and sleep. The medievals, like the poets of antiquity, hankered after a lost golden age in which, as Gnaeus Pompeis Trogus wrote: 'Nobody was a slave and nobody had any private property either; all things were held in common and without division, as though there was one single inheritance for all men.' They therefore introduced customs that tried to re-create a kind of communality. It was the era of 'love thy neighbour' and the 'brotherhood of man'. Such ideas now seem revolutionary. The modern commonsense myth – 'You're on your own in this world' – was unknown. 'Love thy neighbour' has been replaced with 'keeping up with the Joneses'; fraternity with covetousness.

Medieval buildings were the result of a vast collective and creative effort on behalf of the various guilds of the city: 'A medieval building appears – not as a solitary effort to which thousands of slaves would have contributed the share assigned to them by one man's imagination; all the city contributed to it,' wrote Kropotkin, who goes on to quote the words of the Council of Florence: 'No works must be begun by the commune but such as are conceived in response to the grand heart of the commune, composed of all the hearts of all the citizens, united in one common will.'

In less developed countries today, you see people moving around in large groups – not alone as we do on our underground trains and buses. In Mexico, for example, trucks go by containing twenty people. Kids play in large gangs. Whole families sit outside their shops all day. Even in the supermarkets – those terrible institutions which tend to make make shopping such a lonely experience – Mexicans chat and laugh and gossip. In old-fashioned Catholic societies, we can catch a glimpse of what medieval life in England must have been like.

A new approach to life emerged in the seventeenth century, when Calvin and others insisted that man was engaged primarily on a lonely journey towards salvation. The principal text that created or reflected this new loneliness in the UK was John Bunyan's bestseller, *A Pilgrim's Progress* (1678–84). Bunyan lived from 1628 to 1688 and was imprisoned for twelve years for preaching without a licence. In *A Pilgrim's Progress*, probably the most widely read of all the Puritan literature, Christian actually abandons his family in his search for salvation, crying, 'Life, eternal life' . . . I remember staring with horror at the pictures in the copy we had in our house of Christian bent over with that terrible, ugly burden on his back. A purposeful, methodical journey through life, a lonely struggle. This approach is mirrored in the bourgeois conception of work and money-making. Boswell reports that Dr Johnson thought *A Pilgrim's Progress* was a great work of the imagination, which it may well have been, but did it have to be so miserable? Clearly it was the self-denying side of Johnson's character rather than the medieval, pleasure-loving side that approved of the book.

Contrast the gloomy *Pilgrim's Progress* with the jaunty (though admittedly pious) fourteenth-century poem *Piers Plowman*, with its vision of a 'fair field of folk'. Contrast also Chaucer's *Canterbury Tales*. Here, the pilgrimage is not a lonely trudge like Bunyan's but is undertaken as a social event. I think the Protestants suspected that people might actually *enjoy* the pilgrimages and, for that reason, they were a no-no. Pilgrims walk together in a large group, they tell their stories to each other, all ranks together.

There is none of the miserable piety of Bunyan in Chaucer. *The Canterbury Tales* are a celebration of life in all its chaos.

The idea of life as a lonely, even paranoid struggle was also promoted by other Protestant thinkers, such as Baxter and Bailey, as Max Weber reminds us in *The Protestant Ethic and the Spirit of Capitalism*. For Calvin, salvation was not to be found in a constant succession of charitable and creative acts, as the medievals taught, but in a one-on-one relationship with God:

> The Calvinist creates his own salvation, or, as would be more correct, the conviction of it. But this creation cannot, as in Catholicism, consist in a gradual accumulation of individual good works to one's credit, but rather in a systematic self-control which at every moment stands before the inexorable alternative, chosen or damned . . .
>
> Even the amiable Baxter counsels deep distrust of even one's closest friend, and Bailey directly exhorts us to trust no one and to say nothing compromising to anyone. Only God should be your confidant.

In Cobbett's *A History of the Protestant Reformation*, there are some wonderful insights into the 'old ways'. Of course, the destruction of the monasteries and convents meant the destruction of a very visible example of communal living. The monks lived, worked, ate and prayed together, and their way of life was organized around voluntary principles whereby mutual aid was more important than money-making. The monks were by no means all lonely isolationists; they lived alongside the laypeople – indeed, there were the lay clergy, and the monks were often their landlords.

It was the new isolation, the sundering of man from man, which Wordsworth lamented in the *Prelude*. The Romantic poets' sudden interest in nature and man comes at a time when the old ways were being destroyed by the individualist spirit of the Industrial Revolution.

In cities today, we barricade ourselves into isolated apartments and fight with each other in small spaces. 'Here we go, back to our lonely, selfish little flats,' said my friend Marcel one Sunday evening, as a group of us drove back into London after a weekend sharing a rented cottage. It's a truism to say it, but in many cases we no longer know our neighbours. 'Love thy neighbour' has been replaced, too, with 'neighbours from hell'. That is the great thing about the movement of people around the world. When I walk down the Uxbridge road in London, I see Somalians, Indians and West Indians simply hanging out and talking in groups. They are outside their shops, they are at their stalls in the market. But most of the white middle classes hurry through this scene alone, rushing back to the security of their burglar-alarmed terraced houses. We have lost that easy camaraderie of life, and we're lucky that people from other cultures have moved to our cities and are demonstrating a more humane and enjoyable way of living right under our noses.

Life is easier when shared with others. Guests are wonderful things; they entertain us, they bring wine and cheese; they bring their children so our children can play. We talk together about our problems; the women complain together about the men; and the men complain together about the women. Burdens are eased by being shared.

It is the Puritan rejection of 'merry cheer' that leads us to binge and then punish ourselves with guilt and abstinence. The historical reasons for this split are clear. So, not only has society separated man from man, in Wordsworth's phrase, it has also created a split within man. We are radically lonely, in that we are lonely in our own selves. We leave ourselves out. If this internal antagonism and all the energy it wastes could be turned into joyous harmony, then we could do anything we wanted. We see the battle between the new lust for order, discipline and sobriety and the old acceptance of fate and good living dramatized in Shakespeare's *Twelfth Night*, in the battle between the pious Puritan Malvolio and the 'eat, drink and be merry' Sir Toby Belch. And Max Weber says this battle is fundamental to understanding the English:

> Through the whole of English society in the time since the seventeenth century goes the conflict between the squierarchy, the representatives of 'merry old England', and the Puritan circles of widely varying social influence. Both elements, that of a naïve joy of life, and of a strictly regulated, reserved self-control, and conventional ethical conduct are even today combined in the English national character.

Yes, the two are combined; they compete within us. But surely the Puritan strain has been dominant for long enough. It is time to live with people, eat with people, drink with people. We are sociable creatures and we deny ourselves this sociability at our peril. The trials of life are, quite simply, easier to bear if we bear them as a group. Hence the guilds system of the medievals and its large households. I suppose there is a sort of memory of this need for people in some modern companies, which try to encourage 'loyalty to the brand' and take their staff on bonding awaydays. But there is no real freedom within these structures.

Even today, our natural inborn sociability is attacked. I have just taken part in a radio programme to discuss smokers under attack from a professional government body. Having banished smokers from their workplace, it now appears that non-smoking co-workers are developing resentment around the fact that their smoking colleagues are always nipping out for a fag break. These smokers, they assume, are doing less work than the non-smokers. So it is that worker is set against worker; we are encouraged to compete with one another rather than work together.

Well, the way to escape this trap is to embrace community. That way lies the death of loneliness. Neighbours, friends, working for pleasure. Put on parties. Start clubs. I have found that a common purpose, however slight, gives drinking in the pub an extra dimension of pleasure. It means that it is something more than a mere escape from work. That is why I try to organize meetings at 5 p.m. in the pub. Then the meeting is a great pleasure and trickles naturally into the less formal merriment of the evening.

Sociability, merriment, good company: these are the remedies for loneliness, because they can help unite the divided self.

FLING OPEN YOUR DOORS

16 *Submit No More to the Machine, Use Your Hands*

It is questionable if all the mechanical inventions yet made have lightened the day's toil of any human being . . . [machines] have enabled a greater population to live the same life of drudgery and imprisonment, and an increased number of manufacturers and others to make fortunes.
John Stuart Mill, *Principles of Political Economy*, 1848

. . . in proportion as the use of machinery and division of labour increases, in the same proportion the burden of toil also increases, whether by the prolongation of the working hours, by increase of the work exacted in a given time, or by increased speed of the machinery etc.
Marx and Engels, *Communist Manifesto*, 1848

We work, you play.
Advertising slogan for Indesit washing machines, 2005

Faith in the machine as a redeemer and as a kind of automated slave has been the great disappointment of the industrial project. The long-promised technological utopia in which robots do all the work while we give ourselves up to reading philosophy, drinking fine wines and having sex has never materialized. Some of our most radical and anarchic commentators have hoped for a mechanized paradise in which the machines would do all the work. Kropotkin fan Oscar Wilde, in *The Soul of Man under Socialism* (1891), writes: 'Man is made for something better than disturbing dirt. All work of that kind should be done by a machine ... All labour that deals with dreadful things, and involves unpleasant conditions, must be done by machinery.' Man, meanwhile, should loaf. Paul Lafargue, Karl Marx's son-in-law, argues the same point in *The Right to be Lazy* (1883): 'The machine is the saviour of humanity, the god who shall redeem man from the *sordidae artes* and from working for hire, the god who shall give him leisure and liberty.' In H. G. Wells' *A Modern Utopia* (1905), the great sci-fi man envisages a hi-tech paradise, with trains running at 300 miles an hour. In the movie *Sleeper*, Woody Allen imagines butler robots doing the work while the humans lie around pursuing pleasure; and, today, we buy 'household appliances' in the hope of lightening the load.

Well, things didn't quite work out that way. Machines have never liberated us from toil, due to the fact that they need minding by a human being and are owned by the capitalists, in whose hands they become instruments of enslavement and prolonged boredom. Put simply, human beings are employed at low rates of pay to operate machines in order to make profits for the owners of the company. Added to that, the high capital outlay of big machines demands that they be used as intensively as possible, and that means long hours and shiftwork. Even today, though, machines and technology are sold with the same promise. But in trying to escape dirty work in this way, we condemn ourselves to more toil. In the olden days, Jack and Jill simply went up the hill to fetch a pail of water. As they did so, we can imagine that they enjoyed a pleasant walk though nature's bounty and perhaps had a chat on the way. Nowadays, Jill turns on a tap and Jack goes out to work in order to earn the money to pay for taps, plumbers, water rates and the maintenance of an enormously complicated system of tanks, pumps and pipes. Or they buy water in the supermarket, water that has been bottled 500 miles away, sent to warehouses and driven across the country in giant, oil-drinking lorries to huge, cavernous retail centres staffed and patronized, apparently, by zombies. So, water today is obtained with vastly more toil, sweat, cost, boredom and pain, when you add up the labour of those concerned, than when we collected it from wells. It's also undeniable that wells are less likely to go wrong, simply because there is less to go wrong with a well. A well is more efficient than modern waterworks.

And I would certainly attack Oscar Wilde's rather pathetic revulsion for 'disturbing dirt'. I disturb dirt every day in the garden and very enjoyable it is, too.

Far from machines being our slaves, we are actually theirs. In the workplace, they make us look bad. They don't call in sick, they don't ask for a pay rise, they don't go on strike, they don't stop for tea or lunch, they don't get depressed, they don't split up with their boyfriends, they don't cry in the loos, they don't even sleep. So it is that the industrialist, the employer, does all he can to make people more like machines. Machines are held up as an example of correct behaviour. The accusation 'unprofessional' means 'You did not behave like a machine today.' All those call-centre managers must be looking forward to the day when a computer can make the calls and the managers will not have to deal with troublesome human beings who get drunk and catch colds and have little thoughts of their own. 'The very essence, the great charm of the factory,' wrote Eric Gill in 'Painting and the Public' (1933), 'is that you do not need workmen who want to impose their free wills, their idiosyncrasies, their emotions and sensibilities upon the design and manufacture of razor blades.' And the machines can appear more lively than the robot-humans who are operating the machines. E. F. Schumacher provides this horrifying thought in *Good Work*, from a letter written in the 1970s by a British worker: 'Machines have become as much like people as people have become like machines. They pulsate with life, while man becomes a robot.'

Under the banner of liberation, machines now even enter our personal lives. In the nineteenth century, they had steam; today, we have digital technology and all its empty promises. Take that unspeakably awful new gadget called the Blackberry. Quite apart from its terrible crime, which it shares with two other manufacturers of digital technology, Apple and Orange, of exploiting the name of a delicious fruit to make profits, the Blackberry is also to be feared, shunned and cast out of polite society because it allows slave labour further to invade our everyday lives. Blackberries can send and receive emails from anywhere. Therefore, you can take it to the beach and work there. You can work in the pub. The boss can ask for a report when you're three pints down, thus completely ruining your evening. Again, what is truly amazing is that we buy these electronic tagging devices, these digital manacles, at our own expense. We increase the profits of another in order to allow our few leisurely moments to be interrupted by some self-important jackass on the other side of town, or of the world. Laptops and mobile phones have already ruined dreamy train journeys; now, even the time walking to the station can be used to check your Blackberry. Years ago, I bought a digital organizer at great expense. I spent hours typing in my address book. Two weeks later, I dropped it and it broke, losing all the information. I then realized that for the price of this characterless gizmo, I could keep myself in Smythson Featherweight diaries for about twenty years. The Smythson Featherweight is a beautiful leather-bound pocket diary that gives immense pleasure every time you use it.

When the frenzy for digital technology began, in the mid-nineties, I have to admit that I was a fan. I loved computers and the early days of the Internet. To me, at first sight, the whole thing seemed liberating: the idea that, via the web, you could publish whatever you liked and find some sort of audience without having to pay for printing and all the rest of the palaver that goes with the production and distribution of a physical object. I even liked mobile phones at the outset, foolishly believing that they could facilitate loafing by freeing you from the office. Instead, of course, they mean that you take the office with you wherever you go; you can be contacted anywhere. So it is that pleasant evenings in the pub are spoiled by bosses on the phone.

The fever surrounding digital technologies is precisely analogous to the fever surrounding emerging technologies of the past, such as the railway. Initially the technology appears to promise new kicks and freedom from existing restraints. A few misty-eyed pioneers get excited about it for its abstract possibilities. Then, the commerical people, the men of business, move in and exploit it. Naysayers and cynics are condemned as enemies of progress. Academics write books about a 'new way'. The media reports on a bright new dawn. The fools on the streets – people like me – buy it. A bubble forms, expands and bursts. The City boys run away to count their spoils, the little investors blame their own stupidity, and 90 per cent of the companies vanish. But 10 per cent remain, and they dominate the technology. Thus it is that the Internet, once heralded as an exciting new medium of communication, is now little more than a vast mail-order catalogue. Yes, you can consult encyclopaedias online, but then, you used to be able to consult encyclopaedias at home or in the library! And you may very well have had a pleasant walk there and back. Digital technology may supply you with what you want, but it won't supply you with what you need.

When it comes to freeing ourselves from faith in machinery and technology, one answer is to go backwards. I have discovered that it is very easy to live like a millionaire, if you simply go back in time a little. Super 8 cameras from the 1960s, for example, cost about £1 and are much more fun than the dreaded camcorder. Who wants to watch one and half hours of children playing on swings? The Super 8 films are mercifully short at three minutes each and, better, they are silent. I tend to play a three-minute pop song with them, something vaguely appropriate to the subject matter. And not only do you feel like Paul McCartney in 1966 with the latest gadgets, everyone on the film looks like Paul McCartney in 1966. Or Jane Asher. The quality of the film is very kind.

The longer you wait, the cheaper the technology becomes. You could probably get a video recorder for free these days, while, in 1966, when all the Beatles bought a video each, they cost the equivalent of thousands of pounds. If you can wait even a year or two, you will find that you can pick up gadgets for very little.

And the further backwards you go technology-wise, the more enjoyable life becomes. I have just bought, for next to nothing, a hand printing-press with ten drawers of lead type and a box of bits and bobs. This device allows you to set type by hand, letter by letter. It sounds tedious, but in fact there is a real pleasure in considering and placing each letter. I made some beautiful, if a trifle wonky, headed paper, and it only took a couple of hours. Yes, I could have done something similar on the computer in about five minutes, but there would have been far less pleasure in the process for one thing, and for another, the end result would not have anything like the charm of what I managed to create. The letters were crooked, the ink unevenly distributed, but I loved my paper. It was manmade, unique, individual. It was a craft. I plan to go backwards yet further and give up my strimmer for a scythe, write with a quill and inkpot. Certainly it is a great pleasure to write a letter with a fountain pen on good paper rather than firing off an email. It is also a joy to receive a real letter from a friend, perhaps with beermats, postcards and magazine cuttings tumbling out of it. Goodbye, email, hello, Royal Mail.

The Arts and Crafts movement held out no hope for steam and large-scale machinery as the saviour of humanity. Quite the opposite, they saw that the machine *de natura* as enslaving. When machines first made food, they were held by many to be an improvement on mere manmade stuff. Eric Gill remembers the legend 'CLARK'S MACHINE-MADE BREAD' on the roof of his local factory-bakery. When Gill returned as an older man, it seems that Mr Clark had recognized an error in marketing, and now Gill read the 'monstrous proclamation: CLARK'S FARMHOUSE BREAD'.

London's Victoria and Albert Museum recently put on an Arts and Crafts exhibition. What struck me about the show was that the movement was not merely the private passion of a few cranks in Ditchling but a globally influential new way of thinking. There were rooms dedicated to Arts and Crafts in Japan, Arts and Crafts in the US. I was accompanied by my friend Matthew, of the Gentleman's Art Appreciation Society, whose grandfather was Valentine Kilbride, one of the leading lights in the Ditchling branch of Arts and Crafts. He remembers Kilbride talking of visits from the Japanese, who came to check out what was going on in the UK and then went home and rediscovered their own artistic craft tradition. The beauty of Arts and Crafts was that it had no aesthetic agenda beyond making things that were beautiful and useful and making them as far as possible by hand.

The essential idea of Arts and Crafts was quite different from Wilde's idea that machines would make the useful stuff and human beings would make the beautiful stuff. Arts and Crafts sought to combine the two and to restore a dignity to the production of wallpaper, textiles, pottery, glassware and furniture. Art and life, rent asunder by the Industrial Revolution, would be brought back together.

The Distributists, those no-nonsense 1920s Catholics, were also of the opinion that large-scale machinery is by its nature enslaving. In the Distributist world, where families owned their own plot of land and were independent of wage slavery, machinery would take a back seat. Wrote Arthur J. Penty:

> [We] believe that, in the last resort, a man ought to be able to fend for himself, and [we] are opposed to the extensive use of machinery because it prevents him from so doing; the specialization it involves by depriving men of manual dexterity undermines their personal independence and self-respect . . . Certainly we are not so well off spiritually, for not only has unrestricted machinery introduced a tension that fills all our lives with anxiety, but it has de-humanized and de-spiritualized the industrial workers, and has given rise to a spirit of revenge that in these days is finding revolutionary expression. Do not let us deceive ourselves. There is a definite connection between the growth of the revolutionary spirit and mass production.

Anyone who has worked in a big factory, warehouse or office will be familiar with the underlying bubbling of resentful feelings against management. When trapped (or, I should say, self-incarcerated, since I was perfectly free to walk out any time I wanted) in a magazine office I did not like, I spent my spare hours composing in my mind the devastating resignation speech that I would one day deliver to the boss. Of course, I never gave this speech and instead contented myself with moaning in the pub.

The future is always about machines. But I don't think about the future; I think about the present. The future is a capitalist construct. The past teaches us that the future has let us down, and let us down many, many times. Dreaming of some kind of technological utopia in which the machines will do all the work has failed us before, and it is failing us now, with our new faith in digital technology. 'When we speak of the future, we speak of man's *hope* for the future, which he is living, now,' is a line I heard repeated once on a pop record. The 'future', so called, is in fact part of the anti-life system: we are essentially kept quiet by means of the idea that, at some point in the 'future', things are going to get better, as per the theme song of the Labour Party's victory over the Conservatives. The future is part of the classic Protestant notion of deferral of pleasures. Pensions, for example, are sold with the idea of a brighter future. I believe that things can get better from the present moment, right here, right now.

The Arts and Crafts movement was criticized for being nostalgic and sentimental about the past. Well, maybe it was. But the fact is, the past is a great treasure store of good ideas for living, ideas that were actually applied and whose results we can see. The problem with ideas of the future is that they are untested; they are all speculation, fantasy. The future has not happened yet. So it is, in actual fact, less woolly minded to look to the past for inspiration than to look to the future. Right now, for example, there is a move towards re-creating medieval technology such as windmills and water mills as sources of power, because we are finally recognizing that buying power from a centralized source rather than producing our own is hugely expensive and wasteful. And as to anyone who defends the industrial system, I merely ask them to compare Florence with Swindon. I think that even the most determined relativist would agree that Florence has the edge when it comes to beauty. Florence was built by individual human beings who used machines, not by machines who used human beings. It emerged from a federal, small-scale form of government. Any good that happens today in work, art and life has happened despite the system that we inhabit, not as a result of it.

That is why I say: throw out the machines. They have let us down. They are noisy, expensive and they create loneliness. Think not, 'what do I want' but 'what can I do without'. On our farm, the farmer spends all day driving his tractor to and fro, alone, carting muck. In the old days, this job would have been achieved by a group of men working together, chatting, taking breaks, using their bodies. Machines separate us from our very selves. Tools, however, are quite a different thing. The spade, the chisel, the sickle, the pocket-knife: these are instruments of liberation.

USE A SCYTHE

17 *In Praise of Melancholy*

A bad and peevish disease, which makes men degenerate into beasts.
Melanelius, quoted by Burton

Great is the force of imagination, and much more ought the cause of melancholy to be ascribed to this alone, than to the distemperature of the body.
Arnoldus, quoted by Burton

The greatest enemy to men, is man, who by the devil's instigation is still ready to do mischief, his own executioner, a wolf, a devil, to himself, and others.
Robert Burton, *Anatomy of Melancholy*, 1621

For guidance on the vexing issue of melancholy, depression, black bile, we must turn to the world expert, renowned scholarly reflector and gentle intellect, Robert Burton, who wrote that most cheerful and cheering of books, *An Anatomy of Melancholy*, in 1621. Boswell reports that the melancholic Johnson described it as 'the only book that ever took him out of bed two hours earlier than he wanted to rise'. In its day, it was a huge bestseller, running to at least eight editions, by which, my edition reports, 'the bookseller got an estate.' Throw away your Prozac and buy this book.

That the book was a big hit should come as no surprise, because it came out during a miserable period in history. Merry England was dead or dying. Burton's book, 780 pages of the most delightful misery, happily written when bipolar disorder was still called melancholy, was published roughly halfway between the Henrician Reformation and the Industrial Revolution, those two major disasters for lovers of life and liberty. Old medieval values were still widespread, but the age of anxiety, Puritanism, individualism and money-grubbing was gaining momentum. Merry England was under attack from the new Puritan middle class. A population increase had led to a massive rise in poverty. The Tudors were cracking down on beggars and idlers, on wandering musicians and strolling players. The old religious festivals had been banned by Cranmer. Merry-making on Sundays was attacked. The fun was being drained from national life. It is, therefore, safe to assume that there were more melancholy people in 1624, than, say, in the fifteenth century, when such a book did not need to be written. The book is also almost contemporary with Shakespeare's study of isolation, *Hamlet*, and Marlowe's study of ambition, *Dr Faustus*. It was also written during the great expansion of government power of the sixteenth and seventeenth centuries.

The meat of Burton's book is thousands of quotes on the

subject of melancholy from classical sources (for this reason, it has traditionally been plundered by writers looking to make themselves look clever with Latin quotes). This would suggest that the Ancient Romans and Greeks suffered from melancholy, too, which doesn't surprise me, as the Romans, particularly, lived in a rapacious, warlike, exploitative oligarchy, much like Britain and the US today. Some of them might have enjoyed this, but it led to misery on a grand scale for the mass of the citizens and slaves.

It may also be true that, aside from external factors, melancholy is just a fact of life. Indeed, says Burton, when reflecting on the causes of melancholy, it seems to have been a curse of man ever since the Fall. So, it's simply tough luck, Burton appears to be saying: deal with it. Melancholy is part of what it means to be human, and it's been part of the human condition since God first condemned us to delve and spin rather than just loaf around in the Garden of Eden:

[Man's] disobedience, pride, ambition, intemperance, incredulity, curiosity; from whence proceeded original sin, and that general corruption of mankind, as from a fountain flowed all bad inclinations and actual transgressions which cause our several calamaties inflicted upon us for our sins . . . melancholy, therefore, is a punishment for evil: Paul, Rom ii, 9: 'Tribulation and anguish on the soul of every man that does evil.'

So, there is no escape. Even the wise, lucky and prosperous, Burton says, suffer from melancholy:

From these melancholy dispositions, no man living is free, no stoic, none so wise, none so happy, none so patient, so generous, so godly, so divine, that can vindicate himself; so well composed, but more or less, some time or other he feels the smart of it . . . Q. Metellus, in whom Valerius gives instance of all happiness, 'the most fortunate man then living in that most flourishing city of Rome, of noble parentage, a proper man of person, well qualified, healthful, rich, honourable, a senator, a consul, happy in his wife, happy in his children,' etc, yet this man was not devoid of melancholy, he had his share of sorrow . . . for a pint of honey thou shalt here likely find a gallon of gall, for a dram of pleasure a pound of pain, for an inch of mirth an ell of moan; as ivy doth an oak, these miseries encompass all our life.

This itself is massively cheering: if you are depressed, he is saying, there is nothing wrong with you. It's natural!

In the Middle Ages, the sin of sloth came very close to melancholy. The original term for the seventh deadly sin was *'acedia'*, which meant something closer to unhappiness. As Thomas Pynchon puts it in his 1993 essay, 'Nearer, My Couch, to Thee', on the subject:

'Acedia' in Latin means sorrow, deliberately self-directed, turned away from God, a loss of spiritual determination that then feeds back on in to the process, soon enough producing what are currently known as guilt and depression, eventually pushing us to where we will do anything, in the way of venial sin and bad judgement, to avoid the discomfort.

Acedia was a radical giving-up on life, and it was used to apply to a monk who felt that nothing was worth it, he was losing his faith and becoming slack in his observances, wailing, 'Oh, what's the point?', when a brother tried to get him out of his cell. Sloth was the worst of all sins, since it would lead to the other sins.

So, in other words, depression was a sin – which must have made it doubly difficult to cope with: for not only were you depressed, you were also conscious of the knowledge that you were committing a deadly sin by being depressed, a fact that surely would have only made you more depressed, making you more sinful, and so on and so forth right into the seventh circle of hell.

Among the causes of melancholy, Burton lists bad diet. Pork, goat, beef, venison, fish, pulses, root vegetables, cucumbers, gourds, bread and wine . . . it seems that everything is bad for you. Beer, perhaps, gets off most lightly: ''tis a most wholesome (so Polydor Virgil calleth it) and a pleasant drink, it is more subtile and better, for the hop that rarefies it, hath an especial virtue against melancholy, as our herbalists confess.' I, personally, also find beer to be an effective antidote against black bile.

One of Burton's other solutions is merriment: 'In my judgement none so present, none so powerful, none so apposite as a cup of strong drink, mirth, music, and merry company.' He calls music 'a roaring-meg against melancholy, to rear and revive the languishing soul'. This is the power of jazz, or rock 'n' roll, or modern dance music. It gets us into ourselves; it is the precise opposite of a distraction. All the other things are distractions because they are about hopes or regrets. Music brings us into the present. It can literally transform. And the blues, of course, the soundtrack to slavery, forges something good and life-affirming from the rough materials of misery.

A similar approach to melancholy appears in medieval texts, which recommend joyful thoughts for good health and promote what historian Linda Paterson calls 'a wilfully cheerful disposition'. The thirteenth-century troubadour Peir d'Alvernhe, for example, wrote:

> For gloom and deep brooding produce no goodness or acts of prowess, but only damage and disruption; for just as all harmful frustration arises from greed, so all black deeds soaring from habitual moroseness. Anyone who desires joy should therefore keep to the straight path, and leave gloom and vile looks to villains and base churls.

Today, gone are good company, good cheer and good beer as cures. Melancholy has been professionalized, commodified, industrialized. It was been transformed into a 'condition' with a costly chemical cure. In come the new top five: Prozac, Zoloft, Paxil, Wellbutrin and Effexor, all of which sound like the names of far-off galaxies in an episode of *Star Trek*. Otherworldly; manna from heaven, and certainly charmless, sterile, antiseptic, coldly rational, unromantic, pleasure-free. These pills make the most gigantic profits for their dealers, the drugs giants like GlaxoSmithKline, Wellcome, Pfizer and the rest. Depression is big business. In 2000, sales of prescription anti-depressants reached over $10 billion in the US, and that figure rockets every year. It is estimated that one in twenty-five people in the UK are on anti-depressants, as well as 60,000 children, the emerging market. It's a growth industry. Buy shares in depression! Money from misery! Profits from pain! While this is all excellent news if you a director of or shareholder in one of the pharmaceutical giants, it produces an enormous bill for the NHS in the UK and for individuals in the US with their private healthcare insurance (and their private healthcare insurance in turn keeps people in jobs they hate). And are they doing any good? One recent study even linked anti-depressant use to suicide, and there are apparently so many of us taking them in the UK that they have entered the water supply through our excrement and urine, raising the possibility that even more of us are on them than is thought.

Other drugs such as Ativan and Xanax are being sold as anti-anxiety drugs, drugs to help you fight panic. No one ever suggests, of course, that the fault for your depression may lie not with you but with the things that you are expected to do in our hyper-competitive, meritocratic, money-based, godless society. Yes, you are depressed, but that's the fault of the world, not you. So don't change yourself to fit in with an unhelpful world; instead, change your world.

One friend of mine who 'suffers' from 'depression' is John Moore. In his case, the condition has been named 'bipolar disorder', but I think it more elegant, respectful, noble and enjoyable to call it melancholy. In a previous book, I described John as the laziest man in the world. What I did not mention before is that John is of chronically atrabilious temperament. His bile is black. When his now ex-wife would try to get him out of bed in the morning, he would reply: 'I'll get out of bed when there's something worth getting up for.' As Burton says: 'It is a received opinion that a melancholy man cannot sleep overmuch . . . nothing offends them more, or causeth this malady sooner, than waking.' Yes, well, idlers know the feeling: Victoria chides me daily for being grumpy on waking.

John has been on anti-depressants for over four years. He says he started taking them as a result of peer pressure; his melancholy made him unsuited to working in the world:

> I think I started taking them to be seen to be taking them, as I was being told that my depression was unacceptable. I needed to show that I was taking steps to become one of the TV-watching classes. You need to be on medication to watch *Pop Idol* and *X-Factor*.
>
> I want to get off them but I am physically addicted. Therefore I would need to go cold turkey, but it's hard to find the time to do that when you're on the working treadmill. My doctor told me that I didn't need to get off them, that some people took them all their lives.

Doctors would say this. The pharmaceutical industry in the US spends 17 per cent of its turnover on marketing and advertising. In 1998, that amounted to $7 billion. That's mainly golfing trips to Barbados and an endless supply of ballpoint pens and notepads to those publicly funded drugs salesmen called GPs.

> The mental effect is subtle: if you were feeling a depth of emotion before, it flattens things out. But they don't do anything to solve

the problem. To me they are like a sticking plaster, a bodge job: anti-depressants are synonymous with botched workmanship and low quality.

The vision of a whole world on anti-depressants is a depressing one indeed: anti-depressants smooth off the rough edges where the life is. They add blinkers. They seek to remould everyone into the same shape so we can continue functioning in society, continue working uncomplainingly and unreflectively. This remoulding itself makes us ill and depressed, and so it goes on. Norman Mailer wrote about the forties hipsters who were fighting 'a slow death by conformity with every rebellious and creative instinct stifled (at what damage to the mind and the heart and the liver and the nerves no research foundation for cancer will ever discover) . . .'

Moore is of the view that we should embrace our black bile, accept it and learn from it. He says in his case that, as surely as spring follows winter, the miseries will last a few months and then he will return and embark on a period of happiness and creativity:

You get so much more clarity about things. It's like fishing, you go beneath the surface and bring things back which are very useful. There'd be no Keats, Byron or Shelley if they'd been on Prozac. Society needs manic depressives, it needs people potholers, to bring back their treasures from the underworlds, and to polish them and turn them into things that are beautiful and glittering.

What the orthodox solution of pills and blotting-out completely misses is the truth that there can be something pleasurable and even useful in melancholy. Burton's description of the pleasures prefigures the romantic poets wandering around in the wilds and then recollecting the emotion in tranquillity:

> . . . most pleasant it is at first, to those who are to melancholy given, to lie in bed whole days, and keep their chambers, to walk alone in some solitary grove betwixt wood and water, by a brook side, to meditate upon some delightsome and pleasant subject, which shall affect them most . . . a most incomparable delight it is to melancholize, and build castles in the air, to go smiling to themselves, acting an infinite variety of parts, which they suppose and strongly imagine they represent.

So, instead of rejecting it, a useful way to deal with melancholy would be to embrace it. In fact, I think that even simply renaming depression 'melancholy', which is so much more colourful and expressive a word, can do a lot to disarm it. 'Bipolar disorder' sounds like the enemy. There is something quite cool about melancholy; it has an air of candles, romantic love, garrets, pages of half-finished manuscript falling from the hand, a wistful sighing, billowy white shirts, the death of Chatterton the boy poet. Melancholy is depression re-created. Instead of saying, 'I'm depressed,' just say, 'I'm feeling atrabilious today, so I think I'd better stay at home or go for a walk in the orchard.' Then re-create your misery as a creative act.

I also think that the problem with drugs, therapy and self-help books is that they place such a heavy burden on the individual. They say that *you* are disordered, at fault, wonky, abnormal, suffering from a chemical imbalance, off-centre, skewed, and therefore must be cured and made to fit in with society. But could it not equally be true that it is not the individual who is at fault but the society he or she is living in, with its blasted ringtones and work obsession? The world is crazy, not me. The revolution of the individual as free from the collective has led to a tightening of the mind-forg'd manacles.

It may be objected here that I am presenting a contradiction: I blame our depression on society and not on the individual; I blame capitalism, the Thing, the Construct, the Combine – whatever we call it – for our misery; then I go on to say that each man is individually responsible for his own life and that the blaming must stop. Well, in this paradox is the truth: both of these are true. We are both the cause and effect of capitalism. When I blame society, I also blame the individual, since we as individuals are complicit in the creation of the very society that oppresses us. Therefore, we are our own oppressor, and that is why it is simultaneously most definitely not our fault and most radically our fault. By the way, we can also congratulate ourselves on the creation of the good things of society.

The simple answer is to accept responsibility and act accordingly. Quitting your job, refusing to vote, not taking pharmaceutical drugs: these are acts not of apathy but of a radical re-engagement with society and with your own self. It is, in actual fact, lazy and apathetic to be employed, to vote and to take Prozac, because in doing these things we are handing control over our lives to others and implicitly accepting that we are more or less useless unless we contort our very selves to conform to a pre-planned model of how we should act. These are acts of giving up. Once you disengage from the structures that bind you, you find that you begin to re-create a life of self-reliance. And self-reliance, rather than the sticking-plaster method, will help you to come to terms with your melancholy, rather than trying to banish it with drugs. In any case, the drugs don't work: study after study confirms that placebos have the same effect as the pills and recovery is made by the body itself. Good doctors also help: when the patient trusts the doctor, the body is more likely to heal itself.

A very simple trick for those looking for an antidote to melancholy is to engage in some physical work. Baking bread, gardening, carpentry: all these things are productive, creative and use the body. They unite body and soul; they are acts of harmony. You may be surprised to hear an idler recommending the benefits of physical labour, but it undoubtedly helps. We need to replace soul-destroying work with soul-creating work.

Keats, in his 'Ode on Melancholy' (1820) advises not getting wasted (which he calls Lethe) and not taking anti-depressants (which he calls wolfsbane and nightshade). Instead, he suggests going for a walk and gazing at the flowers and recognizing that melancholy is a sister to joy and must be embraced:

In Praise of Melancholy

1.

No, no! go not to Lethe, neither twist
Wolf's-bane, tight-rooted, for its poisonous wine;
Nor suffer thy pale forehead to be kiss'd
By nightshade, ruby grape of Proserpine;
Make not your rosary of yew-berries,
Nor let the beetle, nor the death-moth be
Your mournful Psyche, nor the downy owl
A partner in your sorrow's mysteries;
For shade to shade will come too drowsily,
And drown the wakeful anguish of the soul.

2.

But when the melancholy fit shall fall
Sudden from heaven like a weeping cloud,
That fosters the droop-headed flowers all,
And hides the green hill in an April shroud;
Then glut thy sorrow on a morning rose,
Or on the rainbow of the salt sand wave,
Or on the wealth of globèd peonies;
Or if thy mistress some rich anger shows,
Emprison her soft hand, and let her rave,
And feed deep, deep upon her peerless eyes.

3.

She dwells with Beauty – Beauty that must die;
And Joy, whose hand is ever at his lips
Bidding adieu; and aching Pleasure nigh,
Turning to poison while the bee-mouth sips:

Ay, in the very temple of Delight
Veil'd Melancholy has her sovran shrine,
Though seen of none save him whose strenuous tongue
Can burst Joy's grape against his palate fine;
His soul shall taste the sadness of her might,
And be among her cloudy trophies hung.

THROW AWAY THE PILLS

18 Stop Moaning; Be Merry

It is . . . senseless to think of complaining since nothing foreign has
decided what we feel, what we live, or what we are.
Sartre, *Being and Nothingness*, 1943

Sir, I have never complained of the world; nor do I think I have reason
to complain. It is rather to be wondered at that I have so much.
Dr Johnson, in Boswell's *Life of Johnson*, 1781

When making my way through *Being and Nothingness* by Sartre,
I was surprised to find just how practically useful the existential
philosophy is when applied to your life. At first sight, the book
seems terribly abstract and technical, all the talk of being-for-
itself and being-for-others, of facticity and essence. But at the
heart of the project is a simple plea for us to take responsibility

for our lives and recognize that we choose how we react to situations and that we can choose to be free if we so wish. If there is a nothingness at the heart of man, a view which is also taken by Aquinas, then it is up to us to create meaning. Lazily, we perceive that the only meaning available to us is the one which happens to dominate in society, the myths that are handed down to us, the bourgeois construct. But even a cursory glance at societies in history and in other cultures around the world should be enough to persuade us that the way we do things in the industrialized West is only one way of doing things out of an infinite number.

I cannot complain, for example (although I do), about being exploited as the author of this book. In offering these words to a large business, I have accepted that I will receive 10 per cent of the cover price and other people will share among themselves the remaining 90 per cent. This will be divided up by various profiteers hoping to make extra money from my words. These are the publisher, the wholesaler and the retailer. I could complain about that but, since I have chosen to enter this system, it is meaningless to. I could take full responsibility for my book and choose instead to self-publish. I could drive around the country and visit bookshops and suggest that they make an order.

Moaning means a shirking of responsibility. And people make money from it, particularly lawyers. In divorce, lawyers encourage each partner to blame the other completely for the problems in the relationship that led to the divorce. Lawyers are experts at removing responsibility from the plaintiff, telling their client that they are completely blameless and that the other party is clearly off their rocker. This sort of thing becomes addictive;

'Lawyers are like heroin,' says my friend Bill Drummond, and in my experience this is true. They make you feel good, they make you want more and more of what they offer and they are very, very expensive.

I tell my son Arthur that he actually doesn't have to go to school if he doesn't want to. There are other ways of educating him and bringing him up. If he goes to school, then that is because he has chosen to do so. A soldier has chosen to accept that he may be called upon to fight in a war and therefore the possibility of death or injury.

Nevertheless, we all do moan. I moan constantly, for example, about tax and bureaucracy. To be sure, there can be pleasure in moaning. My friend Murphy objects: 'But I like moaning.' Well, that's all right, I suppose. If you like moaning, then, in fact, you are taking responsibility for your moaning, and you are recognizing it as moaning and not a rational, objective response to the reality around you.

We can be justly shocked at levels of exploitation and brutality and control. We can complain about them. But we also need to be aware of our complicity in creating this situation. If you complain about your job, then you should quit it and create your own job.

I recently discovered something shocking about women. It appears that when they moan, *they are not looking for solutions*. They simply want to moan and to have their husband commiserate, sympathize and agree how awful things must be for them. The last thing they want is what husbands generally give, which is advice. They do not want to be told to 'go on a course' or 'get a job'. They just want to moan. To the more straightforward male, this seems insane. But there you are. And perhaps the acknowledgement that the moaning is in some sense pleasurable is good, because it celebrates the moaning. Victoria says that my equivalent to moaning is swearing. By swearing, I release my anger, and then I go back to normal.

The answer is to keep some of your moans to yourself and simply replace the things you hate with things you love. So, instead of going to supermarkets, I now have a vegetable garden, and friends to stay, books, a horse and people I have chosen. Avoid the dross. Ignore it. Yes, the world is crap and filled with the worst quality of produce imaginable. So ignore it and create a joyful world of high-quality produce.

If I have a bank account, then I can't complain about paying interest and charges to the bank, but it is obvious that, being a bank, it is going to try and make as much money out of me as it possibly can. It is a bank; that is its nature. I could instead choose not to have a bank account or a credit card.

One of my great moans is service stations. I find that when I visit these hellholes of pricey rubbish, I experience a wave of snobbishness around the other people. Poor suckers, I think, falling for all this crap. Then I realize that I am falling for all this crap, too, so what on earth gives me the right to feel superior to the others? 'Who on earth are all these people?' we moan when stuck in traffic. Well, they are us. We cannot separate ourselves from others. At other times, when I have chosen to be in a cheerful mood, I sit on the bus going down Oxford Street and absolutely delight in the variety of life around me.

Moaning is perhaps the first step. But there are different sorts of moaning. There is moaning which merely shifts blame and shirks responsibility, and then there is responsible moaning, or positive moaning, as we might call it. As Penny Rimbaud has put it: 'Our lives are uniquely and instrinsically our own. It is a responsibility that few seem willing to bear.' If moaning leads to an acceptance of responsibility, then it can be a positive act, a step in the right direction.

A new expression has appeared in the UK lately, a little phrase which pops up with great regularity in conversation and which I don't remember hearing before three or four years ago. At first sight, it sounds glibly positive but, on reflection, it seems to me to demonstrate an existential celebration of everything about life. The expression is: 'It's all good.' It is generally used directly after a moan. So I will moan away for ten minutes to a friend, and then say, 'Oh, well, it's all good,' meaning, it's all part of life, and who am I to say that one thing is better than another? Is Florence really better than Swindon? One great advantage of being a writer is that when bad things happen, I just think: 'Oh, well, that's good material.' So it was lately that, when I had to go to court for driving without insurance, I decided to lap up the experience rather than complain about it. Celebrate the bad, celebrate the good, as they may even be the same thing. I got off, anyway.

COUNT YOUR BLESSINGS

19 Live Mortgage-Free; Be a Happy Wanderer

You will see from my few words of explanation that the propositions,
God is evil, and Property is theft, are not mere paradoxes. Although I
maintain their literal meaning, I no more want to make it a crime to
believe in God than I do to abolish property.

Pierre-Joseph Proudhon, 1864

Oh, to be free of this cursed mortgage! When I give talks about
the pleasures and advantages of idleness, I am always asked:
'What about the mortgage?' People cite their mortgages as the
prime reason for doing work they don't want to do. 'It's all very
well to talk about sitting around doing nothing,' they say, 'but
I've got a mortgage.' Clearly, the mortgage has become a symbol
of repression. 'I just need to pay off the mortgage, then I'll be
free,' they say. There it is, the monstrous elephant of a mort-

gage, sitting in our way, holding us back. Property, promiser of liberty and deliverer of slavery!

Now, what is a mortgage? It is simply a very large debt which you take out in order to be able to live in a house or flat. Because the debt is paid back over twenty-five years, the interest rates are relatively low compared with shorter-term loans. We commit ourselves to a certain monthly payment on the debt. We base the size of this payment on our current earnings and perhaps on our hope of higher earnings in the future. Having a mortgage is supposed to be the sensible thing to do, because, the idea goes, at the end of it, you will own a property outright. Underpinning the mortgage, therefore, is a notion of a nation of property-owners. But, in chasing this ownership dream, we give the lion's share of our property to the bank. So the idea that we own this house is a myth – the bank owns it, while we pay the bank. Interest payments on the loan will total more than the actual loan by the end of the term. On a £200,000 mortgage, for example, you will have paid well over £240,000 in interest by the end of the term. Therefore the bank has sold you £200,000 at a price of £440,000 – quite a mark-up. And all the above assumes that interest rates are fairly low and fairly constant – but it is possible that, through absolutely no fault of your own, interest rates could rise. For a while, we were suckered into the endowments system, whereby an extra payment was made each month and invested on the stock exchange. This was later (much later and too late for many) revealed to be a massive con. People object to renting in principle because, they say, you are 'throwing money down the drain', but the mortgage system is an organized way of throwing money down a different drain, the one owned by the usurers.

The very thing that we take on board in order to provide us with security – a home – seems to offer instead only anxiety and a feeling of being trapped. Now, why should this be? The conventional wisdom (I might say the 'brainwashing', as, in our arrogance, we sometimes think that we have come up with this idea all on our own) is that you are supposed to take on the biggest mortgage you possibly can. I read of a nauseating Tory couple in Notting Hill who said that they 'stretched every financial sinew' in order to buy their modest terraced house in fashionable West London. Apart from the fact that they should be cast out of polite society for coming up with such a puke-making phrase as 'stretched every financial sinew', the idea behind it seems ridiculous: make your life a perpetual misery in order to pretend that you have enough money to live in a smart part of town.

And because homeowners tend to sort out a mortgage that is just beyond what they can really afford, the wealthy make themselves feel poor. I have lost count of the successful, high-earning middle-class couples I've met who choose to live in vast palaces financed by giant debts and then complain about the mortgage and money and the terrible suffering of their lives, *as if they had no choice in the matter.*

Well, there are many alternatives, both practical and attitudinal. We will look at the practical alternatives to mortgages but also at the way we have forged of the mortgage in our own minds a manacle, and see that freeing ourselves from it is in reality the work of a nanosecond. And I'm also going to recommend, here as elsewhere, the low-cost, low-effort, high-fun approach to life known as Permaculture.

Renting is, of course, the obvious alternative to taking out a mortgage. We've been renting our house in Devon, while renting out a house in London, for four years, and while one potential downside is that you don't do the place up to the same extent that you might if you owned it, it has the advantage of being extremely cheap, since although the rent may compare or even be greater than the mortgage interest payments, there are no maintenance costs, no boilers to replace and so on. The land-lord looks after those.

Renting would be a perfectly reasonable alternative to buying were leases longer and rents lower. What has happened over the last twenty to thirty years is that market forces have eclipsed any humanitarian considerations. We are all exposed to the slings and arrows of the outrageous marketplace, and we all have to become mini-capitalists – i.e., building up a small amount of capital and then taking out huge loans to finance expansion – in order to play our part in the pushy meritocratic society. Rents have shot up and leases in general can be terminated at a month's notice. As a renter, you are completely subject to the unpre-dictable whims of market capitalism. This makes it hard to put down roots. If we had a system of longer leases, say, thirty or forty years, and lower rents, renting would be a fine alternative. The Bloomsbury Group, for example, rented Charleston and took responsibility for its upkeep. John Seymour rented his tumble-down cottage from a farmer. He did all the repairs himself and paid a modest rent. The CRASS people at Dial House in Essex rented it for thirty years. Renting also means that you do not have to find the initial deposit. The getting of this deposit creates a lot of unpleasant work for a lot of people.

It is not so much ownership that we want as a place where we can live without the fear of being thrown out at any moment, somewhere to plant fruit trees and grow vegetables, somewhere we can keep chickens. In the Middle Ages, rents tended to be low, as the properties were administered by the monks. Even the manor houses tended to be kinder landlords than is generally considered. In *The Common Stream*, Rowland Parker's history of the Cambridgeshire village of Foxton, we read of annual rents of one penny for a twenty-seven-acre smallholding, a sum which could be a hundredth of the peasant's annual income. Imagine paying £300 a year today for a ten-acre farm. Land was more evenly shared: in Foxton, 27 families shared 840 acres. Manor house owners and monks weren't like today's property developers; they did not buy and sell properties in the hope of making vast capital profits. They were long-term stewards of the properties and the lands that went with them. The institution – whether family or monastery – was bound to outlive any individual. Therefore, sustainability was built into the programme. Rowland Parker finds examples of rents unchanged for five hundred years; there were also peppercorn rents, meaning, nothing. As in other areas of life, the maintenance of a healthy community, a commune, was more important than money-getting, and low rents with long leases tended to promote local harmony.

In *Masterless Men*, his study of vagrancy in the period 1560–1640, A. L. Beir notes that:

. . . in the high Middle Ages the poor were comparatively firmly rooted to the land. Before the mid-sixteenth century, they retained gardens and crofts where they still grew some food . . . they kept livestock on the commons; and they supplemented their incomes through casual labouring and cottage industries. When times were bad, they no doubt received assistance from relatives, neighbours and friends.

It was in the late sixteenth and early seventeenth centuries that this system began to be dismantled. Says Beir: 'the whole pattern of agriculture in open-field villages was altered from a communal pattern to an individualistic one.' In the sixteenth century, he says, the new landowners increased rents and imposed new duties, and 'by 1600 the English people had had the country's major resource seized from their grasp.' The Middle Ages saw an almost communistic spread of property ownership or tenantship. In Chippenham, for example, the proportion of landless householders rose from 3.5 per cent in 1279 to 32 per cent in 1544, and up to 63 per cent in 1712. Uprooted from the land, the peasant poor 'were no longer part of a manorial economy'.

Before 1600, the average peasant was living very well. He was more free than is generally thought. He was living exactly the life to which today's stockbrokers aspire: a big house in the country with horses, animals and land. It's just that the peasant didn't have to slave in the city from 7 a.m. every weekday to get it: he just had to work for a day or two each week on the manorial land. Every tenant peasant had his own arrangement with the manor house. Here are two thirteenth-century examples from Rowland Parker:

Thomas Vaccarius holds 9 acres of land with a house, and he must do each year 100 days work, plough one acre and do carting service when required. He shall receive one hen, and shall mow and stack. His services are valued at 10s a year, and he pays a rent of 3d.

John Aubrey holds 18 acres of land with a house, and he must do 52 days work a year, must plough for 2 days, do 2 boon-works at harvest, mow the meadow for 2 days, cart the hay, repair the roof of the hall, harrow the oat-land along with his fellows, and he shall receive one hen and 16 eggs. His services are valued at 9s 8d and he pays a rent of 2s 6d.

Thomas Vaccarius paid a tiny fraction of his wages in rent for his nine-acre holding. He worked just two days a week. John Aubrey had eighteen acres of land and a job which only required him to work one day a week and which, in today's values, pays him thirty grand a year (putting his rent at £7,000, a modest amount for such a considerable property). The rest of the time, John and Thomas would be working on their smallholdings and practising a craft or several crafts by which they earned more money.

Then came the dastardly Henry VIII/Puritan attack on the old ways. The mortgage, which puts all the burden of buying a house on the individual, is the logical outcome of the individualization of ownership. But the reality is that in being sold the idea that we should all own our own house, we have simply given into a giant usury con.

We need to diffuse land ownership, ban usurious mortgages, stabilize rents and bring house prices right down. We could perhaps do this by simply losing interest in money-making. And landlords need to reinvent themselves as kindly patrons uninterested in profit. A good role for the rich would be to let property to the rest of us at low rents and with long leases. We also need to stop constantly wanting bigger houses. One of the great attractions of Permaculture is that it shows you how to make the most of what you have and to enjoy where you are rather than blaming your problems on lack of space or money or time.

Until that magical day comes, you might like to consider squatting. Squatting makes a lot of sense to the freedom-seeker. Squatters simply occupy empty buildings and live in them. This can work beautifully. One group of friends had a squat for over five years. They gradually did the place up, learning building skills in the process. They paid no rent and there were no mortgage payments to make, so one of the primary motivations for taking unpleasant work was eradicated, leading to a high level of freedom.

The great Mutoid Waste Company made squatting into an artform in the 1980s and 1990s. They lived in squats all over London, then in Berlin and across Europe. They would move into a large warehouse, where they would spend the days making fantastic sculptures out of scrap and the nights partying; truly, the Troubadours of their day. Like St Francis of Assisi, they rejected money in favour of travelling the world as fools and truth-tellers.

Another realistic option is communal living. Get together with a few friends and share a house. You could even buy a house together and share out the loan. Or join an existing commune.

According to *Diggers and Dreamers*, a book which lists communal living experiments currently operating in the UK, there are at least 2,500 people living in over 100 communities in the UK, and I don't doubt that the real figure is very much greater than this, since more informal arrangements will not be listed. Find four terraced houses in a row and knock the walls down like the Beatles in *Help!*

As students, many of us share houses, and it's a system that, besides the inevitable grime that spreads when four irresponsible and useless young adults live together, works reasonably well. When we grow up, we come to decide that one of the benefits of wage slavery is our own little flat, perhaps shared with a partner, and escaping from the houseshare situation becomes a status issue. But think how well domesticated young adults might be able to live together.

We have today the living example of Dial House in Essex. It is a five-bedroom cottage with an acre of land, and up to twenty people have lived there at any one time, although, right now, there are just three. The house demonstrates what can be achieved with people rather than money: by any standards, the place is beautifully decorated and the gardens simply splendid. The inhabitants have built sheds and extra rooms in the gardens. It is an efficient blueprint, the only surprise being that more people have not picked up on the idea, an idea which, after all, is just a group of friends renting a house together. The house is now owned by a syndicate, which bought it when the house was under threat from property developers.

The idea behind the CRASS house was that it should operate an 'open house' policy: in other words, all were welcome, and all would be given hospitality and shelter. In this sense, it is a secular equivalent of a medieval monastery, a place of peace and refuge, which is also a thriving working environment – cooking, baking, growing things, making things. Penny Rimbaud is a secular priest, while fellow artist and house-dweller Gee Vaucher is Mother Superior. Penny's latest project is a wood-boarded shed with a bell tower and stained-glass windows. It looks suspiciously like a chapel. Perhaps an even closer similarity is with the Brethren of the Free Spirit, those bohemians of the fourteenth century who lived in groups in what they called Houses of Voluntary Poverty.

Penny Rimbaud envisaged a new network of such houses across the country, all within a day's walk of one another. I think more of us should follow its example and declare our own houses open to travellers.

Another option would be to buy a very cheap house in the middle of nowhere. You can always travel to the big city for trips and stay with friends. Then you will have a tiny mortgage. Or build your own house. I understand that houses built of cob and thatch are making a comeback. Buy two acres of land and build a little house for yourself. Then make it bigger as the years go by. Be an architect. Share the cost with friends. The other question to ask yourself is: do you need such a big house? I know many successful city types who, in their desire for a big house in the country, have saddled themselves with the most enormous mortgages, meaning that they are literally enslaved to the job. Despite earning what would appear to most of us to be a fantastic salary, they feel burdened by the debt and therefore will resort to all sorts of Machiavellian strategies in order to keep their job or get promoted. They earn a lot of money but are still freighted by anxiety. But what is the purpose of the big house? Certainly it saddles you with a lot of expense. The bigger the house, the more work there is to do. More cleaning, more furniture to find, more costs, more toil, more encumbrance.

Again, I would recommend taking a look at the *Permaculture* magazine, which is full of examples of people who have created low-cost living styles for themselves, sometimes building their own houses out deep in the woods. The problem they often encounter is planning law. For some crazy reason, planners will allow any number of wasteful supermarkets to clog up our cities, but if you try to get permission to build a log cabin in a wood, it is practically impossible. Clearly, the authorities cannot stand people who want to be free.

A further alternative is vagabondage. Rid yourself of the mortgage and take to the streets. Vagabondage, as we've seen, was actually socially approved in the Middle Ages, largely because of the example of St Francis and his mendicant friars. Jesus never seemed to struggle with monthly mortgage repayments; he was a wanderer, throwing himself on the hospitality of others. In India today, we have the example of the sadhus, the crazy holy men who come into the village, are fed and sheltered for a few days, and then move on. The Indians do not put the sadhus on restart programmes and try to get them into work. They do not pity them as homeless and make efforts to incorporate them into straight society. So it should be here when the Mutoid Waste Company comes to town: we should welcome them with open arms, not try and force them to get proper jobs.

The problem with vagabondage is that big governments can't stand it. They hate the chaos, the unruly elements, the sense that people are wandering around the country doing what they like. When governments increase in power, they all have a resentful way of cracking down on vagabonds. After having been left alone or even positively encouraged for 900 years, the intrusive, centralizing, ordered, ordering governments of the Tudor period introduced a number of laws against vagrancy. That vagrancy had become a problem can be explained by two factors: the first is that, following the Reformation and the Enclosure Acts, thousands had been thrown out of work by a process that today we would call privatization. The old collective ways of operating had been attacked. So there were more beggars. Secondly, the beggars were no longer looked after by the monasteries and the great aristocratic households. On the one hand, the monasteries had been stolen by the new avaricious poshies, and on the other, the Catholic tradition of hospitality was being undermined by the emerging Protestant individualism.

A different work ethic also failed to understand the social purpose of the wanderer. In 1565, government man Sir Thomas Smith writes: 'Not having rent or living sufficient to maintain himself, does live so idly, he is inquired of, and sometime sent to gaol, sometime otherwise punished as a sturdy vagabond: so much our policy does abhor idleness.' When the prisons had been filled with such sturdy beggars, the authorities decided to send them off to the new plantations in Jamaica, where they would be indentured for seven years. It is reported that they were treated worse than the slaves, because the slave owners had an interest in ensuring that their slaves were well fed and reasonably happy in order that they would give a lifetime of service, while the indentured exiles would leave in seven years and there was therefore no interest in keeping them healthy or even alive.

Houses of correction were the Elizabethan equivalent of Nazi concentration or work camps: an act of 1576 promoted the notion that 'youth may be accustomed and brought up in labour and work' – and lazy children aged five to fourteen were put in the stocks or whipped. Other categories of men viewed with distrust by the authorities were 'pedlars and tinkers, soldiers and mariners, entertainers, students, unlicensed healers, fortune-tellers, wizards'. Gypsies and the Irish were treated as vagrants and an act of 1572 ordered the Irish, associated with 'Popery' and rebellion, back to Ireland. It's the familiar story: government cracks down on idleness.

Perhaps the most important question is: what do we mean by 'home'? It is possible that the homeless wanderer can be more at home than the mortgage-bound banker. Putting a lot of time and money into mortgages and the 'dream home' is never going to be more than a distraction from the real issue, which is you, and your state of mind. The mortgage is a commercial exploitation of our longing for home. You'll know when you've found what you're looking for when you stop looking.

But the final answer to worrying about the mortgage is simply not to worry about it. It is a fiction. Don't let the debt get you down. Who cares about the debt? Are you ever going to be homeless and starving? Unlikely. So how bad can things get? The Thing loves you to be in debt. The money-getters in the City who own your debt love your debt; they are not doing you a favour, much as their promotional material would have you believe otherwise. They are exploiting you. The usurers are having a field day; do not for God's sake let them make you feel guilty. They're the ones who should feel guilty because they are sinners, condemned to the eternal flames! Yea!

SHARE YOUR HOME

20 *The Anti-Nuclear Family*

Leave the children alone. *Pitch them out into the street or the play-grounds, and take no notice of them.*
D. H. Lawrence, 'Education of the People', 1918

We hear a lot about dysfunctional families. The family, which should be a source of pleasure, fun, cosiness and nourishment, seems everywhere to produce misery, anger, door-slamming, shouting, cruelty, fighting, death and abuse. We are stuck living with one another. Something is seriously wrong. I believe that families, by and large, are, very simply, too small. They are also uncreative entities.

All too often, 'family' now just means four completely different and mutually hostile people living under the same roof. The households of old were creative, functioning, productive units.

Stitching, knitting, mending and growing herbs and lettuces were not necessarily drudgery (and they are certainly not drudgery compared with working in a call centre or supermarket all day). Self-directed work, productive work, autonomous work, creative work: that can be a joy. Drudgery is only drudgery if we call it drudgery. The mind makes it drudgery. When the household was a living, breathing organism, providing food and clothing as well as shelter, we, to a large extent, created our own jobs. The family home offered work, merriment, raiment and sustenance.

As businesses have grown in size, families have shrunk. Megacorporations take on the role of community-makers. The central importance of the household as a productive entity has virtually disappeared, and the home is now a purposeless crash pad, a chill-out zone and place of refuge, somewhere to watch TV. Families used to work together; now, our families have become passive and radically uncreative. The modern family merely represents a financial burden – in other words, an inducement to take jobs you don't like. I recently read of a mother who went out to work in a supermarket, a job she hated, solely so her kids could buy expensive trainers and computer games and keep up with their friends. That is the sort of defenceless slave-like thinking that we need to escape from if we are to pursue liberty.

It is actually possible, believe it or not, to combine useful and enjoyable activities with the dreaded 'childcare'. The commodification of childcare is another of the unhelpful effects of capitalism. You earn money doing something you don't like in order to pay someone else to 'do the childcare', i.e. look after your children. The dysfunctional family also creates a giant, parasitic industry of professionals, drugs, therapy programmes and bestselling books by John Cleese. These palliatives don't help much; in fact, by acknowledging, naming and wittering on and on about the problem, they may well make it worse. By confirming the existence of a problem, you create a market. That is why the pharmaceutical industry is forever creating new illnesses; that is why the insurance industry is forever creating new fears; that is why the government is forever creating new enemies. There is an urgent need to deindustrialize.

Much better to ignore all the highly prized advice and help of 'experts' and instead introduce child labour into your house. Get them helping. Make your children into producers and creators. At home, I have found that children can enjoy helping in the garden, for example. Some afternoons, we go to the workshop with a saw, a chisel and a piece of driftwood and make something. We have emerged with an elephant, aeroplanes, rockets and one abstract piece, 'Wild Wood', two pieces of wood nailed together into a cross and covered with scraps of newspaper, which now hangs in the kitchen of a certain well-known artist. This is what I have done with absolutely no talent or ability. I have to confess that these toys do not seem to have been quite as popular with the children as, say, the remote-control Dalek or the chocolate-coin maker. But children are constantly a finger-click away from being helpful and creative. When I summon up the energy to turn off the TV, they moan for a few minutes and then they adjust, and I'll soon find them playing or drawing or building some fantastic creation out of old cardboard boxes.

Another simple solution is to split the family into smaller groups. This can defuse the nuclear tension. I find that the children behave beautifully when I take them out alone. They have my attention, as I'm not trying to chat to Victoria. I also take total responsibility and, therefore, I am not hoping that Victoria will, for example, change Henry's nappy.

Avoid family days out. There is nothing more certain to lead to disaster than cramming four or five people in a Vauxhall Cavalier and going for a Family Day Out. Family Days Out usually mean spending money – at the theme park or the bowling alley – in an attempt to save the family, to do the right thing. They are inevitably disappointing. We think that money means love, but money can lead to squabbles and accusations of unfair conduct from one's children. We have become radically disabled as parents. We plead for help. 'Help me!' we scream, and the consumer culture comes back and says, 'In return for £9.99 entrance fee (or £9.99 monthly direct debit), we will help!' We end up doing ridiculous things. For example, instead of playing in the woods, fields, moors, valleys and beaches near where I live, we drive them half an hour to the nearest town and put them in a giant padded warehouse of plastic tubes called Bumper Back Yard, at great expense.

Another easy answer is to invite more people around. Share the burden. Do swaps. Fill the house with other people's children. Drink in the kitchen with their parents while the kids riot around the house or in the garden. If we invite two or three other kids to come and play, the gang of them just vanish off together, and I can get on with some work. We employed a nanny for three years, borrowed against the house to pay for her. The big benefit was the expansion of the household; we behaved better when she was around; she brought fun and a good spirit; we were able to catch up on sleep. But the downside was a shifting of responsibility on the part of Victoria and myself. A friend noticed that the kids were bad with us and good with Nanny.

One major problem of the nuclear family is that we are too much in each other's faces. This is certainly the problem we had with Arthur. At five, he had become reliant on constant entertainment, whether it was TV, company, playing games or the computer. He was not self-sufficient, in that he constantly sought external stimuli. The other day, he said to me, in anger: 'I need . . . some . . . *entertainment!*' In other words, he is in danger of lacking the inner resources to play. This is in sharp contrast to our other two children, who have inevitably been more left alone than Arthur, because they were the second and third children. So they have been able to develop self-reliance. Arthur's mode of self-expression, his public demonstration of his freedom, is to scream 'no' when asked to do something.

The wonderful thing about children is not their so-called innocence but their passion, their passion for life and living. This can take the form of tears or laughter, and we need to get it into our heads that tears and laughter are both to be welcomed. You can't have one without the other. They may even enjoy it – like the medievals, who seemed to embrace all extremes of passion. It is this passion that we need to find in ourselves.

There is a very powerful piece of childcare advice in D. H. Lawrence's long essay 'Education for the People', written in 1918. It is a simple approach to family life, which involves less work at no cost with better results. 'First rule: leave them alone,' he says. 'Second rule: leave them alone. Third rule: leave them alone.' Lawrence argues that there is something wrong with cloying, sentimental mother-love. He sees it as disabling. So the advice, 'Leave them alone,' which I repeat as a mantra to myself every day, seeks to allow the children to grow up in their own way. It is the patronizing and interfering, done in the name of love, which causes the problems. It is the attempt to impose order on nature that causes mental and physical sickness. We are told these days that we need to 'spend quality time' with the kids. 'Make time for play every day.' Such rules and to-do lists have a negative effect, for the simple reason that they transform parenthood from something done out of love into a duty. It makes it into a job, something to be skived off from and avoided. It makes childcare into drudgery, when the goal should just be to live your own lives together. If you please yourself first and avoid the trap of doing things out of duty and then resenting them later, you find that you start playing with them at odd, unscheduled times, quite naturally.

Lawrence's advice, the 'leave them alone' philosophy, also indicates a greater degree of respect for the child than rampant over-scheduling, the guilt-and-duty approach. Maybe the children don't actually want their parents in their face all the time? When a male politician announces that he wants to spend more time with his family, the question in my mind is always, yes, but do they want to spend more time with you? And just as children should say, 'Leave us alone,' to their parents, so we adults should say, 'Leave us alone,' to our governments. Because, of course, the very same process is at work here: by allowing ourselves to be looked after too much, we become completely lacking in self-reliance, and habits of uselessness and dependence build up.

'Benign neglect' was the other lovely phrase I heard to describe this approach. Let them get on with it.

One thing that depresses me greatly is the argument I hear trotted out with tedious regularity by other parents, usually said about boys. 'He'd better toughen up, because it's a tough world out there. It's a competitive place . . .' Why not say, 'It's a wonderful world out there, so let's make him wonderful!' The solution to the world being full of arseholes is not to add to the problem by making your own son into an arsehole. Set a good example!

In actual fact, it is only a tough world out there if you choose to make it so. If you see life as a race or a competition then that's what it will be. If, on the other hand, you choose to see it as a place of wonder and magic, then it will become that. By telling our children that everything is awful and tough and unfair, we are adding to the problem.

We are fatally over-scheduling our children and creating a nation of useless dependants unable to do anything for themselves apart from the spectacularly useless and costly occupations of computer games, tennis and ballet. We are creating a generation of children who don't know how to play. I remember a *New Yorker* cartoon showing two kids standing next to each other with their Palm Pilots out. 'OK,' one is saying. 'I can fit you in for unscheduled play next Thursday at four.' Most of these so-called activities are mere distractions, diversions, bagatelles, and we should just let children play with each other and create their own games, which they will readily do if left to their own devices. And you can do your own thing while they do theirs. In order not to resent looking after children, I tend to carry a book around with me. This means that when they are playing together nicely, I can enjoy a couple of pages of Boswell's *Life of Johnson* or whatever it happens to be.

An example of child-based scheduling lunacy in my own life is that Victoria organized tennis lessons a half-hour drive from our house for Arthur on Saturday mornings at 9 a.m.! Finally, we have one morning when we don't have to rush to get him ready for school, and she creates an early appointment for him – at great cost, too! She found a school replacement! How crazy is that? Rampant over-scheduling must die! Leave them alone!

We are throwing money at the problem. We are delegating the care of our children to experts. Mothers shriek, 'I'm such a bad mother.' Dads grump around the house and shout at their infants. And why? Because we are radically helpless; households are too small; we have no manners. Get them working for you, that's my advice! But, really, since all is futile, it doesn't matter what you do. The kids will sort themselves out. So beat yourself up no more.

LEAVE THE KIDS ALONE

21 Disarm Pain

GSK's biggest contribution to society is the discovery and development of medicines that help people to do more, feel better and live longer.
from GlaxoSmithKline's website

Life, at all times full of pain, is more painful in our time than in the two centuries that preceded it. The attempt to escape from pain drives men to triviality, to self-deception, to the invention of vast collective myths. But these momentary alleviations do but increase the sources of suffering in the long run.
Bertrand Russell, '"Useless" Knowledge', 1935

Pain means profit: that, in a more honest society, would be the slogan of the pharmaceutical monsters GlaxoSmithKline – because that is the simple truth, unvarnished: the more pain you are in, the more pills you will take, and the quicker their share price will rise. And the more pain there is in the world, the more profit, too. The logical step, therefore, is to create pain, to cause misery, depression and bipolar disorders in order to sell the solution to that misery. New disorders create new markets. And this, in a sense, is precisely what happens. We are oppressed by boring work, by blaring screens, by impossible desires. There is a great Damien Hirst installation called *Looking forward to the Total and Absolute Suppression of Pain* in which four TV monitors simultaneously and at ear-splitting volume play four different commercials for Nurofen, Solpadeine and other headache tablets. The solutions to pain are precisely the things that cause the pain in the first place. The same system that causes the pain promises to take it away.

The goal of a complete suppression of pain, never achieved, is a very profitable one. The chairman of GlaxoSmithKline, Jean-Pierre Garnier, receives an annual salary (including bonus) of $4.5 million. In addition to that, the company makes massive annual contributions to his pension scheme and, of course, he has enormous shareholdings. As if that's not enough, in 2003, he wanted a package worth $22 million, but the idea was voted down by other shareholders. GSK's annual turnover is £20 billion and its profits come to £6.1 billion. Much of this profit comes from its anti-depressant drug Wellbutrin.

Of its 100,000 staff, 40,000 are employed in sales and marketing. The big drugs companies also have a huge 'unpaid' band of salesmen in the form of GPs, who are in fact paid – by UK tax revenue. They will prescribe Amoxicillin and Wellbutrin at the drop of a hat. The CEO of GSK bears a startling resemblance to Mr Burns of *The Simpsons*. A new addition to the board is Sir Chris Gent, who made a fortune working for grotty mobile-phone pedlars Vodafone.

GSK's slogan, quoted above, pretty much sums up the depressing ambitions of modern man: 'Do more, feel better, live longer.' Apart from the fact that these are all hopelessly woolly relative terms and therefore completely without meaning, the lack of passion for life they exhibit is worrying in the extreme. 'Do more' – as if doing were in itself a good, and more of it better. Surely there's far too much 'doing' going on in the world. The responsible response to a world in which interfering has created terrible health and environmental problems is to do less, not more. It is doing that has caused all the problems. And why is 'doing more' for its own sake meant to be a worthy goal? Hitler and Stalin 'did more' but, clearly, it would have been a lot better if they had done a lot less. 'Feel better' – well, there is the idea of suppressing pain. Pain is seen as an impediment to 'doing', whereas I see it as a welcome chance not to 'do' for a few days or hours. Surely, all we should do when ill is retire to bed with a pile of books and some fruit salad? And, as for 'live longer' – there lies another problem. Quality of life has been sacrificed to quantity of life. Living as long as possible rather than living as well as possible – that seems to have become the goal.

The GSK chairman's report exhibits an odd mixture of boasting about profits and boasting about the charitable intentions of the company. The world of pills, the modern sacrament, is vast and frightening. The corruption of the medieval Catholic Church is a tiny drop in the ocean compared with the vast size, unimaginable profits and sharp practice going on across the world among the global pedlars of snake-oil and poison, constantly opening up new markets in their restless need to grow.

Well, so much for the profits of pain, which I have outlined merely in the hope that it will become easier to free ourselves of pain when we realize that the creation of it is useful to the profit system. Therefore, it is rebellious to be merry and enjoy yourself.

But fear of pain may well be an impediment to living life well. Fear of pain, indeed, might be seen as fear of life, since life is pain. It would therefore make sense to embrace pain and hardship. One of Damien Hirst's party tricks is to ask you what you love about life. 'Erm, not sure,' you say. Then he will say: 'I love all of it.' He loves *all* of it, the highs and the lows. He does not subscribe to the perfectionist ideal of removing all pain and suffering from the world. Life *is* pain and hardship. Every up seems to have an accompanying down. As the gloomy Robert Burton writes:

> In adversity I wish for prosperity, and in prosperity fear adversity
> . . . what condition of life is free? Wisdom hath labour annexed
> to it, glory, envy; riches and cares, children and incumbrances,
> pleasure and diseases, rest and beggary, go together, as if man
> were therefore born to be punished in this life for some prece-
> dent sins.

I wonder if it might be possible to enjoy pain. Certainly this seems to have been the case in the Middle Ages, when people positively revelled in their woes. Life was lived with an intensity that is hard for us rational republicans to imagine. In *The Waning of the Middle Ages*, Huizinga writes of the passionate spirit that led the medievals to queue up all night to hear a preacher whose stirring sermon would send the entire congregation howling and sobbing from the church door in the morning. Then, of course, there were the thirteenth-century flagellants who deliberately imposed pain on themselves for its mystic properties. They also provided great theatre. And their pain, indeed, had positive ends, as Norman Cohn reports:

> It was in the crowded Italian cities that organized flagellant processions appeared for the first time. The movement was launched in 1260 by a hermit of Perugia and spread southwards to Rome and northwards to the Lombard cities with such rapidity that to contemporaries it appeared a sudden epidemic of remorse. Led usually by priests, masses of men, youths and boys marched day and night, with banners and burning candles, from town to town. And each time they came to a town they would arrange themselves in groups before the church and flog themselves for hours on end. The impact which this public penance made upon the general population was great. Criminals confessed, robbers restored their loot and usurers the interest on their loans, enemies were reconciled and feuds forgotten.

Public pain led to positive outcomes for the community. I somehow can't imagine the same thing happening today in our pain-phobic society. I just can't see Bono and Geldof whipping themselves outside Westminster Abbey. Nietzsche was of the opinion that the rejection of pain is a rejection of life. In *Ecce Homo*, he writes:

I was the first to see the real opposition, the degenerating instinct that turns against life with subterranean vengefulness (Christianity, the philosophy of Schopenhauer, in a certain sense already the philosophy of Plato, and of all idealism in typical forms) versus a formula for the highest affirmation, born of fullness, of overfullness, a Yes-saying without reservation, even to suffering, even to guilt, even to everything that is questionable and strange in existence.

It is the nay-saying, Nietzsche maintains, the pushing away of all that is awkward, painful and difficult which leads to our lives being drained of colour. Even cruelty, he argues, was part of a certain joy in life:

> It is not long since princely weddings and public festivals of the more magnificent kind were unthinkable without executions, torturings, or perhaps an auto-da-fé [the public burning of heretics in the Inquisition], and no noble household was without creatures upon whom one could heedlessly vent one's malice and cruel jokes.

To modern eyes, this sort of behaviour looks unimaginably cruel, but Nietzsche offers a crumb of comfort: 'Perhaps in those days – the delicate may be comforted by this thought – pain did not hurt as much as it does now.'

I recently decided that, instead of avoiding hardship and pushing it away with central heating and air-conditioning, it might be sensible to embrace it. Yes, that might sound like a strange idea coming from the pen of an idler, but could embracing hardship be the path to freedom? For example, I recently considered buying a draughty old Land Rover to replace my old, luxury American van, partly because, in the Land Rover, you are better exposed to the elements. This is not to deny the pleasures of the log fire; indeed, the pleasures of the log fire are all the more intense when you have just been out in the snow to chop up the logs for it. This is a pleasure that those with underfloor heating cannot experience. This is what the medievals enjoyed – the harsh contrast between hardship and pleasure. The fire is all the cosier when you've been for a long walk in the cold.

Some pain I can do without, and thank heavens for Ibuprofen when the headache strikes, although lying in bed for hours can have the same effect. In a less work-orientated time, as the Middle Ages incontrovertibly were, you might have had the time just to go to bed with your headache rather than take a pill and soldier on with your work. There was more time to recover. Things took longer. Doubtless also there were medicines available for pain at the time, too, folk medicines and herbs and so on. These sorts of things are scoffed at today; but ask yourself, who does the scoffing serve? The scoffers who sneer are mere dupes of the capitalistic project. When you scoff at the free chemicals which leap out at you from the hedgerow, you are simply playing into the hands of those who want you to spend, spend, spend on their own factory-made snake oils. In any case, the doctor's art is the same as it has always been, which is to amuse the patient while the body heals itself. Placebos, I repeat, are possibly as effective and certainly less harmful than the real drugs, as long as you trust your doctor, or imbue him or her with some sort of magical power. So many modern pharmaceuticals are merely a costly and dangerous nonsense.

Pain will never leave us. Live with it. Instead of putting energy into destroying pain, we need to put energy into creating pleasure. Pleasure for yourself and pleasure for those around you. Sex, music, dancing, beer and wine, good company, good work, merry cheer: these are the antidotes to pain, and they are of course only pleasures because we know pain. Without pain, there would be no pleasure.

EMBRACE HARDSHIP

22 Stop Worrying about Your Pension and Get a Life

Humanity knows nothing at all. There is no intrinsic value in anything, and every action is a futile, meaningless effort.
Masanobu Fukuoka, *The One-Straw Revolution*, 1978

In the olden days, the word 'pension' referred to an annual sum that some benevolent beneficiary gave an individual in recognition of public service. Dr Johnson, for example, was granted a pension of £300 a year from King George III in 1762. This annuity was made principally to thank him for having created his great Dictionary, and was unconditional: the prime minister, Lord Bute, told Johnson: 'It is not given you for anything you are to do, but for what you have done.' Soldiers, too, have traditionally received pensions, and that is right, because once a soldier has grown too old to be useful to his army, why should he be callously thrown aside?

I've nothing against money for nothing. The idea of receiving money and not having to work for it is a very attractive one. But I wonder if the government-run and City-run pension systems really benefit the individuals they are supposed to serve. In both cases, there is a vast industry providing jobs and wealth for those inside it but seemingly nothing for those putting their money into it. In the case of government, we are forever hearing of a 'pensions crisis' (but not of a 'defence crisis' or a 'too many civil servants crisis'). This means, once again, that the trusting individual, who foolishly believed that the state would look after him or her with a nice pension on retirement, has to carry the can for another giant foul-up.

In the case of private pensions, you never know when some Maxwell type might come along and steal your money. At the very least, it is obvious that the City boys make a lot of money out of pension funds. Just compare the house or houses of your average pension-fund manager with your own humble dwelling. Well, that's your money he has bought his champagne with. There is also an ethical consideration here: the pension funds create giant pots of cash, drawn from the poor people's monthly contributions, which are moved around world markets, from GlaxoSmithKline to HSBC to arms dealers and other unsavoury money-making enterprises. You really have no idea what your little contributions are being used for. Much better to ignore the empty promises of state and business and make your own provision or, better still, to create a life that you won't want to retire from.

The artists among us should look to benevolent private individuals. Providing pensions of the old-fashioned sort – money for nothing – should be the role of monarchy and the aristocrats today. Having been attacked by the middle classes, armed with meritocratic ideals and demands for inheritance tax and removed from the House of Lords, the aristocrats are searching for a role, and the answer is simple: they should be providing pensions for great writers, poets, philosophers, musicians, artists – in other words, for idlers. In the eighteenth century, there was a fashion for employing a hermit to live in a grotto in your garden. I should think that 'hermit' would be a nice job for someone. The rich should also open up their houses and dole out bread and beer and tasty sweetmeats in the grand tradition of hospitality. Their role has been usurped by professional corporate outfits such as Bloomberg and the sellers of mobile telephones.

The pensions industry does its damnedest to instil fear about the future in us poor consumers. Trapped on the train platform or on the bus, we are blasted by their anxiety-inducing messages. Anything can happen, they say, so it makes sense to plan ahead. But, of course, it is easy to sell products on the basis of events that haven't yet happened, because you have virgin territory in which to stir up all sorts of fears. The shape of the future can be bent to the will of the ad men. The phrase 'What if . . . ?' should be banned from polite society. The simple fact is that you could die in a motor-car accident tomorrow and all your pension-planning and careful saving would be lost. Therefore, the really responsible thing is to shout, 'Stuff your pension,' as Philip Larkin longed to have the courage to do in his famous poem, 'Toads'. A great insult recently was the government raising the retirement age, as a result, it said, of the 'pensions crisis'. This 'pensions crisis' has been talked about for years, and then, just when everyone has become really worried – wham! – the state comes in with its solution, which is to work harder and longer! (Once again, the state comes in to correct the problems caused by the state.) Can you imagine what it must feel like if you are one of the ones who thought they had three years to go before retirement suddenly to be told that this period had extended to six? Now we are faced with the undignified spectacle of eighty-year-old men working on the check-out in the supermarket, men who should be taking naps, drinking beer and pottering around in the allotment. This is accompanied by patronizing twaddle in right-wing newspapers and magazines about how jolly these 'sprightly' eighty-year-olds are in their work. (Have you noticed how eighty-year-olds are always 'sprightly'?) It's humiliating.

And what has the retirement age to do with the government anyway? When I retire or do not retire is really nothing to do with them. Our retirement age should be a matter for private contract between ourselves and our employers or, even better, something that we decide for ourselves.

The rise of the pension as a sort of earthly reward for having suffered for forty years or more in a job you didn't like – this is something new. Likewise, pension as a kind of national entitlement. A pension has become something that you work for rather than something you get after working. In other words, it is an expression of reward by the authorities for good work, the 'secular afterlife', in the words of my friend Matthew de Abaitua. Suffer now; enter paradise later.

Private pension plans claim to sell you 'peace of mind', i.e.

freedom from fear, but the reality is the opposite: they sell us fear and then sell us the apparent solution to that fear – money. But that solution never works. In the case of pensions, you will dutifully squirrel away little bits of money, causing suffering for you today, in the hope of better tomorrows, because you believed the fradulent message of the ad men. When bombarded by pension advertising, we should repeat the wise words of the Troubadour Cercamon, who sang, in 1140:

> All your fine words at less than a farthing I rate. Better a quail held fast in my bosom here than a whole poultry-house locked up by someone else. Rely on another's gifts and you gape at empty air.

Yes, I, too, would rather have a quail now than the vague possibility of a poultry-house tomorrow. Pensions are about empty promises. They are devilish. Meanwhile, the capitalists are swanning around using *your* money to buy infernal Blackberries and sit in the back of cabs feeling important: but they are mere *stock-jobbers*! It's time to reverse the status of things. Look down on the money-makers and elevate yourself! No, I will never take out a pension. Any money I make, I would like to keep for myself. Put it under the bed! Or buy something you like! In my case, this means books. I would always rather spend £50 a month on books than give £50 to a City broker. The inbuilt greed of the pension-fund managers also means that they are vulnerable to scammers. A lawyer friend has just told me how a group of City boys scammed £80 million out of a pension fund with promises of huge returns. Therefore, your pension is the very opposite of what it claims to be: far from being safe, it is a catastrophically insecure place to put your money. To invest in a pension, in actual fact, shows irresponsible recklessness.

So, when it come to pensions, I am firmly of the 'eat, drink and be merry, for tomorrow we may die' school. Belief in pensions produces a kind of slavery. If you don't believe in pensions, then you believe in yourself and you believe in looking after yourself. This makes you free. I would rather have my money now and let tomorrow look after itself. Again, we can't complain if, in our greed, we entrust our money to a gang of speculators and they throw it away on flaming Ferraris.

The other point to make about pensions is that security itself is a phantasm. It simply doesn't exist. It's a construction of the mind, a mere hope, a will o' the wisp. Things are unpredictable. How do you know what is going to happen tomorrow or even in the next minute? A natural disaster could wipe out your savings – or a stock-market crash. If you've got money, for god's sake, spend it. Life is change, flux, flow, process. Security is the desire to fix, to be certain, to be safe. It is a fiction and, although worrying about such things is often referred to as the 'real world', it is, in fact, the precise opposite. The real world is the one we live in, that chaotic, confused, insecure and wonderful place.

Worrying about the future is a useless act; it does nothing to improve the present. Funnily enough, the people who encourage others to worry about the future are those who want your money now. They themselves are not worrying about the future; they are maximizing their profits today.

Make your own provision. Continuing to work could be one.

Owning a property could be another. Selling your house could be another. Another option is simply to give up and let God provide, and when I say 'God', I mean friends, relatives and neighbours. Financial institutions make us feel scared and lonely in order that we pay them for security. But we forget the power of family, friends and community to help out when times are tough.

If you worry about how you will survive in the future, then why not consider simply selling your house when you retire. If you think that 40 per cent of its value will end up in the Treasury anyway, it makes sense to sell it and live off the money. There won't be much of an inheritance, but then, why can't your children look after themselves?

Throw caution to the wind. Even if you look at pensions from a rational, sensible point of view, they are dangerous, because the market is so unpredictable. Your pension is all mixed up in the stock market, so if the stock market crashes, your hard-earned money will simply vanish into thin air, leaving you waving worthless bits of paper at the gates of the bank. Investing in stocks and shares is really the triumph of hope over experience, as Dickens and Edward Chancellor show so clearly.

I would abolish retirement altogether. It is an absurd notion: if I enjoy working, then why would I want to retire? In cases where we can simply no longer work, then our own trade should provide us with a living; and this would be another argument for a return to something like the guilds system. The guilds looked after their own; when a member was ill and unable to work, his work was covered by other guild members. The members of the guilds also paid dues, which went towards looking after the families of dead members. They looked after themselves, and provision for disaster was made on a local level and by private agreement between groups, not as a result of fear-inducing advertising campaigns.

Well, in my case, in a sense, I retired at thirty-five in order to write a book and, God willing, I shall never have to go to work again. I think this should be our responsibility: rather than waiting for the glory days of retirement, let us take our pleasures now. Let us not delegate our future to an outside agency, whether that is government or pension-fund manager. Let us not hand over our money to someone else to manage. Far from providing security, to do so is a highly dangerous operation.

We need to look after ourselves, and rejecting the empty promises of the evil pensions industry is a positive step on the way. To reject pensions is to embrace yourself; it is to stick two fingers up at the silver-tongued money-men.

SAY YES TO LIFE

23 Sail Away from Rudeness and towards a New Era of Courtesy, Civility and Grace

Men are evil, wicked, malicious, treacherous, and naught, not loving
one another, or loving themselves, not hospitable, charitable or sociable as
they ought to be, but counterfeit, dissemblers, ambidexters, all for their
own ends, hard-hearted, merciless, pitiless, and to benefit themselves,
they care not what mischief they procure to others.
Robert Burton, *Anatomy of Melancholy,* 1621

There is a great book to be written called *Rudeness and the Rise of Capitalism.* The two are practically synonymous. Puritanism and its brother, money-getting, are rude by nature, because they require a simple inability to see the point of view of another because of an earnest exaltation of profit above any other consideration. This failing leads Puritans to acts of spectacular rudeness.

Cancelling Christmas, as they did in 1649, is an extraordinarily impolite thing to do. Indeed, the more extreme Puritans were so rude that, in the end, we packed some of them off to the States, where, notwithstanding an excellent Constitution, they were able to build a whole new nation free to be as rude as it pleased. They continued their battle against fun and life over there, in the Civil War, the rude North against the courteous South.

I imagine we all know someone who fits the following description, by gentle Bertrand Russell, in his essay 'The Recrudescence of Puritanism', of the Puritan cast of mind: intrusive, morally superior, ascetic, humourless. Certainly it describes very well Britain's prime minister in the later 1990s and early 2000s:

> We must learn to respect each other's privacy, and not to impose our moral standards upon each other. The Puritan imagines that his moral standard is *the* moral standard; he does not realize that other ages and other countries, and even other groups in his own country, have moral standards different from his, to which they have as good a right as he has to his. Unfortunately, the love of power which is the natural outcome of Puritan self-denial makes the Puritan more executive than other people, and makes it difficult for other people to resist him.

For Russell's word, 'executive', substitute 'bloody bad-mannered'. It may be literally rude to *do* things, because the things that you do will not necessarily be the things that suit others. Above all else, idleness is polite. It is polite not to shine too brightly, it is polite not to be too successful, it is polite not to work too hard, it is polite to *leave others alone*. The idler makes other people around him feel good, because he behaves as if he is worse than they are, not better. Behaving as if you are better than others shows a lack of regard for other people. Zealous ambition is rude; Homer Simpson is polite. Government, which started life as a polite phenomenon designed to protect the people from plunder, has turned into a very rude institution which kills people, tells them what to do and how to live, and spies on them. All those Google searches you've performed and all those emails you've sent: before long, government will give itself the power to examine them whenever it feels like it. And the people are heartily fed up with this interference. I was chatting with our postman, a lifelong Labour supporter, and he is livid at the extension of state powers into every tiny corner of our lives. 'They're everywhere,' he said. 'You can't get away!' Computers, CCTV cameras, storecards, credit cards: every move you make, they're watching you, recording everything on vast databanks.

Just as the capitalist ethic grew up alongside Puritanism, so money and rudeness are bedfellows. Manners come second to money. When you owe someone money, it seems to give them licence to treat you with the utmost contempt. When you delay paying the capitalists, they turn very nasty very quickly. Those same people who had previously courted, flattered and seduced you so assiduously, until you gave in and handed over your credit-card details or returned the direct-debit form, suddenly lose all courtesy and respect when you owe them money. Courtly manners do verily fly out the window, and in fly threatening letters and hectoring emails. When my mother's long-time partner died, she called the gas company to tell them that they would settle his bill once probate had been arranged. Her letters were ignored, and an unstoppable stream of increasingly unpleasant letters poured through the dead man's letter-box threatening disconnection, bailiffs, court appearances, destruction of credit ratings and all the rest of the battery of modern power. The size of the gas bill? £34.80.

Salesmen are rude. Telephoning people at home on a Sunday morning to sell them some new telephone deal is downright rude and an abuse of my freedom. True freedom is not the freedom to interfere with the pleasures of others. It is the right to enjoy one's own pleasures and create one's own life; it is also about guaranteeing that right to others.

While writing this page, I received a cold call. At noon on a Friday.

'Hello, is that Mr Hoss-king-son?' The line was crackly, the accent Indian. Clearly some poor guy in a Delhi call centre.

'Erm . . . yes?'

'Can I just ask you, do you use a mobile phone?'

What can you say? I wished I didn't have a mobile phone so I could simply say 'no' without lying. These cold callers presented me with an awkward dilemma: you want to tell them to go away, but then you don't want to be rude to another human being. So how do you get rid of them without screaming, *'Leave me alone!'* or slamming down the phone, as I tend to do when grumpy?

'I'm sorry, but I don't want these calls. You've just disturbed me while I am trying to work. Thank you. Goodbye.'

As I put the phone down, I could hear him continuing the sales patter.

Another frequent call is the one about home improvements. Some poor, desperate, commission-only single mum will call on a Sunday morning, saying: 'We've got representatives in your area and wonder whether you'd be interested in a free consultation.' Oh, they try to sound chirpy as they read from their script. It makes me want to break down and weep. These people are motivated by a manager who will give them a pep talk about how, just six months ago, he had nothing. Then he started selling, and now he's driving a Porsche. I once overheard some young lads on the train who, I deduced, had been peddling mobile-phone tariffs door-to-door. The conversation centred around some figure, almost mythical, they knew of, who was making 'silly money'. This is how it works in sales jobs: a pot of gold is created in the mind, a huge pile of cash at the end of all this unnecessary and soul-destroying rudeness, and always just out of reach. And, in the UK, sales is the worst paid of all areas of work. The best, by the way, is healthcare. The doctors, those peddlers of antibiotics and other pills and potions, have got it sewn up.

Email *de natura* seems to produce bad feeling. The medium without doubt affects the quality of the message, and we seem to give ourselves licence to be terribly offhand in our emails to one another, abandoning grammar, spelling, and sentences in favour of staccato and telegram-like abbreviations. All elegance of expression vanishes. You cannot imagine the Collected Emails of Seamus Heaney. And because email does not convey nuance well, it is easy to come across as more abrupt and lacking in manners than you had intended. Sometimes you sense a bad vibe building up over an email correspondence and decide to speak to the other party on the telephone. And, when chatting properly, the bad feeling will vanish. The answer is to introduce elaborate courtesies back into our emails, opening them with,

'My Dear . . .' signing them off with, 'I shall remain ever your faithful servant . . .' The contemporary loss of formality in every-day communication can lead to hurt feelings. Politeness respects the sensitivities of the other person. Let's also bring back letter-writing: what a joy it is to compose and to receive a real letter! Pen, ink, paper, post: these are inexpensive joys. People complain about the mail, but I have always found it miraculously good. A hard copy of your letter delivered anywhere in the country the next day for the price of a stamp! And you can send objects in the post. You can put stickers, badges and newspaper cuttings in there. Many of my friends are now rejecting email. They find it liberating to live without it.

In societies where money does not play such a central role, the people are more mannerly. For example, in Mexico, it is expected, upon retiring to bed, to say to the assembled company, '*con su permiso*', meaning, 'with your permission', a delightful phrase. In good manners and civility, we see a playful linguistic element at work. Kropotkin mentions the good manners and charm of primitive societies, and in Mayan civilization, courtesy was paramount. Confucius, of course, put a lot of stress on good manners as the oil which ensures the smooth functioning of society. It makes perfectly logical sense that in societies based on a collective ideal, manners and rituals are of the highest impor-tance, whereas in societies based on a competitive ideal, manners are useful only as a means of getting what you want. We read in Cobbett and Hardy of the 'old manners', meaning the cour-tesy and respect with which people used to treat each other before the shoving, pushing, interfering, money-based Calvinists came along and ruined everything.

The most polite man who ever lived was probably that great visionary vagabond of the twelfth century, St Francis of Assisi. He was a bright young man about town when young and a member of the charming literary-musical movement of the twelfth and thirteenth centuries, the Troubadours of Occitania, South of France. Later, though, he took a vow of poverty and chastity and rejected money. This itself is supremely polite, because it is guaranteed to make others around you feel good, whereas the flash millionaire with girls on his arm excites envy and is behaving with bad manners. For Chesterton, one of the great qualities of St Francis of Assisi was his manners: he was unfailingly courteous to everyone he met and took a sincere interest in their inner life. 'We may say if we like that St Francis, in the bare and barren simplicity of his life, had clung to one rag of luxury, the manners of a court.' He did not set himself up above others; he was of the world, and he knew that the world had room for a limitless variety of people. He played in the space between this world and the other-world.

Good hospitality was also expected in the South of France, the home of the Troubadours. The Troubadours were not simply wandering minstrels but a large group of composers and musicians from all walks of life who held up courtly love as an ideal. The word 'troubadour' comes from the Latin '*tropator*' meaning, 'discoverer'. And what they invented was a new kind of vernacular love poetry set to music. Their lyrics were sometimes satirical, sometimes pastoral, sometimes bawdy; sometimes they sang of chivalry, many times of joy. They were Romantics ahead of their time, the pop stars of their day. They played drums, lutes, pipes and the wonderful hurdy-gurdy, or versions thereof. And as they travelled, they rated houses and courts on the fare they offered. An ideal dinner would consist of venison, wild boar, game and fish, plain and spiced wine, fritters and biscuits, also bustards, swans, cranes, partridges, ducks, capons, geese, hens and peacocks, rabbits, hares, wild bear, roots and fruit. There are frequent complaints in Troubadour poems about the stingy rich who offer but a poor table. Thankfully, there are musicians around today who are re-creating their energetic music, and of an evening I like to sit in my pub, the Green Man, with some pounding Troubadour beats on the stereo. (I can particularly recommend the work of the Unicorn Ensemble.)

The Troubadours, above all, praised merry living and courtesy. In the words of 'Tant m'abelis' by the twelfth-century Troubadour Berenguier de Palou:

> *Tant m'abelis jois et amors et chans*
> *Ert alegrier deports e cortezia*

> (So much I love joy and love and song,
> mirth, sport and courtesy)

Good manners and hospitality were also important to the early artisanal middle class, who formed themselves, as we have seen, into the guilds. The early middle class of tradesmen and artisans needed to prove to the nobles and the clerics that work could be carried out without offending customs of politeness. A high standard of craftsmanship for a fair price was polite; to rip people off with shoddy goods was rude.

It was simple good manners to look after the poor and to look after each other. Henry VIII, Cranmer and the Protector

Somerset introduced new and shocking standards of rudeness. They systematically dismantled all the polite innovations of medieval society: the shared fields, the monasteries, the guild lands, the custom of open house. One of the great attractions of the medieval age was that it combined a childish intensity of living with a giant effort to behave well to one another.

The problem today for rebellious types is that, since the Victorian age, good manners have been associated with servility. Unfortunately, manners became warped in the nineteenth century by an undue emphasis on etiquette, based more on a respect for your betters than genuine courtesy. While the lower orders were expected to be courteous to their superiors, it seems that no such duty weighed on the upper echelons. And manners became not so much about consideration for others as an expression of subservience. Therefore, to be ill-mannered would be seen as a sign of rebellion against authoritarian values.

A moment's reflection, however, will reveal that the opposite is the case and that it is, in fact, rebellious and anarchic to be well mannered. Good manners are anti-capitalist. My friend the impeccably dressed Gavin Clarke runs a brilliant magazine called *The Chap*, which evokes a world of pipe-smoking gents tipping their hats to one another. Yet the staff and readers of the magazine will sometimes rouse themselves to rebellious actions, such as marching into McDonald's and ordering kedgeree and lapsang souchong. *The Chap*'s slogans include 'Civilize the City' and, for them, dressing in tweeds and brogues is an expression of defiance against ringtone culture, branded tracksuits and the deadening blandness of the modern world. *The Chap* stands up for eccentricity in a world of uniformity.

I see hope, too, in the movement of immigrants around the world. Immigrants with more old-fashioned cultures bring their civility to the UK as part of a process that has been going on for centuries: Sir William Temple observes that, through the Norman Conquest, we 'gained more Learning, more Civility, more Refinement of Language, Customs and Manners, from the great Resort of other strangers, as well as Mixture of French and Norman'. Strangers can help us to live well.

We need to reclaim good manners. *Idler* contributor Josh Glenn wrote a regular etiquette column for the magazine in which he, for example, promoted the idea of Apology Cards, which would be sent the day after a party at which you had disgraced yourself. Somehow, we need to learn how to behave: charm, civility, courtesy, thought for others. Too often, these are considered virtues only if serving a commercial end. But they should be ends in themselves.

What I have tried to do at home (with no success thus far) is to introduce politeness competitions. The idea is to channel our competitive energies into a battle of manners: who can be the most absurdly over-polite? 'Good morning, Pater. Could I possibly trouble you to help me find my pants? Mater appears to have mislaid them.' 'Certainly, my child. It would be a pleasure and a privilege and please don't mention it. By the way, when you are ready, and in your own time, breakfast is ready.'

Disintegrating manners are the sign of a disintegrating society. The late Romans were rude; the contemporary American government is rude. It is rude to kill 27,000 Iraqi civilians. Interference is rude; governments are rude; professionals are rude. As the old society falls apart, we need quietly and modestly to re-create a new one alongside it. The old, battling ways will quietly destroy themselves. Competition will eat itself. Our task is to start to create a well-mannered society. When you declare yourself to be free, you also declare others to be free, and that means that you will not interfere with them. You will not abuse them.

Don't bother setting up free republics or moving to a country which offers more liberties. Simply declare yourself to be an independent state. Do not involve and coerce others. This is the only way we will effect a proper revolution. Once each of us recognizes our own freedom and our own responsibility, then the chains that bind us will fall away. To be free from bad manners, we have to be mannerly ourselves, and then we have to ignore the bad manners in others.

Hospitality is its own reward. If we put people up here at home, then they will open their doors to us if we need it. Being good to people is the only insurance policy you need; just as you will help out friends and neighbours in times of need, so they will help you when the boot is on the other foot. One of my plans is to offer open house every full moon. Friends and neighbours will all be aware that they can pop in on that day and enjoy good company, good wine, good beer, good food, and good cheer.

To be polite is to register a protest against all the many rudenesses of everyday life. Mobile phones are rude. The other day, I was in the pub with a friend, who was lecturing me about the wonderful communications revolution of mobile phones. He then received a text, and we sat in silence while he composed a reply. A new horror, worse perhaps than mobile phones on trains, is TVs on trains. Train journeys used to provide an oasis of calm, a time for reading and gazing out of the window. Now, they are installing TV screens on every seat back, so you are bombarded with news and advertising during your journey. Surely that is rude? It is like having a salesman sitting down next to you and trying to sell you stuff for the entire trip. There is a feeling of being shouted at wherever you go.

We can easily change this by avoiding shouting ourselves. Be cordial. Find freedom in manners.

BE GRACEFUL

24 Self-Important Puritans Must Die

One of the symptoms of the approaching nervous breakdown is the belief that one's work is terribly important & that to take a holiday would bring all kinds of disaster.
Bertrand Russell

Puritanism leads to self-importance. Once you take on the doctrine of predestination, the notion that there is an elect in the world and damn the rest of them, and once you take on the idea that worldly success and wealth are outward signs of God's approval of your conduct, then you can very easily start to turn into an insufferable prig and power-crazed zealot.

The approach to life of the existential, anarchic, medieval roustabout, however, is very different. If all is vanity, if life is absurd, then why not live in the moment? The medieval laughs at life; he does not have the spiritual arrogance of the Puritan. The medieval theology was close to the philosophy of inaction promoted by Taoism. For the Taoist, the aim is to stop making any effort at all, since all action is futile and vain. Man is supremely unimportant. The battle between the two strains of the human spirit have been fighting it out for many centuries and, indeed, the battle was symbolically represented during the English Civil War by the life-loving Cavaliers and the earnest Roundheads. 'In our army,' said a Cavalier general to Roundhead boss Lord Fairfax, 'we have the sins of men, drinking and wenching; but in yours the sins of those devils, spiritual pride and rebellion.'

In Shakespeare's *Twelfth Night*, the arrogance of the Puritan is satirized in the figure of the priggish Malvolio, whose self-importance blinds him to the impossibility of the idea of Viola taking a fancy to him. He is therefore easy prey for the practical joke that Sir Toby Belch and Maria, representing the 'eat, drink and be merry, for tomorrow we may die' attitude to life, decide to play on him. Here is how Maria describes Malvolio's character:

> The devil of a puritan that he is, or any thing, constantly, but a time-pleaser, an affectioned ass, that cons state without book and utters it by great swarths: the best persuaded of himself, so crammed, as he thinks, with excellencies, that it is his grounds of faith that all that look on him love him; and on that vice in him will my revenge find notable cause to work.

It is Malvolio's very 'grounds of faith' to believe he is a sort of superior being. Maria and Belch forge a love letter to Malvolio from Viola, in which she tells the Puritan that she would like nothing better than to see him dressed in yellow stockings with cross-garters. So it is that the medievals famously humiliate the Puritan, but we are left with Malvolio's chilling warning, 'I'll be revenged on the whole pack of you,' and so indeed he was: the Puritan strain has thoroughly dominated the medieval strain ever since.

That's not to say that the anti-Puritan never gets a look-in. One man who could never be called a prig was the aforementioned Lord Wilmot, Earl of Rochester. Wilmot was a Restoration dandy, a reckless, sex-addicted libertine, friend of Charles II and one of the 'merry gang', as contemporary Andrew Marvell called Rochester and his literary mates. I was lucky enough recently to have his poem '*Régime de Vivre*' recited to me from heart by a visitor:

> I rise at eleven, I dine about two,
> I get drunk before seven; and the next thing I do,
> I send for my whore, when for fear of a clap,
> I spend in her hand, and I spew in her lap.

That gives you an idea of Rochester's priorities in life. But there was more to Rochester than bawdy. He exhibited a fine nihilistic, Sartrean view of the world as essentially absurd and meaningless. In 'A Fragment of Seneca Translated', he maintains that all myths of the afterlife are merely phantasms, created by man from his own imagination. He also condemns Malvolio-style self-importance in the figure of the 'ambitious zealot':

After Death nothing is, and nothing, death,
The utmost limit of a gasp of breath.
Let the ambitious zealot lay aside
His hopes of heaven, whose faith is but his pride;
Let slavish souls lay by their fear
Nor be concerned which way nor where
After this life they shall be hurled.
Dead, we become the lumber of the world,
And to that mass of matter shall be swept
Where things destroyed with things unborn are kept.
Devouring time swallows us whole.
Impartial death confounds body and soul.
For Hell and the foul fiend that rules
God's everlasting fiery jails
(Devised by rogues, dreaded by fools),
With his grim, grisly dog that keeps the door,
Are senseless stories, idle tales,
Dreams, whimseys, and no more.

Here we see the link between libertinism and liberty: the libertine believes that all morals are mere manmade fictions, and, therefore, it doesn't matter what you do. We are told that another nihilist, Samuel Beckett, loved booze and prostitutes. And since we are all going to end up as nothings, why worry? The libertine, above all, lacks self-importance.

The mystery is how the Puritan strain became so powerful. The answer, I think, is resentment. Puritanism gave the resentful lower orders a way to feel powerful. In order to get power for themselves, the new bourgeois stirred up the grumpiness of the lower orders. This conclusion would certainly be suggested by the popularity of the early Puritan, the Florentine monk Savonarola. In the late fifteenth century, Savonarola made a name for himself with thundering sermons which attacked the corruption, profligacy and vanity of the Church, of society in general, and of the Medici family, who more or less ran things in Florence. 'Rethink you well, O ye rich,' he thundered, 'for affliction shall smite ye. This city shall no more be Florence, but a den of thieves, of turpitude and bloodshed.' He urged his followers, who became known as the Weepers, to go to their houses, pick up their Dantes and Petrarchs, their paintings of naked ladies, their soaps, silks, mirrors, chessboards, harps and jewellery and heap them up in the square and burn them. These symbolic rejections of luxury were called Bonfires of the Vanities. However, the people soon changed their mind and, on 23 May 1498, Savonarola was tried for heresy, hanged and then burned on the same spot in the Piazza del Signoria where he had held his bonfires.

Savonarola's success was achieved by manipulating the resentment of the people, and so it was with the Reformation. Calvin, Luther and the Wesleyites blathered on about corrupt priests and how the clergy lived in luxury in order to bring the people round to their side. It's clear also from Chaucer that hostility to the clergy – for being lazy and bloated, benefiting from the toil of the people and selling indulgences and so forth – had become widespread in Europe by the fourteenth century. This chink in the system allowed the Malvolios to move in and take over. But what happened was that a new meritocratic, bourgeois élite replaced the old élite of the aristocrats and the clergy and, as

Bertrand Russell, Chesterton and many others have argued, the new Puritans were actually more brutal and exploitative than the old medievals.

So, resentment leads directly to self-importance. If you are not of a resentful cast of mind, then you are unlikely to envy the riches of another. In this sense, revolutions can be seen as puritanical in spirit. In Orwell's *Animal Farm*, the pigs stir up the resentment of the animals against the men: why should you toil so they can live in luxury? By the end, as we all know, the pigs and men become indistinguishable from one another. One tyranny is replaced by another. The Puritan is simply jealous.

Today, it is consumer products and the job system which have taken the place of the Puritans. They promise to 'big up' the user, in the modern vernacular. They promise to make you feel like someone. A big car is a sign of being a worthwhile person. It is an outward sign of God's favour. The job system, with its rigid hierarchies of juniors and seniors, deputies and directors, executives and managers, also feeds self-importance. No, you are not just a quintessence of dust, a speck of nothing, you are Senior Branch Manager! You are a product manager! You are a *somebody*!

The old aristocratic system of rank and title has given way to a bourgeois system of promotion and self-promotion. Anyone who believes we are living in a non-hierarchical age has never worked in an office – all offices and workplaces seethe with hierarchy. How many marketing meetings have I sat in where the people seemed genuinely to feel that they were doing something important! Madness! And, as Bertrand Russell wisely points out, this madness, that mistaken apprehension that we are indispensable is likely to lead to a nervous breakdown. Mobile phones, too, make everyone look like a somebody; they trade on self-importance, that is their genius. At first, it was only the rich and very busy who had them. Gradually, we all decided that we were important enough to have a mobile phone, despite having managed for an eternity without them. Now, we are tethered to these absurd and expensive nothings.

However, let's not follow Savonarola and burn our phones. Then we will turn into the enemy. Following leaders will always disappoint. Their promises are empty, they are devils, profligates in disguise, all bound for the high table. Instead, it is far more sensible to recognize the anarchist idea 'There is no authority but yourself,' and, in the words of Kropotkin, to 'act for yourselves' and to eat, drink and be merry.

Self-importance is a trap, because the moment we start to think that we actually matter is the moment when things start to go wrong. The truth is that you are supremely unimportant, and that nothing matters. All of man's striving is for nothing; all effort is wasted. To realize that everything is meaningless is tremendously liberating, since it then leaves us completely free to create our own lives and ignore the plans that others have for us.

WE ARE NOTHING

25 Live Free of the Supermarkets

The consumer cannot and must not ever attain satisfaction.
Raoul Vaneigem, *The Revolution of Everyday Life*, 1967

Supermarkets are evil. That is a statement of fact. A friend once said to me, 'Tom, I think it's a bit more complicated than that.' But the longer I have looked at the question and the more I have researched it, the simpler my views have become. Supermarkets combine many evils into one big evil. They are gluttonous and have recently added usury to their list of sins by offering loans and bank accounts. Tesco's operates nearly five million personal bank accounts. They want everything. They want to control what we eat and where we shop, and now they want to profit from our poverty. According to a recent interview with chief executive, Terry Leahy, Tesco's latest plan is to move into holidays, thereby exploiting our leisure time. Having created a host of crap towns by driving small high-street shops out of business, creating hundreds of thousands of miserable jobs, they now want to offer low-rent holidays. Where we live, where we work, where we enjoy our leisure: they want it all. They exploit labour. They dissemble and lie. They produce the most appalling quality of goods. They are expensive. They offer a bad service – in fact no service at all, being, as they are, merely giant cash-and-carry warehouses which charge retail prices. The food on offer is tasteless and very possibly harmful. A recent report to parliament in the UK showed that small retailers are closing at the rate of 2,000 a year and that, as a sector, they will be completely wiped out by 2015. The supermarkets are greedy devils, monsters devouring everything in their path. They spend millions upon millions every year on advertising in order to persuade us that, far from being profit-driven, hungry carnivores of the forest, they are, in actual fact, a public service, a sort of charity with only the consumer's best interests at heart. Recently, Leahy has even claimed that, with their small high-street outlets, Tesco's are regenerating communities. 'Our new staff walk to work, and they love it,' he said. Having destroyed communities, they now advertise themselves as community-builders.

This is the way of the world. Our interfering creates problems, which we then try to solve with more interfering. The answer is to stop interfering. It is as the wise Masanobu Fukuoka writes in his book *The One-Straw Revolution*, which I would urge each and every one of you to read. It is the wisest book I have ever read. *The One-Straw Revolution* details Fukuoka's experiments in natural farming in Japan from 1935 to 1978, a period when Japan was introducing chemicals and machinery into agriculture. With his 'no-work' methods, which involved allowing nature to do as much of the work as possible and refraining from intervention, he achieved the same yields as the most productive fields in his area, with the added bonus of constantly increasing the richness of the soil. Well, here is what he has to say about the modern way of operating:

> Human beings with their tampering do something wrong, leave the damage unrepaired, and when the adverse results accumulate, work with all their might to correct them. When the corrective actions appear to be successful, they come to view these measures as splendid accomplishments. People do this over and over again. It is as if a fool were to stomp on and break the tiles of his roof. Then when it starts to rain and the ceiling begins to rot away, he hastily climbs up to mend the damage, rejoicing in the end that he has accomplished a miraculous solution.

The supermarkets constantly tell us how great they are through hypnotic advertising, and we believe them. Even Henry VIII, as he plundered the nation, didn't run an ad campaign to tell the people how great he was. Cobbett himself, or Morris or Ruskin, none of those men could have imagined the horror of the supermarket culture. Near us, in Devon, there is a fantastic vegetable farm called Riverford, which operates a box scheme. Each week, we are delivered a box of vegetables, fruit, milk and eggs, all of the best quality. Guy Watson, who runs Riverford, tells the story of the discussion he had about becoming a supplier with one of the big supermarkets. A meeting had been arranged for a Friday. Watson called and asked if the meeting could be moved to Thursday, as he needed to be back on the farm. The phone went dead. Assuming there had been a fault, Watson called back and said, 'Oh, I think something went wrong with the phone.' 'Listen,' came the voice at the other end. 'This is Sainsbury's. When we shout, you jump.' Watson vowed never to deal with a supermarket from that day on.

Here are some facts about Tesco's:

Pre-tax profit 2004–5: £2.03bn
Number of stores in UK: 1,779
Number employed in the UK: 251,000 (twice the size of
    the army)
Stock market value: £24.7bn
Number banking with Tesco's: 4.9m
Chief Exec's annual wages: £2.97m
Percentage of UK population which shops at Tesco's
    each month: 66

Tesco's is omnipresent, omnipotent, omnivorous and, through its loyalty card scheme, which records everything you buy, omniscient. The medieval clergy were nothing to Tesco's. There was a cartoon in *Private Eye* recently which showed a shop giving directions: 'You'll find us on the High Street, between Tesco's and Tesco's.'

In the UK, Tesco's takes £1 in every £3 spent on groceries. The poor work for them and then spend their money in them. We slave all day, and then, after work, we pour our wages back into the system at the supermarkets. We must stop it now! Are we sheep? Have we forgotten *Small Is Beautiful*? Did Schumacher never exist? How did we let this happen?

First, we have to admit our complicity in creating this situation of dependence. By shopping in them for the last twenty years, by buying their insurance policies and falling for their endless cons, we have given the supermarkets the huge power that they are now starting to abuse so thoroughly. The supermarket system is enslaving, as it is motivated solely by ever-escalating profits, as amoral shareholders are interested only in growth in order to sell shares at a higher price. Felicity Lawrence, author of *Not on the Label: What Really Goes into the Food on Your Plate*, quotes the director of the Soil Association on the supermarket dynamic:

> It's not a food chain so much as a fear chain. The supermarket directors live in fear of losing their market share and not being able to deliver endless growth to their shareholders. The supermarket buyer lives in fear of not meeting his or her targets and always wants to buy cheap and sell expensive, the packer lives in mortal fear of having his goods rejected or the price falling below the costs of production. How do you rebuild trust in a chain which is dominated by aggressive players and practices? This is what happens with the twin pressures of globalization and concentration of power. It's a crisis affecting every farmer in the land.

This is to say nothing of the sheer hell of shopping in supermarkets. Stressco's and Strainsbury's, my friend Gordon calls them. Wheeling your lonely trolley around the aisles, hundreds of people walking side by side in total isolation, talking to no one. And the sad, defeated countenance of the people on the check-out, who are similarly isolated from each other. I cannot imagine the stress of working on a check-out, the feelings of uselessness, powerlessness and tedium. Compare the drab, expressionless faces of the check-out girls with the animated faces of market-traders, those independent men and women who still believe that small is beautiful. They are free, and it shows in their faces. When I walk down Leather Lane market in London, I see wit and life among the traders. Their faces are alive because they are in control of their own business.

The supermarkets have sold us a myth of cheapness, convenience and variety. But the reality is none of those: they are expensive, a hassle and you are forced to buy from someone else's selection. And, worst of all, they condemn thousands to boring jobs. Lost, lost, lost.

How different things were in the early days of trade when the guilds controlled quality and prices, and profits were spent not on the Chief Executive's salary but on feasting, merriment, fantastic buildings, art and alms. Tesco's feeble modern-day equivalent of such public spirit is to 'take kids off the dole' in return for planning permission for yet more supermarkets.

So: don't sell to the supermarkets, don't buy from them, don't even look at them. Forget about them. They are history, a strange blip in recent history, which, one day, we will, I hope, look back on with a weary shake of our heads in incomprehension that we could have allowed a force so utterly against nature to happen to us. I would like to bomb them, but it's probably more effective to boycott them.

The wonderful thing is that freeing oneself from the supermarkets is so very enjoyable. The alternative is not an expensive, time-consuming, self-denying life of shopping in pious and over-priced health-food shops. It is rather a rich existence of pleasure, ease, quality and a lot less driving around. Reject the supermarket and embrace life.

Shop in proper shops, where the owner and staff are proud of the things they make and sell, not places where exploited workers peddle rubbish. It is easy to tell the difference. They offer good quality; they combine manufacture with retail. Let us turn to craft historian Norman Wymer, who paints a portrait of how things used to be in his study *English Town Crafts*:

Down to the time of the Industrial Revolution, and for quite a while afterwards, the retail shops of an average town presented an entirely different spectacle from what we know today. Not only were many of the goods offered for sale made on the spot, but, more often than not, the craftsmen themselves could actu-ally be seen at work. Sometimes, where conditions permitted, they might be seated in their shop windows in the full gaze of passers-by, but, more usually, they would occupy a back room or, perhaps, a room at the top of rickety stairs, immediately above their shop. In any case, they were always at hand, ready to discuss the particular requirements of a customer, and to make any piece in strict conformity with those requirements . . . Their code, from start to finish, was ever to turn out the best and always to satisfy a customer even if to do so sometimes meant making a second attempt and working for a negligible profit, or even, on occasion, maybe, at a loss. The very trade signs outside the shops – painted by a local sign-writer, very often – seemed to give a kind of guarantee of the pride that must, surely, be found within.

This style of retail is not entirely dead. In the London district of Clerkenwell, near my office, there are watchmenders who sit in the windows of tiny workshops and work. There are tailors. There are good independent Italian delicatessens. There is a magic shop where all the staff are excellent magicians. I worked for a year in a skateboarding shop which was independently run and where we put the skateboards together in the shop. Such shops can act as social centres. In my nearest village, there is a fantastic butcher and a dressmaker who works in the window of her home. Small hardware stores seem to have retained their independence, notwithstanding the encroachment of the unspeakable B&Q and its ilk. In the country, the trade of blacksmith is enjoying a renaissance, and their traditional handiwork can fetch good prices.

Indeed, small is beautiful.

If you want to live free of the supermarkets, try the following:

1. Bake your own bread! Pour two and a bit pints of warm water into a bowl. Throw in a handful of yeast, a handful of sugar and a handful of salt. Add around a kilo of flour. Mix in very well till all the flour is wetted. Leave for a few hours. Cover a table with flour. Pour the mixture on top. Knead, throwing on more and more flour. When it gets sticky, add more flour. Do not wash your hands. Throw on more flour. Now divide

the dough into six piles and half-fill six bread tins. Then leave
in a warm place for an hour or so until they've risen. Put in
a hot oven for about twenty minutes to half an hour. There
you have it: bread. And if you can make bread, you can do
anything. It's amazing how much confidence baking bread
gives you.

The whole process is easy and pleasurable and, at the end
of it, I have six delicious loaves of bread which last us two
weeks at a price of about £1, less than 20 pence per loaf. And
this is proper bread, Cobbett bread, sustaining bread, not
factory pap.

2. Grow your own vegetables. Growing our own vegetables –
well, at least some of them – has been one of the great discov-
eries of the last couple of years for me. I never imagined how
enjoyable, easy and satisfying it could be. It is also terribly
therapeutic. When I started digging up a patch of ground in
preparation for planting seeds in it, I was going through a
hellish time with a publishing project. Lawyers were involved,
and every time the phone rang, there seemed to be more bad
news. Well, in the middle of all this, it was immensely comfort-
ing to go and do an hour or two of physical work in the
garden. Outdoor physical work brings harmony to the spirit.
Then there was the amazing and magical fact that the seeds
did actually grow into something you could eat. While London
media projects collapsed, here was something that worked.
For virtually no cost whatsoever, in that first year I grew
onions, garlic, potatoes, leeks, parsnips, radishes, carrots, beet-
root. In a world where fun is usually purchased, growing

vegetables combines fun with productivity. It is enjoyable and useful, and gives you a pleasant feeling of taking care of yourself.

Growing your own vegetables is also far more efficient than depending on the supermarket. For one thing, you can grow a variety of your own choosing, some weird old Victorian runner bean, perhaps, which supermarkets won't go near because it is uneconomical. So there is a sudden new freedom there.

Also, there is no need to go shopping; the vegetables are right there on your doorstep. Forget driving out of town and picking over a few shiny, tasteless, plastic-wrapped vegetables before wheeling them to the check-out and handing over yet more cash to the megamachine. Instead, your vegetable shopping means an intensely enjoyable walk around the garden. And you are dependent on nobody but yourself; no suppliers, no warehouses, no staff, no lorries, no farms in New Zealand, no food miles.

The other wonderful thing is that your vegetable patch is uniquely your own; there are no two patches in the world that are the same; they are like fingerprints. You choose the vegetables, the varieties, the layout, the fruit. You are in every earthworm and every bit of soil, every nettle and every weed.

Becoming a gardener also opens up a new community of other gardeners. You go and get tips from each other's patches, swap seeds, swap vegetables. It is profoundly creative, whereas supermarket shopping is profoundly uncreative. In the veg garden, you do everything. In the supermarket, everything has been done for you. Your job is simply to hand over your credit card. It now seems completely ridiculous to buy fruit and vegetables in a supermarket: it is time-consuming, and they are expensive and of extremely poor quality. Vegetables grown in the soil near your front door are not only the tastiest you will ever eat, but they are also a medicine as well as a food.

3. Shop wholesale. This is one of the great hidden secrets of the modern age. Thanks to the initiative of a neighbour, we have teamed up locally with one or two other families and, every month or so, we make a big wholesale order. We buy sacks of flour, tins, pasta, rice: all the staples. They also offer household items like washing powder and loo roll. Some of the wholesalers have a minimum order of just £100. They all have catalogues, so you sit at home of an evening flipping through the price list and deciding what you want to buy. Then they deliver it to you. No shopping! No queues! No driving! No car parks! More time for loafing!

   By getting together with other people in this way, you can make your life easier and cheaper. This sort of sharing attitude to life is precisely what the big companies want to keep a secret. They want to communicate directly with you via the television. They do not want us to free associate in little groups. They are against self-government and federalism. We need to free ourselves from the grip of giant institutions, whether they are supermarkets or governments.

4. Shop locally. This point is so obvious it barely needs repeating. Patronize your local butcher's, greengrocer's, corner shop

and market stall, and do it now or you may well see it disappearing, to be replaced by the horror of another Tesco Metro. Remember also that when you shop locally, the money stays in the local community. When you shop at Tesco's, the money is sucked away and into the pockets of the directors and shareholders, who laugh at us fools as they order fine wines and buy new houses. Damien Hirst once wrote an article for the *Idler* called 'Why Cunts Sell Shit to Fools', and I think that pretty much sums it up. The answer? Don't be a fool and don't buy shit.

We should tear down the supermarkets, at least in our minds. Boycott them for ever. Forget them. We should raze these edifices of oppression and slavery to the ground and replace them with allotments. Remove the ugliness and dependence and replace it with beauty and self-sufficiency. Make the land green and pleasant. Look after the soil.

GROW YOUR OWN

26 The Reign of the Ugly is Over; Long Live Beauty, Quality, Fraternity!

Beauty is truth and truth beauty,
That is all ye know and all ye need to know.
Keats, 'Ode on a Grecian Urn', 1819

Go forth again to gaze upon the old cathedral front . . . examine
once more those ugly goblins, and formless monsters . . . for they
are the signs of life, the life and liberty of every workman who struck
the stone; a freedom of thought and rank in the scale of being, such
as no laws, no charters, no charities can secure; but which it must be
the first aim of all Europe at this day to regain for her children.
John Ruskin, *The Stones of Venice*, 1906

Things used to be more beautiful. That is fact. The industrial process can be seen as a process of uglification, as everything becomes objectively uglier when it submits itself to the rule of mass manufacture, cheap labour and profit. Noble, contemplative Quality is murdered by venal, avaricious Quantity. In the UK, it was in the nineteenth century that things began to get really ugly. It was when art was taken away from the people, when the people were reduced to mere operators of machines and the professional classes stole the responsibility for building and creating for themselves. So-called miracles of science produced hideous metal bridges, with no fun and no life. It was in the nineteenth century, that most prosaic and work-obsessed of periods, that our novelists first began to rail against ugliness. You just do not get that complaint in literature before around 1800. But one hundred years later – how ugly had things become. As wide-eyed D. H. Lawrence put it:

> The real tragedy of England . . . is the tragedy of ugliness. The country is so lovely: the man-made England is so vile . . . it was ugliness which really betrayed the spirit of the man, in the nineteenth century. The great crime which the moneyed classes and promoters of industry committed in the palmy Victorian days was the condemning of the workers to ugliness, ugliness . . . The human soul needs actual beauty even more than bread.

We have a duty to Beauty. We have scorned her and left her writhing in the gutter, and her vengeance on the ugly-makers will be swift, sudden and terrible.

Things get uglier and uglier, and so do we. After reaching a height of finery in the fifteenth century, clothes seem to have become progressively plainer as the centuries have gone on. The flowing curves, parti-coloured tunics and gowns, green houppelandes decorated with golden birds and crowns, wide sleeves embroidered 'like a meadow', ermine trims, long pointed shoes, elaborate hats and rich colours were replaced in the nineteenth century by black cylinders, everywhere cylinders, pipes, tubes and chimneys: hats looked like black chimneys, trousers looked like black chimneys. The medievals were like children; they loved dressing up. They didn't have trousers and they didn't dress in black. They did, literally, have rings on their fingers and bells on their toes. Curves vanished, to be replaced with straight lines. Clothes today are work-clothes. Sportswear has taken over. Puritan black is the number one colour, despite the unending attempts in fashion to create a 'new black'. We need to reintroduce impracticality into clothing. Thank God, then, for Vivienne Westwood. Thank God for the punks and hippies, who loved to dress up in fantastic colours, like the medievals, like children.

Again I blame the Puritans. They consciously attacked the colourful clothing which was favoured by the medievals and introduced blackness. Colour was pointless, vain frippery. Look at the old religious paintings and marvel at the colour and life in the clothes, remembering that it was the custom in medieval art to put bibilical figures in contemporary fashions. Then, in the words of Max Weber:

> Asceticism descended like a frost on the life of 'Merry old England' . . . The Puritan's ferocious hatred of everything which smacked of superstition, of all survivals of magical or sacramental

salvation, applied to the Christmas festivities and the May Pole and all spontaneous religious art . . . The Theatre was obnoxious to the Puritans . . . in favour of sober utility as against any artistic tendencies. This was especially true in the case of decoration of the person, for instance, clothing. That powerful tendency toward uniformity of life, which today so aids the capitalistic interest in the standardization of production, had its ideal foundations in the repudiation of all idolatry of the flesh.

In other words, first Henry VIII and then the Puritans started the Uglification revolution, the Boredom revolution, the Ascetic revolution, the Funless revolution: Goodbye, colour; hello, blackness. He and Cranmer, and later the Protector Somerset, did literally tear the beauty from the heart of the country, by smashing or stealing all the art which had sat undisturbed in the churches for hundreds of years: screens, altars, statuary, gold and silver ornaments, stained-glass windows, crosses and the like. The excuse was that such beautiful things were vain, idolatrous and irrelevant to religion, which was to become simple and unencumbered. So we can see why artists and writers traditionally tend towards Roman Catholicism, while Protestantism is the religion for the serious man of business, the practical man.

Beauty and variety were also attacked by the Enclosure movement, which replaced the strip-filled medieval fields and common lands with large monotonous expanses for sheep-grazing. The Industrial Revolution further attacked beauty, replacing it with utility. Giant, smoke-belching factories running on fossil fuels replaced the water mills and windmills that had dotted Britain before. I often think of how charming the countryside must have looked when windmills were everywhere. We think we are being clever when we talk about wind-energy, but of course this was a central part of life for the eco-friendly medievals living before coal, nuclear power and electricity.

William Morris complained of the unattractive nature of the Victorian age. In *News From Nowhere*, he describes the London underground as a 'vapour-bath of hurried and discontented humanity', and we might reflect that little has changed. Morris also complained of the ugly iron bridges across the Thames. When his hero wakes up in the post-revolutionary England of 2005, he sees that all the iron bridges have been torn down. Indeed, sheep roam Piccadilly Circus, and money has been abolished. It is a beautiful fantasy.

Machines create ugliness; human hands create beauty. And the belief in utility over beauty destroys beauty. Here is John Seymour on tins *versus* pots:

> I used to think that an old petrol tin was as good for carrying water in as an earthenware pot. One day I read something written by [the poet] Tagore, in which he touched on this very comparison. He said – yes – an old petrol tin is as good for carrying water as a chatti, or one of the beautiful pots that Indian women carry on their heads, except for one thing: the petrol tin is mean. It is grudging. Because it just serves the utilitarian purpose – and no more. It carries the water all right. So does the chatti. But the chatti is delightful to look at, delightful to feel and to touch, pleasant to have around. Every time you look at it you think of the love and care with which it was made, by the hands of a human being. Every time you look at the petrol tin you think of

a huge, ugly, clanking, dirty machine, mindlessly slamming out ugly objects. For no machine-made artifact can be beautiful. Beauty in artifacts can only be put there by the hands of the craftsmen, and no machine will ever be built that can replace them.

I understand that there is a tradition in Chinese pottery deliberately to create a slight imperfection in the object to ensure that every piece is different and unique. Perfectionism itself is a kind of death; the machine can turn out thousands of perfect objects, but they have no life.

So, what can we do about the uglification of life? Well, there is an easy answer. Avoid ugly things, ignore them and instead embrace craft, which is what the Arts and Crafts movement was all about. Let each man and woman master one or two or three crafts. I look forward to a craft revival. Crafts are people-based, pleasure-based; they represent an equal society, they represent quality and joy in the making. Crafts mean the triumph of quality over quantity, of self-government over exploitation. Bring beauty into your home. A pot of geraniums on the windowsill. A Pelican paperback. Make your own clothes. Sew red diamonds on your sleeves. With less time given to work and the Thing, the Combine, the Construct or the Man, you will have more time for yourself and more time to be creative, more time to produce rather than consume.

Only buy beautiful things. Only make beautiful things. It is surely better to buy one shirt of high quality each year than to buy five cheap ones which will be in the garbage within months. And things that you make, however ugly, are always more beautiful than the mass-produced option, simply because they radiate care even if they are wonky and erratic and funny-looking.

For one thing, everything – I mean, absolutely everything – these days appears to be made of plastic. It's just as Woody Guthrie predicted in his song 'Talking Columbia', trains, clothes, furniture. White plastic is covering the nation like an unbiodegradable shroud. Plastic is the triumph of quantity over quality, of factory over handwork. Plastic is cold, sterile, humourless, poisonous, ugly, wasteful, unrottable, unburnable; it is a stinking nothing made of oil and money. Plastic drips greed, like that friend of Ben's parents in *The Graduate* who famously advises him on what business to enter: 'Plastics, Ben, plastics.' Recently, a fortune was made by the man who sold Tetrapaks to the world, thus creating a hideous mountain of unburnable rubbish. Not that long ago, we all had our own lovely milk churns, which we would take to the farm. In parts of France, this is still the case. Let's create our own world, made of wood and carved with chisels.

It is one of the terrible ironies of the age that something as expensive as plastic, which relies on limited supplies of oil, has become cheaper than wood, which is endlessly renewable. However, using some ingenuity, wood can be found very cheaply or for free. We collect bits of timber from nearby woods. We pick up driftwood from the beach. We then use it to make things. I carved a toy elephant the other day out of an old piece of driftwood. My elephant, while not exactly elegant, will outlast all the plastic crap that our children have.

Beauty feeds us. Anarchy is beauty. We are against the grey people. We want to decorate, like those fantastic Indian lorries which are covered with flowers. Beauty must conquer the lust for order; order is ugliness. The Nazis were ugly, and Florence is beautiful. Nazi Germany was a bureaucracy, and Florence was created by a federal system of self-government. That is all the proof you need: industrialization created Swindon, and medieval independence created Florence. Take your pick.

It is up to the individual or to groups of individuals to make of something ugly something beautiful. This is precisely what skateboarding does: it takes the apparently unappealing straight lines and concrete banks of modernity and works a kind of alchemy on them, transforming car parks, hand rails and corporate steps into objects of beauty, promise and fun. Skateboarding brings beauty into the city. In other words, you don't have to leave the city to escape from it, because you can re-create your own city. This idea is obvious, too, in the Permaculture approach to growing fruit and vegetables: a windowsill on the fourteenth floor can become a herb garden; wasteland can become allotments. Let us surround the tower blocks with carrots, parsnips and onions; away with the arid green lawns that dot the estates. Dig up the land, start your own vegetable patch. Make your own city.

HAIL THE CHISEL

27 Depose the Tyrant Wealth

Tolle querelas
Pauper enim non est cui rerum suppetit usus
Horace, 65–8 BC

Then cease complaining, friend, and learn to live.
He is not poor to whom kind fortune grants,
Even with a frugal hand, what Nature wants.

Sometimes I think that what we need is not more wealth but more poverty.
It is wealth that causes the problems, wealth that causes the inequalities.
Satish Kumar

I have nothing – nothing! – and I love it.
Keith Allen

Superficially, to the freedom-seeker, money is very attractive. It can certainly be pleasant to have money. It appears to promise comfort, ease, plenty, fun, happiness and, above all, it appears to promise freedom. Freedom of movement, freedom from interference by others, freedom from doing work that we don't want to do. Or, at least, some very large amount of money – exact amount unspecified – appears to offer freedom. What would you do if you had a million pounds? This is the question that's debated in every school playground. You could give up your job, go on the holiday of a lifetime, buy a Ferrari. You could live like the fantastic lottery yob Michael Carroll, brimming with Asbos, sticking two fingers up at authority and having 'Crazy Frog' painted on the bonnet of your Beemer.

And what about 'fuck-off money'? This vulgar but expressive phrase refers to having so much money, being so very rich, that you don't have to think about money, and that you can exit the world of Powerpoint presentations, business plans and pitches and all the kowtowing that is generally involved in getting money. Vast wealth, in theory, means you are free from enslaving yourself to another, as you have enough money to do as you please; you do not have to tug your forelock in order to get a job or a piece of work from someone else. You can say 'no'. In other words, the idea is that you make a lot of money in order to escape from money. I daresay this approach can be successful. In fact, I know of one or two people for whom it has worked well. But it's a risky game. Most money-making schemes fail, and you are always going to be at the mercy of unpredictable market forces. In the UK today, there are something like 8,000 of these mega-rich people, out of a working population of 30 million. That gives you a one in four thousand chance of joining them, odds no gambler would ever go near. With the odds so highly stacked against you, is it really worth the effort?

It doesn't make much rational sense to propose money-making as a solution for everybody, because it is in the nature of wealth that only a few can be wealthy, since one person's wealth depends on other people's lack of it. We cannot all be rich. As Ruskin puts it in *Unto This Last*: '. . . riches are a power like that of electricity, acting only through inequalities or negations of itself. The force of the guinea you have in your pocket depends wholly on the default of a guinea in your neighbour's pocket . . .' He goes on to say: 'The art of becoming rich . . . is the art of establishing the maximum inequality in our own favour.'

We are all supposed to want to become rich. Wanting to be rich is one of the motors of a competitive world. Wanting to be rich is what keeps us striving, working, fighting, struggling, competing, conning and abandoning morals. And wanting to be rich is the precise impulse that is exploited by the people who actually do become rich, the usurers and the investors, the market manipulators, because they exploit our greed for their own ends. Wanting more money removes us from enjoying the present; it is therefore a Puritan trait. We should celebrate what we have. Wanting to be rich is actually the first desire that must be cast off in the pursuit of freedom.

The problem is that, now, unlike during the Middle Ages, no one wants to be poor. It is seen as a sign of failure. As William Godwin puts it: 'The manners prevailing in many countries are accurately calculated to impress a conviction, that integrity, virtue, understanding and industry are nothing, and that opulence is everything.' What, in 1793, Godwin called 'manners', i.e. the means by which a dominant ideology is spread among the people, today, we would call 'the media'. There is another way of looking at this, and it's called 'counting your blessings'. Real riches are a question of mental attitude. As Robert Burton writes:

> One of the greatest miseries that can befal a man, in the world's esteem, is poverty or want . . . yet if considered aright, it is a great blessing in itself, a happy estate, and yields no cause of discontent, or that men should therefore account themselves vile, hated of God, forsaken, miserable, unfortunate. Christ himself was poor, born in a manger, and had not a house to hide his head in all his life, 'lest any man should make poverty a judgement of God, or an odious estate.' And as he was himself, so he informed his Apostles and Disciples, they were all poor, Prophets poor, Apostles poor . . . 'As sorrowing (saith Paul) and yet always rejoicing; as having nothing, and yet possessing all things.'

There are rich and there are poor; there are good rich, good poor and bad rich and bad poor. One or the other should carry no moral judgement with it. It is completely immaterial to freedom. The key phrase in the passage above is 'if considered aright'. To be poor is only a disgrace if you decide that it is a disgrace, if we as a society agree to see it as a disgrace. There are no absolutes in this. There is a readily available moral approach that says it is good to be poor, and we are equally free to choose that attitude.

In any case, being rich comes with many burdens. There are the bickering relatives and dependants, the sharks who gather around you with their generous offers to relieve you of your cash, the clubs for rich people, the private healthcare, the pension plans and investment programmes. Certainly, when I look back on periods in my life when I have had money, the way I wasted it makes me feel quite queasy.

For the Puritans, worldly success was a sign of religious success. If you were rich, it meant that God favoured you. However, you were not to enjoy your money; better to save it, keep hold of it. Here is Max Weber's description of the Puritan attitude to wealth:

> Wealth is thus bad only in so far as it is a temptation to idleness and sinful enjoyment of life, and its acquisition is bad only when it is with the purpose of later living merrily and without care. But as a performance of duty in a calling it is not only morally permissible, but actually enjoined. The parable of the servant who was rejected because he did not increase the talent which was entrusted to him seemed to say so directly. To wish to be poor was, it was often argued, the same as wishing to be unhealthy; it is objectionable as a glorification of works and derogatory to the glory of God. Especially begging, on the part of one able to work, is not only the sin of slothfulness, but a violation of the duty of brotherly love according to the Apostle's own word.

I would precisely reverse the Puritan attitude, stated at the start of this passage, and assert that wealth is only good when it leads to 'living merrily and without care'. Picasso famously said, 'I want to live like a poor man with lots of money' – by which he meant, he would spend it generously, freely, joyfully. A beggars' banquet. This is living free with wealth, whereas, for the Puritans, wealth and possessions were another burden.

The evil Methodist leader John Wesley said: 'We must exhort all Christians to gain all they can, and to save all they can; that is, in effect, to grow rich.' Today, we see the same attitude to money among the Christian right in America: riches means God loves you, quite the opposite attitude to riches to the one that Jesus proposed. What I object to in all this is the restless effort and the meanness rather than the wealth itself. If your money comes as a side-effect of doing what you want to do, then it would be perhaps foolish to send it back, however convinced one might be of the holy advantages of poverty. But to seek it for its own sake – although, God knows, having it might ease some burdens – seems dangerous, if it is freedom you really seek. For Burton, wanting more cash was itself enslaving, and he wrote of merchants:

> . . . they are all fools, dizzards, mad-men, miserable wretches, living beside themselves, *sine arte fruendi*, in perpetual slavery, fear, suspicion, sorrow, and discontent, *plus aloes quam mellis habent*; and are indeed, 'rather possessed by their money, than possessors', as Cyprian hath it, *mancipati pecuniis*.

Instead of trying to be rich, we might try to be poor, simply by embracing thrift and rejecting consumer gewgaws. Not needing money by reducing our needs can have the same liberating effect as not needing money by making a lot of it. Learning to live within limited means gives a great sense of security, because you become free of wanting more and therefore free of struggle. Also, the less money you need, the less you have to work. This way of escaping money has the great advantage over the high-earning route in that it is very much easier to achieve. But, with being poor, there is no risk attached and most of us would probably find it a fairly simple process to work less and earn less.

I now earn less than half the amount I earned four years ago but, having learned to live within this sum, I am free to pursue my own work. For sure, there are hardships involved. But we manage. Our relative poverty was originally involuntary, but we have learned to accept it and indeed to embrace it and enjoy it. Living with fewer needs, living humbly, frees up an enormous amount of time for reflection and pleasure. That itself is a lucky state to be in. If I can continue to live without having a job, then I shall count myself extremely lucky.

To be free from poverty, then, we need paradoxically to embrace poverty. If we were all poor, then we would all be rich. The answer is to be creative with what you have rather than to resign yourself to the slavish state of constantly wanting more.

Eric Gill embraced this kind of self-sufficient poverty, which he called 'positive poverty'. In his autobiography, Gill remembers his impoverished father cutting a sausage into eleven slices so each child could have a piece. We need to admire this sort of thing rather than pitying it. Says Godwin: 'If admiration were not generally deemed the exclusive property of the rich, and contempt the constant lackey of poverty, the love of gain would cease to be an universal passion.' This was actually the case in the medieval world, with its constant condemnation of capitalism (usury) and industrialism (slavery). It was not that riches did not exist; of course they did. Some merchants became extremely wealthy; the famous example of Dick Whittington is but one. It is more that the love of gain had not become a 'universal passion'.

We need to recast voluntary poverty as a desirable end. Today, I admire *Idler* contributors Chris Yates, Mark Manning, Jock Scot and Keith Allen, all of whom have more or less voluntarily embraced Lady Poverty, as St Francis of Assisi called it. I say 'voluntarily', because all of them could easily have made a lot of money had they been so inclined, because they are all very talented. But living every day, art and poetry and life, are more important to them than money. These are the people we should venerate, as Godwin suggests. Make poverty cool! (I hope it is obvious, by the way, that I am not promoting famine.)

Freedom from hassle and the cares of cash must surely have been one of the motives of the K Foundation, Bill Drummond and Jimmy Cauty, when, in 1997, they withdrew a million pounds from their bank account, money that they had earned from the sales of various hit records, took it to a remote bothy in the Scottish Highlands and burned the lot. It was a spectacular act and in the tradition, I would say, of Jesus and the money-lenders, and also Abbie Hoffman and Jerry Rubin, who went into Wall Street and set light to five dollar bills, much to the disgust of the brokers. But the K Foundation's act was braver, in a sense, than either. They burned a million quid! Their act is also reminiscent of Savonarola's Bonfire of the Vanities. But where Savonarola's bonfire was a pious attack on pleasure, the K Foundation's fire was a freedom-embracing attack on the belief in money.

One of the nice things about growing vegetables is that you escape from the world of money. You also tend to have a surplus, so you can give stuff away. There are all sorts of ways of escaping from the manacles of money. Freecycle is one, a new system whereby people give each other stuff that they don't need any more. The LETS system is another, where work is carried out on an exchange system. The Permaculture movement is all about creating freedom and self-reliance within your means rather than vainly hoping one day that you will win the lottery. Do it now. Give things away for free and money will lose its power over you.

The answer with money is simply to deprioritize its importance in your life and instead start to create a whole life for yourself. This might mean trying many different projects all at once, some of which earn money and some of which don't, some which will and some which won't. I personally pursue a range of activities, all of which are work and all of which are life. Some – books and journalism – make money, and others – the *Idler* magazine, the village-hall committee, playing with children – do not. Others – vegetable growing, bread-baking – do not make money, but they do produce useful stuff. They save money. Others – ukulele-playing, carpentry – are done for their own sake, and the rest – washing-up, cleaning, cooking, driving – are just as essential. And a very easy and enjoyable way to reduce your dependence on money is simply to embrace thrift, the subject of our next chapter.

WANT LESS

28 Reject Waste; Embrace Thrift

I tell you that the very essence of competitive commerce is waste.
William Morris, 'Art, Labour and Socialism', 1884

Waste is unpoetic, thrift is creative.
G. K. Chesterton, 'The Romance of Thrift', 1910

Make compost, not war.
slogan of Graham Burnett, spiralseed.com, 2005

As an amateur smallholder – or 'chaotic tinyholder' would be more precise – one phrase from John Seymour's book *Self-Sufficiency* rings in my head. It is: 'The dustman need never visit the smallholder.' The first time I read this statement, we were producing perhaps three or four black bin-bags of rubbish every week. My mind boggled when I started to reflect on all the unnecessary work that this waste created. There was the toil of putting the rubbish in the bin, the toil of taking the bin-bag out to the dustbin, the toil of leaving the dustbins out on the right day. Then there was the work of the dustmen, the petrol, the man hours, the labour involved in manufacturing the giant, belching dustbin lorries. Then there was the toil of driving to the dump and shoving all the waste into a huge hole from which more lorries transport it to some toxic dump somewhere in the countryside where it sits for all eternity, loved only by rats, poisoning the soil. This is the result of waste: waste of time, waste of energy, waste of life.

The antidote to waste is thrift. Now, thrift, in the days of high spending and credit cards, is a very unfashionable notion. It's presented to us as a pious, worthy and mean attitude to living, the philosophy of the skrimbleshanks, the miser, the tightwad. In the prejudice against thrift, there is perhaps a residue of the old medieval prejudice against hoarders, against Mr Money-bags, often satirized in medieval statuary, who gets but does not spend, who does nothing of social use with his money.

But being thrifty is not the same as being miserly. It simply means that you don't spend your money on unnecessary stuff. It means, very simply, being creative with your money, and being creative in your household. Etymologically, it derives from 'thriving'. One chicken makes many meals. It makes stock, it makes sandwiches, it makes curries and stews later in the week.

And, since shopping is today seen as our patriotic duty, to be thrifty is actually to be unpatriotic, and therefore it gives one a pleasant sense of rebelling against the state. It is your duty as a freedom-seeker to reject waste, as waste is a necessary part of the capitalist system. Think of the food that supermarkets and sandwich shops throw away each day. There is a new movement out there called 'Freeganism': this refers to the practice of finding all your food for free by raiding dustbins at the end of the day. It seems like an excellent scheme. Live in a squat, get your food for free and there will be absolutely no need to waste your time by working. It's amazing what people throw away. Thrift allows you to escape the consumer culture and to replace working-earning-spending with creating.

In a superb essay on 'The Romance of Thrift', Chesterton makes the case that economy and thrift, far from being prosaic and dull, are, in fact, romantic notions:

> Economy, properly understood, is the more poetic. Thrift is poetic because it is creative; waste is unpoetic because it is waste. It is prosaic to throw money away, because it is prosaic to throw a thing away; it is negative; it is a confession of indifference, that is, it is a confession of failure.

This sort of passionate thrifting is quite distinct from the Puritan, Smilesian, Methodist notion of thrift, which was simply an expression of the greed of the manufacturers. They preached the importance of sparse living to the factory workers, teaching them how to live within their pitiful wages, as a cost-saver which would increase their own profits. It is not thrift as self-denial and the preaching of sobriety, industry, frugality and virtue to the lower orders that I am recommending; it is more a spirited reclaiming of one's own finances. And, the thriftier you are, the less money you need, and the less money you need, the less paid work you will need to do. Therefore, thrift equals idleness. Thrift is freedom, freedom from bosses, anxiety and debt.

We should also be thrifty with our time, and that means not rushing through things and not wasting our time by giving it to an employer. That is the one aspect of being employed full time that used to annoy me beyond all others: the waste of time. Whether or not there were seven hours of work to do, you still had to sit there for seven hours. To sit staring at a screen pretending to work while the sun shone outside seemed crazy. I could have been doing something useful, like making a daisy chain or learning the ukulele.

In the area of fashion, my friend Kira Jolliffe's magazine *Cheap Date* has protested against the sheep-like buying of the latest thing and instead promoted thrift-shop clothes and charity stores. To be able to find an odd item that looks good from a second-hand shop proves that you have real style and are not a mere follower of fashion. Style is about being yourself, and fashion is about being like the others.

The Mutoid Waste Company demonstrated the creative power of thrift. By taking vehicles that were destined for the scrapheap and making them into amazing sculptures, they made a radical statement against waste.

Now, having been shocked into action by John Seymour's line about the dustmen, I decided at home to try to cut down on the waste we were producing. His idea really is that the smallholder creates a friendly cycle in which nothing is wasted. Food waste turns into compost or is fed to animals, old meat is fed to animals, animal waste fertilizes the fields, there is precious little packaging, since most things are produced at home, jam jars are endlessly useful, paper and cardboard can be burned or shredded for compost. Bottles can be reused or recycled. Old clothes can be made into patchwork quilts. Wood can be used to make things or burned. Even household slops can be made into compost rather than being piped off into costly sewage works. So things would have been on the medieval smallholding: no waste, no rubbish; no dependence on councils and their elaborate waste-disposal systems. Rubbish provides us with another example of how the system toils hard to correct the problems it has itself created. We create problems like waste and plastic, and then congratulate ourselves on inventing unwieldy structures for removing the waste. We should simply not create it in the first place.

Our first step was to make compost, which is the process of keeping organic waste and decomposing it to turn it into useful food for the soil. There are many books on the art of compost, but if you get it right, the compost heap will heat itself up and the rubbish will turn into juicy compost in only a few weeks. And even if you don't get it right, you will still get compost in a year. And if you can't be bothered with all that, then simply dig a ditch in your veg patch and chuck the waste in that. It will rot in the earth and return all its organic splendour to the soil.

Plastic can be a problem. However, it can have its uses. I use see-through plastic pots as cloches in order to protect small seedlings. If you plant out small lettuce plants, for example, they will be destroyed by slugs. But, inside a little upturned plastic yoghurt pot, they will thrive. Cardboard should not be thrown away. Cardboard boxes can be cut up into wonderful shapes. The other day, we made ice-cream shops out of cardboard boxes. Cardboard is good when shredded into the compost heap, as it soaks up excess moisture. It can help when clearing new ground for cultivation; simply put a layer down over the grass and weeds, and then put a layer of compost, straw and anything else organic on top. Newspaper can be used for lighting fires and as litter for your pets. The other bonus for the responsible idler is that the more of these sorts of policies you pursue, the less work you are creating for the rest of the world. It is the duty of an idler not only to make his own life as work-free as possible but also to avoid adding unnecessary burdens to others. Most of work is waste, and therefore the idler is extremely efficient.

Of course, it goes without saying that the medievals were Permaculturists: in an age without oil, all energy was renewable, money was kept circulating in local communities, there was no waste. Everything had a use and went back into the household in a friendly cycle.

The traditional objection to anarchist ideas is: 'Who will do the dirty work?' Well, the simple answer is that you will do the dirty work. We will do our own dirty work. And if the work is your own work, it doesn't seem so dirty.

Take shovelling shit. In my experience, shovelling shit is not the most unpleasant task in the world. There is also a world of difference between shovelling your own shit and shovelling someone else's shit. If you forced me to shovel shit in a factory for seven hours a day, then I would, before too long, hate the sight of it, dread the job, detest every moment. But shovelling your own shit around your own property at a time of your own choosing and making good use of it – well, that is a pleasure. I am delighted when I see chickenshit and horseshit lying around the place, because I know that it is fantastic stuff for the soil. And it's free. Therefore, to collect it will be a huge pleasure.

It is, after all, remarkable that the stuff that comes out of the back end of a horse or cow or chicken should be precisely what the earth needs to remain fertile. We might as well make use of this fact. To be free, use free stuff. To embrace thrift is to embrace freedom; waste is for the slaves and the fools, the dupes of the capitalist system.

SHOVEL SHIT!

29 Stop Working, Start Living

Idler: Can one live without working?
Vaneigem: We can only live without working.
'In Conversation with Raoul Vaneigem', *Idler* 34, 2004

What, then, is the right way of living? Life must be lived as play, playing certain games, making sacrifices, singing and dancing, and then a man will be able to propitiate the gods, and defend himself against his enemies, and win the contest.

Plato

If you really enjoy your job, if you go to bed on Sunday night full of joy, if you leap up on Monday morning full of excitement and anticipation at the pleasures the day will bring, if you love your boss and love your work, then you can skip this chapter.

If, on the other hand, you find your job a drag, if you find it exhausting, stressful, boring, frustrating, enraging, humiliating and badly paid, then read on. You are not inevitably stuck in it. *You do not have to do it.* There are alternatives. Work and life do not necessarily need to compete. They can meet in the idea of play.

The tragedy of the nineteenth century was that Western man came to see himself, first and foremost, as a worker. Life became a serious business. Frivolity, mirth, play, ritual, dance, music, merriment, dressing up: those childish pleasures, all central parts of life for the nobles, priests and peasants of old, had been under constant attack since the middle of the sixteenth century.

Before the Reformation, England was one non-stop party. It really was merry. Ronald Hutton, author of a splendid book called *The Rise and Fall of Merry England*, writes of the all-year-round festivities of the merry English. Christmas, for example, lasted a full twelve days, during which time you were not allowed to do any work. This was quickly followed on 2 February by a holiday called Candlemas and then more merriment on St Valentine's Day on the fourteenth. Then came Shrovetide, which started on the seventh Sunday before Easter and lasted for three days. Easter lasted a full ten days, till the festival of Hocktide. There was just time for a bit of work. Then there was St George's Day on 23 April, another day off. A week after that came May Day, of course, which marked the first day of two months of merry-making and sex in the woods. Then there was 24 June, or Midsummer Eve, and the feast of Corpus Christi. Then came St Peter's Eve on 28 June, followed by Lammas on 1 August, opening a season of summer fairs and harvest suppers. In November came Martinmas, followed by the fasting of Advent, and then it was back to Christmas once again.

Merry old England was, says Hutton, 'a society in which ritual and festival was utilized for many different purposes at many different levels'. But, he writes: 'Then came a direct ideological challenge from early Protestantism, which stood not merely to reform the physical and ideological context of worship but to destroy much of the festive culture with which the old Church had been bound up.'

Following the Puritan attack on fun, the nineteenth century came up with a new idea: instead of banning it, they decided to sell fun, and therefore make money out of it. Our need to play was sold back to us as a product. The record industry, for example, represents the industrialization and commercialization of music. It is the making of something that is by its very nature not-work into work. Industrialization is the process of taking life, splitting it up into little bits and turning them into profit-based industries. Other examples might include the communications industry (pay to talk), the energy industry (pay for wind), the food industry (pay for what nature provides for free), the entertainment industry (pay to be diverted), the leisure industry (pay to play), and so on. These were all areas that once upon a time were voluntary, free-flowing, domestic and, in most cases, literally free.

The line between art and life is still blurred today in more primitive, less serious, more playful societies such as rural Mexico, where the people come down from the mountain farms to the towns in order to sell their crafts in the marketplace. These crafts are useful and beautiful: rugs, ceramics, hats, wooden toys. It is not a slave-like existence, because the craftsman/smallholder takes responsibility for his own life. 'Every workman,' says Eric Gill of the olden days:

> was in some degree a responsible workman – responsible not merely for doing what he was told but for the quality, the intellectual quality of what his deeds effected. He was a more or less independent person who was expected to use, and was paid to use, his intelligence and, therefore (if only to make his work pleasant in the doing – for it says in the book of Ecclesiasticus, 'a man shall have joy in his labour; and this is his portion'), he was a person who did to some extent, either more or less, regard the thing to be made as a thing to be made delightful as well as useful.

Gill talked of what he called 'integrity'. By this he meant not 'staying true to your principles' but 'integrating different parts of your life'. It is the separation of our lives into mutually competing zones that causes the problems, the anxieties, the illnesses, the debts. Our goal should be to bring them together, to integrate them, to harmonize them, so work and life become one and the same thing. Make money out of what you are doing anyway. In my case, I spend each morning writing and reading, and the rest of the day is given up to household work: gardening, cleaning, baking. Gardening is a good one, because there is so much pottering involved. I would say that during one hour of gardening, at least half is spent just staring. Sometimes I succeed in bringing the children to the vegetable patch with me, thereby combining the useful and enjoyable activity of growing food with childcare. The evenings are for drinking, eating and talking.

Indeed, before industrialization, 'beautiful' and 'useful' had not yet been separated into mutually antagonistic categories. They were the same thing. The peasant/craftsman also had a few acres of his own and could therefore produce some of his own food. This kind of responsibility for one's work has been removed from the equation, and work has become an exercise in handing over shifts of one's own life to an overlord in order to get money, and far longer shifts and far more of them than was expected of the most downtrodden medieval bondsman.

In *Homo Ludens*, the venerable Huizinga argues that all cultures are at heart based on a concept of life as play rather than life as work. The Japanese, for example, enjoy their *asobi* and *asobu*, meaning 'play in general, recreation, relaxation, amusement, passing the time or pastime, a trip or jaunt, dissipation, gambling, idling, lying idle, being unemployed'. We might note their similarity to the English social phenomenon given the acronymn ASBO, after Anti-Social Behaviour Disorder, the latest failed attempt by the forces of law to control delinquent youth. Play and its brother, idleness, were once incorporated into work. Even the judges of old didn't over-exert themselves. In *De Laudibus Legum Angliae*, written in 1470, Fortescue actually boasts of how little work the judges do. This leaves them more time for reflection, which will make them better judges:

You are to know, says he, that the Judges do not sit in court to do Business above three Hours in the day, that is from Eight in the Morning to Eleven. After they have taken some Refreshment, the Method is, to spend the rest of the Day in the Study of the Law, reading of the Holy Scriptures, or else it is taken up in some other innocent Amusements, at their Pleasure: So that it is rather a Life of Contemplation, than of Action, free from worldly Cares and Avocations.

To write such a passage would be almost inconceivable today, when most of us spend our time going round telling everyone else how busy we are and how hard we are working. In the internal interplay between the World and the Dream, between the everyday and the otherworldly, the world has been in the ascendant too long. We need to redress the balance. 'Only connect the prose and the passion,' wrote E. M. Forster in *Howard's End*, 'and both will be exalted, and human love will be seen at its height. Live in fragments no longer.' We have fallen off the wall, and we need to put ourselves back together again.

We have lost play, soul, creativity. The great junkie Beatnik Alexander Trocchi writes in his book *Invisible Insurrection*:

Man has forgotten how to play. And if one thinks of the soulless tasks accorded each man in the industrial milieu, of the fact that education has become increasingly technological, and for the ordinary man no more than a means of fitting him for a 'job', one can hardly be surprised that man is lost. He is almost afraid of more leisure . . . His creativity stunted, he is orientated outwards entirely . . .

Education itself is a putting-off, a postponement: we are told to work hard to get good results. Why? So we can get a good job. What is a good job? One that pays well. Oh. And that's it? All this suffering, merely so that we can earn a lot of money, which, even if we manage it, will not solve our problems anyway? It's a tragically limited idea of what life is all about. But we should be mucking about all the time, because mucking about is enjoying life for its own sake, now, and not in preparation for an imaginary future. It's obvious that the mirth-filled man, the cheerful soul, the childish adult is the one who has least to fear from life. Each time I put on a party either at home or at our village hall, a certain grown-up neighbour complains. He is the fearful sort, free of mirth, bound by seriousness. Other people for him exist only as barriers to his cocoon, his 'peace and tranquillity'. He has run away from life.

We have been taught to believe that the new system, in which a service industry has replaced service – or, in other words, we no longer work for the grand houses, we now work for the big companies – is an improvement in terms of personal liberty. But I would question that assumption. No feudal overlord of the past ever had the might, power and wealth of Terry Leahy, the Earl of Tesco's. He earns £10,000 a day, £1,500 an hour, and is lord and master of over 250,000 vassals – that's nearly one in every hundred UK workers, all in thrall to Tesco's, and most taking a year to earn what he takes in a day. It amazes me that we all queue up to serve him and his gang of mega-shareholders. There is no autonomy in employment, no elegance, no grace, no hospitality. Surely the lowliest pot-boy was never so encumbered as the Tesco's shelf-stacker? The supermarkets take all romance and spirit out of life.

We snigger and scoff at the feudal system of work, counting ourselves very lucky today, but a sober examination of the manorial system of the eleventh to fifteenth centuries would suggest that the supposed illiterate, bonded peasants had more freedom, more riches and were more self-sufficient than the average wage slave of today. We saw earlier how John Aubrey of Foxton owed just one day a week's work to the manor. The rest of his time was his own. His income *pro rata* would have been at least £150,000 in today's terms. As it was, he was earning three to four times his annual rent for one day's work a week. He had eighteen acres and his own house. He also would have known one or more crafts: every village needed its shoemaker, mason, carpenter, blacksmith. Now, compare that sort of life with the tedium of the call-centre operative earning £12,000 a year for five days' work a week. The call-centre employee has to work five times as hard for less than half the salary. As for a widespread house-owning class, said to be one of the great economic advances of the recent age, this is another con. If the mortgage company owns 90 per cent of it, how can this be said to be owning your own house? Instead, you are in slavery to two authorities, the employer and the mortgage company. Fall behind on these payments, and the mortgage company will literally take your home from you. Therefore, you will subject yourself to all sorts of humiliations at work out of fear of losing your job. This is surely savagery and slavery far in excess of the medieval system.

If you are thinking of quitting your job, then let me say I can highly recommend it. I think it's much easier to live without a job. For one thing, it's a lot less work. An hour worked at home is equivalent to two in the wasteful office or factory. In the institutional workplace, we perfect the art of doing the smallest amount of work in the longest amount of time. There is a huge amount of time wasted. At home, that process is reversed: we do as much work as possible in the smallest amount of time. So four hours work at home is like a full day's work in the office. In another sense, though, when you work at home and when you manage to bring work and life together into one thing, then you are working all the time. Or you are never working; it's up to you. Writing an article is neither more nor less important to me than digging up a parsnip. It is all part of life; everything is equal, the good and the bad, the money-earning and the not-money-earning.

You also find that, when jobless, you stop spending so much. Gone are the commuting costs, gone are the endless giant coffees – slave no more to Starbucks! Free at last! – gone are the lunchtime sandwiches, gone are the drinks after work with co-workers. You don't even need so many clothes. Your costs plummet. The home worker can easily save £100 a week. That itself reduces the pressure to work.

One objection I hear, another mind-forg'd manacle, is the line: 'I wouldn't have the self-discipline to work for myself.' This is another myth. We are encouraged to believe that we are useless, unable to look after ourselves and hence need an employer to subdue our unruly self and slot it into a strict timetable. When you realize that, in fact, you are free, this problem ebbs away.

A wonderful thing about being jobless is the fantastic sense of freedom and autonomy that you feel every day. I would rather earn £10,000 a year and be jobless than earn £500,000 and spend ten hours a day as an employee. In my mind, there's no contest.

Active joblessness of this sort also leaves time and energy for community projects. Since giving up work, I've been able to join our local village-hall committee, organizing concerts and dinners. I've joined the local music festival and work on booking bands each year. This is all unpaid work and all the more enjoyable for being unpaid.

Relaxing the hold that work has over your life and replacing it with play can be a slow and gradual process. The key to enjoying a life beyond full-time employment is to realize that, once you stop working full time, you start to become a producer, a creative person, rather than a consumer. The earliest forms of work deemed acceptable by the Catholic Church were creative. The monks were allowed to bake bread, brew beer and work in the garden. This is because work, the clerics felt, should reflect God's own act of creation. And they were right: these three forms of work are the most enjoyable. Gardeners, bakers and brewers tend to be happy people.

It is also true to say that you can be a wage slave without being a slave to wages. You don't necessarily have to quit your job in order to be free. You can make your job into something that suits you. One friend, for example, decided to stay on the shop floor, so to speak, in his social-work job rather than move up to management. This is because he could work a shorter week (thirty-three hours, in his case), and the work itself was less stressful. In his job, looking after adults with learning disabilities, he does things he enjoys, such as gardening and playing the guitar. And he still has plenty of time and energy to work in the garden and make things at home and update his website and print magazines. So, he has a job, but he is not wholly dependent on it; and he has taken a creative approach to his job, in that he has made it fit his life, and not the other way around.

Many people I know have chosen to go part-time. Working three days a week gives you a psychological advantage, because the number of days you have to yourself outnumbers the days you are selling to an employer. Reduce your hours of vassalage; reduce your service. Do less.

Another argument for freelancing is that it is much safer than regular employment. Work is dangerous. Four hundred people a year are killed at work in the UK. The vast majority of these deaths occur at the bottom end of the scale, among goods drivers, warehouse staff, fitters, dock workers and so on. Work causes around 30,000 non-fatal injuries per year; half of these are in the service sector. And, according to the Centre for Corporate Accountability, idlers are safe: the figures for injuries among the self-employed are minute.

Anything that helps reduce our dependence on wages is a good thing. My new idea is the three-hour-shift system. The standard working day should be seven hours, and it should be divided into two shifts of three to three and half hours each. Thus, each week would consist of ten shifts. Now, at different times in your life, you could do more or less work. So, at certain times you might do the full ten shifts; at others, you could cut down to just a handful. A freelance economy of this sort would open up all sorts of new avenues for people. Right now, with a forty-hour week, it is just too difficult to see the wood for the trees and to have any energy left over at the end of the day for doing anything creative, making compost, or keeping hens or making honey, or baking bread, or brewing beer, or whatever your pleasures happen to be.

My other idea is Odd Jobs. This is a new service that I have set up on the *Idler*'s website. Noticing that *Idler* readers were struggling with the idea of giving up work entirely and trying to make money solely from their creative enterprises, I conceived Odd Jobs as a way for idlers to find temporary or part-time work in order to support their other activities. So, on Odd Jobs, you can advertise your own services or offer work. One example is a freelance classical musician, a tuba-player, who trained as a plasterer in order to make money during fallow periods in the tuba-playing world. He answered an ad on Odd Jobs, and he is going out to Italy to live for two weeks with a couple who need some plastering done, in return for a free holiday. This is the sort of creative approach that we need to take to the world of work. Odd Jobs escapes entirely from exploitative temp agencies and the disabling professionalization of work, because it simply works on the basis of a private contract between two individuals. Odd Jobs also says: 'We are not going to sit around and wait for government and unions to improve working conditions. We are going to ignore the whole thing and set up our new vital systems for living and working.'

Specialization is a curse. 'Oh, I'm no good at that sort of thing,' we say to ourselves, with our learned sense of uselessness. But crafts are actually terribly easy to learn. Better to be jack of all trades than master of none. Victoria went on a course locally in which she learned how to make the rush matting on one of those Van Gogh-type chairs. Every moment a pleasure and, at the end of it, we had a mended chair, a thing of beauty and utility. Craft unites work and play, and art and life.

Be a jack of all trades; abandon perfectionism. Embrace the creed of the amateur. Do it for love, not money. A spade, a saw and a chisel, that is all you need to be free.

In play is freedom, says Huizinga, because it is self-directed and voluntary:

> Child and animal play because they enjoy playing, and therein precisely lies their freedom. Be that as it may, for the adult and responsible human being, play is a function which he could equally well leave alone. Play is superfluous. The need for it is only urgent to the extent that the enjoyment of it makes a need. Play can be deferred or suspended at any time. It is never imposed by physical necessity, or moral duty. It is never a task. It is done at leisure, during 'free time'. Only when play is a recognized cultural function – a rite, a ceremony – is it bound up with notions of obligation and duty. Here then, we have the main characteristic of play: that it is free, is in fact freedom.

We need to make all of our time free. Do what we like all day long. Do nothing all day long. Muck about all day long.

If you enjoy your work, then it's not work. As my friend Sarah says, the trick to living free is to wake up every morning and screech: *'Morning, Lord, what have you got for me today?'* She

317

maintains that this really works. Freedom can start today, right now. You can change your life in one second. Freedom is a state of mind.

PLAY

Further Reading

Here is a list of some of the books I read while writing this one. I would recommend them for any freedom-seeker's library:

Aquinas, St Thomas, *Selected Works*, ed. The Rev. Fr M. C. D'Arcy (London: J. M. Dent, 1940)

——, *Summa Contra Gentiles* (Notre Dame, Indiana: University of Notre Dame Press, 1975)

Writing in the late thirteenth century, Aquinas was the Jean-Paul Sartre of his day. He believed that 'All is vanity.'

Aristotle, *Nicomachean Ethics* (Oxford: Oxford University Press, 1980)

Aristotle (384–322 BC) was known as 'the Philosopher' by the medievals, and his laid-back approach provided the intellectual motor for hundreds of years of brotherly love and praise of the contemplative life.

Armytage, W. H. G., *Heavens Below: Utopian Experiments in England 1560–1960* (London: Routledge and Kegan Paul, 1961)

From the Reformation onwards, freedom-loving Brits have made noble attempts to escape tyranny via the establishment of communal systems of living. This book traces those experiments.

Arnold, Matthew, *Poetical Works* (London: Macmillan, 1890)

The gloomy Arnold is a strangely cheering read.

Beat, Alan, *A Start in Smallholding* (Holsworthy: Smallholding Press, 2004)

Inspiring account of one family's successful attempt to live the good life.

Beckwith, John, *Early Medieval Art* (London: Thames and Hudson, 1969)

Badly written but with lots of good pictures of the modern-looking, sometimes comical and often cartoon-like religious paintings and carvings of the so-called Dark Ages.

Beir, A. L., *Masterless Men: The Vagrancy Problem in England 1560–1640* (London: Methuen, 1985)

The Reformation produced a vagrancy problem of huge dimensions, which gave the Elizabethan government an excuse to introduce all sorts of new laws to crack down on beggars and wanderers. This excellent study chronicles a decisive attack on Merry England.

Belloc, Hilaire, et al, *Distributist Perspectives* (Norfolk, VA: IHS Press, 2004)

Distributism is the anarchic idea that every family should have its own plot of land in order to produce some of its own food and therefore be independent. The idea was popular in the twenties, when it was promoted by Catholic writers such as Belloc and Chesterton.

Benton, Janetta Rebold, *Medieval Mischief: Wit and Humour in the Art of the Middle Ages* (Stroud: Sutton Publishing, 2004)

Bare bottoms, copulating couples, donkeys playing harps: this book takes a look at the hidden corners of medieval cathedrals and churches.

Biddle, Violet, *Small Gardens and How to Make the Most of Them* (London: C. Arthur Pearson, 1911)

An Arts and Crafts-era gardening guide which promotes originality and fun.

Blythman, Joanna, *Shopped: The Shocking Power of British Supermarkets* (London: Fourth Estate, 2004)

A brilliant exposé of the extent to which the supermarkets rule our lives.

Boswell, James, *The Life of Samuel Johnson* (London: Dent, 1946)

Always a great read.

Bulley, Margaret, *Ancient and Medieval Art* (London: Methuen, 1996)

Good on the craftsmen's guilds and on medieval churches. First published in 1926.

Bunker, Sarah, Charnock, Christine, Coates, Chris, Hodgson, David & How, Jonathan (eds.), *Diggers and Dreamers: The Guide to Communal Living 2004/2005* (London: D&D Publications, 2003)

Directory of communal groups in the UK today.

Burnett, Graham, *Permaculture: A Beginner's Guide* (Westcliffe-on-Sea: Land and Liberty, 2002)

A handy pamphlet which introduces the Permaculture principles of low-effort, high-yield gardening.

Burton, Robert, *Anatomy of Melancholy* (London: William Tegg, 1861)

The seventeenth-century self-help classic and a paradoxically joyful book.

Cash, Arthur H., *John Wilkes: The Scandalous Father of Civil Liberty* (Boston: Yale, 2006)

Biography of one of the eighteenth-century's greatest free spirits.

Chancellor, Edward, *Devil Take the Hindmost* (London: Macmillan, 1999)

Illuminating history of financial bubbles, from tulips to dot-com mania.

Chaucer, *Canterbury Tales* (London: J. M. Dent, 1984)

Portraits of fourteenth-century types, written with light touch and ribald humour.

Chesterton, G. K., *The Man Who Was Thursday* (London: Penguin, 1972)

Tale of scheming anarchists, with a twist. First published in 1908.

——, *The Thing* (London: Sheed and Ward, 1931)

Essays on religion and on escaping the industrial programme. Graham Greene called it 'among the great books of the age'.

——, *St Francis of Assisi* (London: Hodder and Stoughton)

A portrait of the most polite man who ever lived, 'morning star of the Renaissance'.

——, *William Cobbett* (London: House of Stratus, 2000)

Brilliant essay on the importance of Cobbett as a humane thinker.

Clayton, Antony, *Decadent London* (London: Historical Publications Ltd, 2005)

Tales of London's *fin de siècle* aesthetes, Wilde, Beardsley et al.

Coates, Chris, *Utopia Britannica: British Utopian Experiments 1325–1945* (London: D&D Publications, 2001)

Attempts to build Jerusalem on our green and pleasant land.

Cobbett, William, *Cottage Economy* (London: Peter Davies, 1926)

——, *A History of the Protestant Reformation* (London: R&T Washbourne Ltd, 1827)

> A blistering attack on Henry VIII and his destruction of the old ways.

Cohn, Norman, *The Pursuit of the Millennium: Revolutionary Millenarians and Mystical Anarchists of the Middle Ages* (London: Pimlico, 2004)

> A study of medieval bohemian and amoral movements, from Sufis to the Brethren of the Free Spirit.

Dante, *The Divine Comedy* (London: Penguin, 1959)

> Medieval poetry at its best.

Debord, Guy, *The Society of the Spectacle* (Detroit: Black and Red, 1967)

> The free-wheeling Situationist attacks commodity culture.

Donkin, Richard, *Blood, Sweat and Tears: The Evolution of Work* (London and New York: Texere, 2001)

> A pacey account of work through the ages and our changing attitudes to it.

Fattorusso, J. & M. L., *Florence: The City of Flowers* (Florence: The Medici Series, 1950)

> Quaint guidebook.

Fearnley-Whittingstall, Hugh, *The River Cottage Cookbook* (London: HarperCollins, 2001)

> Inspiring handbook for free living and good eating.

Fortescue, Sir John, *De Laudibus Legum Angliae* (London: Hall, 1775)

> The classic fifteenth-century celebration of the English legal system.

Fukuoka, Masanobu, *The One-Straw Revolution* (Mapusa, Goa: Other India Press, 2005)

> Wise and inspiring account of one man's experiment with

'do-nothing farming', where you let nature do the work.

Gandhi, Mohandas K., *Autobiography: The Story of My Experiments with Truth* (New York: Dover Publications Inc., 1983)

Where Mohandas finds freedom through service.

Gardner, Edmund G., *The Story of Florence* (London: J. M. Dent & Co., 1908)

Useful history of the great free city-state.

Gill, Eric, *Autobiography* (London: Jonathan Cape, 1947)

Thoughts on art and life from the letter-cutter turned sculptor.

Godwin, William, *Caleb Williams* (Oxford: Oxford University Press, 1986)

A riveting tale of life on the run.

——, *Enquiry Concerning Political Justice* (Oxford: Clarendon Press, 1971)

Early anarchist theory from Mary Shelley's father.

Gombrich, E. H., *A Little History of the World* (London: Yale University Press, 2005)

Originally published in 1936, this is the noted art historian's brilliantly simple account of how we got to where we are now.

Griffiths, Jay, *Pip Pip: A Sideways Look at Time* (London: Flamingo, 1999)

The essential history of the politics of time.

Hesiod and Theognis (London: Penguin, 1973)

Greek farming advice and gay love poetry.

Hibbert, Christopher, *The Rise and Fall of the House of Medici* (London: Penguin, 1979)

The story of the great banking family which dominated medieval Florence.

Hills, Lawrence D., *How to Grow Your Own Fruit and Vegetables* (London: Faber & Faber, 1974)
    The bible for organic fruit and veg growers by the founder of the Henry Doubleday Research Association.

Hoffman, Abbie, *Revolution for the Hell of It* (New York: Pocket Books, 1970)
    Down with the squares!

Hoggart, Richard, *The Uses of Literacy* (London: Penguin, 1965)
    Study of working-class attitudes.

Houston, Mary G., *Medieval Costume in England and France* (Mineola, NY: Dover, 1996)
    Pointy shoes, bells and bright colours: all medieval finery is here.

Huizinga, J., *Homo Ludens* (London: Routledge and Kegan Paul, 1970)
    The importance of the spirit of play in civilization.

——, *The Waning of the Middle Ages* (London: Penguin, 1955)
    Brilliant portrait of a more passionate age, first published in 1924.

Hutton, Ronald, *The Rise and Fall of Merry England: The Ritual Year 1400–1700* (Oxford: Oxford University Press, 1993)
    Demonstrates how the festive culture of the Middle Ages was gradually eroded by the Reformation and the Puritans.

Hyams, Edward, *Pierre-Joseph Proudhon: His Revolutionary Life, Mind and Works* (London: John Murray, 1979)
    Biography of the great French anarchist.

Illich, Ivan, *Celebration of Awareness* (London: Penguin, 1977)
    Ideas for a brighter future.

——, *The Right to Useful Unemployment and Its Professional Enemies* (London: Marion Boyars, 1978)

An attack on the creed of professionalism.

Ingrams, Richard, *The Life and Adventures of William Cobbett* (London: HarperCollins, 2005)

Contemporary study of the bloody-minded autodidact and radical, by *Private Eye* founder.

Innes, Jocasta, *The Country Kitchen* (London: Frances Lincoln, 2003)

How to make bread, beer, jam and much more besides.

Jameson, Storm, *The Decline of Merry England* (London: Cassell, 1930)

Long essay attacking Puritanism.

Keen, M. H., *England in the Later Middle Ages* (London: Methuen, 1980)

Slighty dull textbook but with valuable insights.

Kesey, Ken, *One Flew over the Cuckoo's Nest* (London: Penguin, 2005)

Nurse Ratched and the medical authorities restrain the free spirit in Kesey's work of genius.

Kropotkin, Prince Peter, *Act for Yourselves* (London: Freedom Press, 1998)

Articles from *Freedom* magazine, 1886–1907.

——, *Mutual Aid* (London: Penguin, 1939)

The spirit of cooperation in animals and man.

Lawrence, D. H., *Phoenix: The Posthumous Papers of D. H. Lawrence* (London: Heinemann, 1961)

Collected essays by the wide-eyed freedom-seeker.

Lawrence, Felicity, *Not on the Label: What Really Goes into the Food on Your Plate* (London: Penguin, 2004)

You'll never buy food from a supermarket again.

Le Goff, Jacques (ed.), *The Medieval World* (London: Collins & Brown, 1990)

    Academic essays by medievalists on knights, clerics and intellectuals.

——, *Time, Work and Culture in the Middle Ages* (London: University of Chicago Press, 1980)

    The birth of mercantile culture and its battle with the Church.

——, *Your Money or Your Life* (Brooklyn, NY: Zone Books, 1998)

    Usury in the Middle Ages.

Lindsay, Jack, *The Troubadours and Their World of the Twelfth and Thiteenth Centuries* (London: Frederick Muller Ltd, 1976)

    Portrait of the pop stars of their day, the literary musicians who wandered from court to court.

Livingstone, Karen & Parry, Linda (eds.), *International Arts and Crafts* (London: V&A Publications, 2005)

McCarthy, Fiona, *Eric Gill* (London: Faber & Faber, 2003)

    The essential biography, which documents Gill's contributions to English culture as well as his sexual peculiarities.

Marcus, Greil, *Lipstick Traces: A Secret History of the Twentieth Century* (Cambridge, MA.: Harvard University Press, 2003)

    Punk and its heritage, from the Brethren of the Free Spirit to Dada to Situationism.

Marsh, Jan, *Back to the Land: The Pastoral Impulse in Victorian England from 1880 to 1914* (London: Quartet Books Ltd, 1982)

    Victorians resist industrialization.

Marx, Karl, *Capital* (London: J. M.Dent & Sons Ltd, 1934)

    Always worth a look.

Michel, John, *Eccentric Lives and Peculiar Notions* (London: Thames and Hudson, 1984)

Lives of a few free spirits.

Mill, John Stuart, *Utilitarianism, Liberty and Representative Government* (London: J. M. Dent, 1944)

Another free spirit in rationalist's clothing.

Morris, William, *News From Nowhere, or, An Epoch of Rest* (London: Routledge and Kegan Paul, 1983)

Morris' charming utopia, in which there is no money and fields cover Piccadilly Circus.

——, 'Art, Labour and Socialism' (London: Socialist Party of Great Britain, 1962)

A passionate plea to reunite art and life.

Mumford, Lewis, *The Myth of the Machine: Technics and Human Development* (London: Secker and Warburg, 1967)

How machines have detached man from nature.

Nietzsche, Friedrich, *On the Genealogy of Morals*, ed. Walter Kaufmann, trans. Walter Kaufmann, R. J. Hollingdale (New York: Vintage, 1969)

Where morals are revealed to be mind-forg'd.

Nuttal, Jeff, *Bomb Culture* (London: MacGibbon & Kee, 1968)

Exhaustive study of sixties underground movements.

O'Brien, George, 'The Economic Effects of the Reformation' (Norfolk, VA: IHS Press, 2003)

Reprint of a 1923 Catholic attack on Henry VIII and the rest, and a celebration of the medieval approach to economics.

Parker, Rowland, *The Common Stream: Two Thousand Years of the English Village* (St Albans: Paladin, 1976)

A history of one village, drawn from court rolls and parish

records, particularly fascinating on medieval judicial and social systems.

Parry, A. W., *Education in England in the Middle Ages* (London: W. B. Clive, 1920)

Which shows that free education is not a modern innovation.

Paterson, Linda M., *The World of the Troubadours: Medieval Occitan Society c. 1100–c. 1300* (Cambridge: Cambridge University Press, 1993)

Academic study with great stuff on medieval childcare.

Penty, Arthur, *The Gauntlet: A Challenge to the Myth of Progress* (Norfolk, VA: HIS Press, 2003)

Catholic writer (1875–1937) attacks industrialization.

Prabhavanda, Swami, & Isherwood, Christopher (trans.), *The Song of God: Bhagavad-Gita*, with an Introduction by Aldous Huxley (London: Phoenix House, 1947)

Proudhon, Pierre-Joseph, *Selected Writings*, ed. Stewart Edwards, trans. Elizabeth Fraser (London: Macmillan, 1970)

Where Proudhon declares: 'I am an anarchist' and 'Property is theft.'

Rackham, Oliver, *The History of the Countryside* (London: Phoenix Press, 2000)

Take a trip into the history of British hedges, ponds, quarries, woods and wastelands with a Cambridge academic who loves the wild places.

Rubin, Jerry, *Do It!* (London: Jonathan Cape, 1970)

Bible for the Yippies. We are asked to 'read this book stoned!' Dated but inspiring.

Ruskin, John, *The Stones of Venice*, Vols. I, II and III (London: George Allen, 1906)

Ruskin's great study of medieval buildings.

——, *Unto This Last* (London: Collins, 1970)
Essays on life and art.

Russell, Bertrand, *A History of Western Philosophy* (London: George Allen and Unwin, 1961)
Handy guide, although a bit rough on the great Nietzsche. Russell was always just slightly too wet.

——, *Sceptical Essays* (London: Unwin, 1985)
Fun-loving Bertie writes on Puritans, education and the loafers of China.

Sartre, Jean-Paul, *Being and Nothingness: An Essay on Phenomenological Ontology*, trans. Hazel E. Barnes (London: Methuen & Co., 1957)
Long and technical but well worth a dip, particularly if you would like to enjoy the washing-up.

——, *Sketch for a Theory of the Emotions* (London: Methuen, 1962)
Where he seems to be saying that emotions don't exist.

Schama, Simon, *A History of Britain, 3000 BC–AD 1603* (London: BBC Worldwide, 2000)
Where the popular historian has some nice attacks on Thomas Cromwell and Henry VIII.

Schumacher, E. F., *Small is Beautiful: A Study of Economics as if People Mattered* (London: Sphere Books Ltd, 1974)
Inspiring celebration of human-scale institutions, needed more than ever in the age of Tesco's.

——, *Good Work* (London: Jonathan Cape, 1979)
Ideas on how work could be fun, creative and satisfying.

Seymour, John, *The Countryside Explained* (London: Faber & Faber, 1977)
A history of agriculture and farming.

——, *The Fat of the Land* (London: Faber & Faber, 1961)

First book from the great smallholder, describing his early days on the farm.

——, *Self-Sufficiency* (London: Faber & Faber, 1973)
Both a great read and very useful for anyone wanting to pursue a free life.

Simons, Arthur J., *The New Vegetable Grower's Handbook* (London: Penguin, 1975)
The classic that emerged out of a series of guides for wartime vegetable gardeners.

Svendsen, Lars, *A Philosophy of Boredom* (London: Reaktion, 2005)
A playful study which argues that boredom is a symptom of modern life.

Tacitus, *The Agricola* and *The Germania* (London: Penguin, 1970)
Where Roman soldier Tacitus praises the social systems of the so-called barbarians.

Tawney, R. H., *Religion and the Rise of Capitalism* (London: Penguin, 1942)
On the transition from medieval federalism and communal living to modern profit-centred living and the role of Protestantism in that change.

Thompson, E. P., *The Romantics: England in a Revolutionary Age* (New York: The New Press, 1997)
On the radical politics of the Romantic poets.

Thompson, J. Eric S., *The Rise and Fall of Mayan Civilization* (London: Pimlico, 1993)
Portrait of a laid-back and creative people.

Tolstoy, Leo, *The Kingdom of God is within You* (London: OUP, 1936)
Tolstoy's great pacifist anarchist essay.

Trocchi, Alexander, *Invisible Insurrection of a Million Minds: A Trocchi Reader* (London: Polygon, 1991)
> The beat poet's finest.

Vaneigem, Raoul, *The Revolution of Everyday Life* (London: Rebel Press, 2003)
> The Situationist's brilliant attack on the empty promises of capitalism.

Weber, Max, *The Protestant Ethic and the Spirit of Capitalism*, trans. Talcott Parsons (London: Unwin University Books, 1968)
> How the competitive Protestants booted out the cooperative Catholics.

Wells, H. G., *A Modern Utopia* (London: W. Collins Sons and Co. Ltd, 1905)
> Techno fantasy of 'swift gliding trains' and 'world unity, world language, world-wide travellings'.

Wenner, Jann S., *Lennon Remembers* (London: Verso, 2000)
> Lennon in candid form.

Whitehead, A. N., *Symbolism: Its Meaning and Effect* (Cambridge: Cambridge University Press, 1928)
> Whitehead was a philosophical mate of Bertrand Russell, and this book discusses our love of symbols.

Wilde, Oscar, *The Soul of Man under Socialism and Selected Critical Prose* (London: Penguin, 2001)
> Wilde's great Kropotkin-influenced essay on political freedom.

Wymer, Norman, *English Town Crafts: A Survey of Their Development from Early Times to the Present Day* (London: B. T. Batsford Ltd, 1949)
> The former importance of crafts in the everyday lives of the English.

Free Resources

Here are a few places that might help on your quest for liberty. Best of all, start your own magazine or website to share ideas. And the Internet is all well and good, but it is no substitute for talking to other human beings.

1 Banish Anxiety; Be Carefree

www.anxietyculture.com
This is Brian Dean's sober and sensible website, which demonstrates that anxiety about crime is merely a convenient fiction
For an admirable celebration of not caring, listen to 'Pretty Vacant' by the Sex Pistols
For fine ales delivered to your door, try Majestic Wine Warehouse

2 Break the Bonds of Boredom

To buy a ukulele, take a look at London's Duke of Uke shop: www.dukeofuke.co.uk
To buy a quality skateboard, take a look at the website of Slam City Skates, the skateboarding shop where I used to work: www.slamcity.com
For tips on making your own stuff, go to www.readymademag.com

3 The Tyranny of Bills and the Freedom of Simplicity

There is a nice site at www.geocities.com/livingsimplynow

4 Reject Career and All Its Empty Promises

Our own website at www.idler.co.uk will help you find the courage and confidence to pursue a life free of fruitless ladder-climbing

5 Get out of the City

The Permaculture movement helps you to turn your home into a productive entity and thereby bring nature into your everyday life, wherever you live. Start at www.permaculture.org or www.permaculture.org.uk

Try the National Society of Allotment and Leisure Gardeners at www.nslag.org.uk and contact your local council to rent an allotment

6 End Class War

To visit the grand houses, check out the National Trust at www.nationaltrust.org.uk

7 Cast off Your Watch

For an insight into a fantastic protest against fast culture, go to www.longnow.org and read about the world's slowest computer, the Clock of the Long Now

8 *Stop Competing*

The Association of Guilds of Weavers, Spinners and Dyers can be found at www.wsd.org.uk. If you are not a weaver, spinner or dyer then you'll have to start your own guild

9 *Escape Debt*

For an excellent definition of usury, the 'queen of sins', go to www.newadvent.org/cathen/15235c.htm
For advice on getting out of debt, try www.nationaldebtline.co.uk or your local Citizens Advice Bureau. The *Idler*'s web forum often discusses such issues

10 *Death to Shopping*

Just throw out the telly and don't buy magazines

11 *Smash the Fetters of Fear*

Ride a horse

12 *Forget Government*

Go to the brilliant Freedom Bookshop in London, online at www.libcom.org/hosted/freedom, endless brain food for the free of spirit

13 *Say No to Guilt and Free Your Spirit*

There's a good piece on the Brethren of the Free Spirit and their notion that 'nothing is sin' at www.totse.com/en/fringe/fringe science/freesprt.html

Otherwise, reading about great rakes and scoundrels can help dent that bourgeois morality, and best of all for revealing that guilt is a capitalist plot is Max Weber's *The Protestant Ethic and the Spirit of Capitalism*

14 *No More Housework*

Force the children to do the washing-up. Try the excellent www.lazywoman.com for advice on that all-important attitude adjustment, and an attack on Martha Stewart-style perfectionism

15 *Banish Loneliness*

Start an association or club. Meet in your kitchen

16 *Submit No More to the Machine, Use Your Hands*

Go to www.luddite.meetup.com to meet others who share your feelings about technology gone too far. Also take a look at the US-based Arts and Crafts Society at www.arts-crafts.com Also check out Danielle Proud's craft site at www.houseproud craft.com

17 *In Praise of Melancholy*

Read the Romantic poets

18 *Stop Moaning; Be Merry*

There is a very good introduction to existentialism at www. interchange.ubc.ca/cree/index.htm

19 *Live Mortgage-Free; Be a Happy Wanderer*

For advice and information on communal living, go to www.diggersanddreamers.org.uk; on squatting, go to www.squatter.org.uk; and on the travelling life, www.gypsy traveller.org or telephone 01273 234777

20 *The Anti-Nuclear Family*

The Alliance for Childhood at www.allianceforchildhood.org.uk appears to have the positive aim of 'leaving them alone' at its heart

21 *Disarm Pain*

Go to SmithKline's website to acquaint yourself with the full horror of the global pain trade

22 *Stop Worrying about your Pension and Get a Life*

There is no pensions crisis. For more, see articles in the *Socialist Worker* at www.socialistworker.co.uk/article.php?article id=7907

23 Sail Away from Rudeness and towards a New Era of Courtesy, Civility and Grace

Listen to the music of the Troubadours, as recorded by Vienna's Unicorn Ensemble at www.unicornensemble.at

24 Self-Important Puritans Must Die

For resources on the joyfully nihilistic Samuel Beckett, go to www.themodernword.com/beckett

25 Live Free of the Supermarkets

A good place to start when growing vegetables is www.spiralseed.co.uk and what used to be called The Henry Doubleday Research Organization but is now www.garden organic.org.uk Try www.suma.co.uk and others similar for buying wholefoods at wholesale prices. Also I would recommend Hugh Fearnley-Whittingstall's website at www.river cottage.net, and, of course, the Permaculture websites. But best of all: talk to neighbours and just do it

26 The Reign of the Ugly is Over; Long Live Beauty, Quality, Fraternity!

Buy a chisel. Learn a craft. Local councils and organizations run courses very cheaply

27 Depose the Tyrant Wealth

For tips on spending less and living more, try www.frugal.org.uk

28 Reject Waste; Embrace Thrift

Keep hens; make compost. Go to www.smallholder.co.uk or www.countrysmallholding.co.uk

29 Stop Working, Start Living

Odd Jobs is a service on the *Idler* forum where you can find part-time or temporary work. Try also Pat Kane's www.theplay ethic.com for ideas on work as play

Acknowledgements

Many thanks to Victoria Hull, Penny Rimbaud, John Nicholson, Simon Prosser, Cat Ledger, John Moore, Gavin Pretor-Pinney, Mark Manning, Clare Pollard, Dan Kieran, Bill Drummond, Brian Dean, Jay Griffiths, Marcel Theroux, Neil Boorman, Jock Scot, my parents, Will Hodgkinson, Gee Vaucher, John Michell, Hannah Griffiths, Joe Rush, Keith Allen, Nick Lezard, Sally and Alan, Sarah Jones, Mathew Clayton, Damien and Maia, the late Jago Elliot, Louis and Murphy, Nick, Rob, Zoe and Mark of the Alabamas, Llama, Anna Ridley, Sarah Day, Francesca Main and Juliette Mitchell.

Find out more about Tom Hodgkinson
in an exclusive interview at
www.penguin.co.uk/tomhodgkinson